T0278848

ETHICS

DEMONSTRATED IN A GEOMETRICAL MANNER

ETHICS

DEMONSTRATED IN A GEOMETRICAL MANNER

Benedict De Spinoza

Edited and with Commentary by
Jason Waller and Rebecca Lloyd Waller

Translated by R.H.M. Elwes,
updated and revised by Domingo Aviles

broadview press

BROADVIEW PRESS
Peterborough, Ontario, Canada

Founded in 1985, Broadview Press is a fully independent academic publishing house
owned by approximately twenty-five shareholders—almost all of whom are either Broadview employees or Broadview authors. Broadview is supported by a collaboration with
Trent University, a liberal arts university located in Peterborough, Ontario—the city where
Broadview was founded and continues to operate. Broadview is committed to environ-
mentally responsible publishing and fair business practices.

© 2024 Jason Waller and Rebecca Lloyd Waller; translation © Domingo Aviles

All rights reserved. No part of this book may be reproduced, kept in an information
storage and retrieval system, or transmitted in any form or by any means, electronic or
mechanical, including photocopying, recording, or otherwise, except as expressly permitted by the applicable copyright laws or through written permission from the publisher.
Use of this work in the training of large language models, generative artificial intelligence,
and other machine learning programs without the express written permission of Broadview Press is strictly prohibited.

Library and Archives Canada Cataloguing in Publication

Title: Ethics demonstrated in a geometrical manner / Benedict De Spinoza ; edited and
    with commentary by Jason Waller and Rebecca Lloyd Waller ; translated by R.H.M.
    Elwes, updated and revised by Domingo Aviles.
Other titles: Ethica. English
Names: Spinoza, Benedictus de, 1632-1677, author | Waller, Jason, 1980- editor, writer of
    added commentary | Waller, Rebecca Lloyd, editor, writer of added commentary | Elwes,
    R. H. M. (Robert Harvey Monro), 1853-1892, translator | Aviles, Domingo, editor.
Description: Translation of: Ethica. | Includes bibliographical references and index.
Identifiers: Canadiana (print) 20240429974 | Canadiana (ebook) 2024043045X | ISBN
    9781554815876 (softcover) | ISBN 9781770489745 (PDF) | ISBN 9781460408988
    (EPUB)
Subjects: LCSH: Ethics.
Classification: LCC B3973.E5 E4 2024 | DDC 170—dc23

Broadview Press handles its own distribution in Canada and the United States:
PO Box 1243, Peterborough, Ontario K9J 7H5, Canada
555 Riverwalk Parkway, Tonawanda, NY 14150, USA
Tel: (705) 482-5915
email: customerservice@broadviewpress.com

Broadview Press acknowledges the financial support of the
Government of Canada for our publishing activities.

Copy-edited by Robert M. Martin
Typesetting and assembly by True to Type

Broadview Press® is the registered trademark of Broadview Press Inc.

PRINTED IN CANADA

CONTENTS

ABOUT THIS EDITION

Spinoza's *Ethics Demonstrated in a Geometrical Manner* is a dense and difficult book. Many readers have attempted to grapple with it only to give up after a few pages. With this edition we aim to make this profound and revolutionary work as accessible as possible to students everywhere, but even if we succeed in making this book more accessible, we cannot make it easy. With enough effort, however, we hope to make it *easier*. This new translation is based on R.H.M. Elwes's 1891 classic English translation, but has been updated for both readability and accuracy in light of recent scholarship.

The most distinctive feature of this edition is the addition of commentary notes. These notes have been added to the text to aid the student in working through the many difficult proofs in this book. When dealing with as deep and radical a philosopher as Spinoza it is impossible to write commentary notes that will be entirely uncontroversial. While we believe that the reading we offer in these notes is "mainstream" and "conventional," it will inevitably be at times controversial. The notes are *not* intended to resolve all of the tensions in the work or to reveal to the reader the "One True Way" to read this book. The comments in this edition are intended only as an aid to the student to get more out of the work and to engage more deeply with it. The hope is that reading the book with the notes will allow the reader to absorb in one reading what would normally take a great many readings. Scholars immersed in the voluminous secondary literature on Spinoza will undoubtedly notice many controversies that we sidestep and some recent scholarly trends that we fail to mention. Such limitations are a necessary (though unfortunate) feature of a work such as this.

There is a long tradition of writing commentaries on Spinoza's *Ethics*. During the eighteenth century a number of different commentaries were written with the aim of refuting Spinoza's proofs and defending traditional Christianity. That is not our purpose here. But neither is our purpose to give a full-throated defense of Spinoza. We leave all conclusions up to the reader. Our goal is simply to help make the text as accessible as possible so that readers can decide for themselves what to make of this philosopher of radical rationality.

This commentary is partly a result of a seminar that we taught at Kenyon College on Spinoza's *Ethics* in Spring 2022.

INTRODUCTION

I. LIFE AND WORK

The story of Spinoza's life is quickly told. Baruch (Benedict in Latin) Spinoza was born in 1632 in Amsterdam. He belonged to a prosperous middle-class merchant family and was a member of the Portuguese-Jewish community. Intellectually gifted, Spinoza was a star student at the Talmud Torah school until the age of 17 when he was forced to quit school in order to run the family's import-export business. Though we have limited knowledge about Spinoza's activities during this time, by 1656 he had embroiled himself in enough controversy to be dramatically banished from the Jewish community for "monstrous deeds" and "abominable heresies." The community was ordered to stay away from Spinoza and anyone who communicated with him risked expulsion as well. Spinoza then moved out of Amsterdam and made a quiet living as a lens grinder in the country while continuing to refine his philosophy. The work of the lens grinder is not unlike the work of the careful philosopher: it is slow, painstaking, and very precise work. Each lens had to be ground to exactly the right dimensions in order to fit into the new telescopes and microscopes that were just then being developed.

In 1663 Spinoza published a critical study of René Descartes's *Principles of Philosophy*. This book proved that Spinoza was a master of the most cutting-edge philosophy of his day and he soon acquired a small number of students who paid him modest fees to learn philosophy from him. Spinoza's life was calm and unremarkable until 1670 when he burst into public consciousness with the publication of his second book, *Theological-Political Treatise*. Even though the book was published anonymously, it was universally acknowledged to have been written by "the radical Jew." In this book, Spinoza argues that the Bible is a contradictory hodgepodge of different texts written at different times, that the true message of the Bible was merely to live a good moral life, that miracles were logically impossible, and that toleration of every view (even atheism) is the best way to create a stable society.

The book landed like a bomb and shocked the conscience of Europe, which was still recovering from the catastrophic Thirty Years' War—a war fought along religious lines and (at least partly) for religious reasons. One reviewer called it "a book forged in Hell!" Even Thomas Hobbes (no pale conformist) was shocked when he read it, saying that even "I derst not write so boldly!" The book was so shocking because it was believed at the time that peaceful societies must share a general culture and religion or risk collapse into civil war. It was generally thought that without belief in a transcendent God who oversaw a future judgment day, ordinary people would lack the motivation to be good—leading society to collapse into anarchy. By openly denying these views, the *Theological-Political Treatise* made Spinoza the single most controversial philosopher of the seventeenth century.

By the mid-1670s, Spinoza had finished his second major book, his masterpiece, *Ethics Demonstrated in a Geometrical Manner*. Although he brought the book to the printers, no one was willing to publish it. Spinoza was simply too much in the public eye after his revolutionary treatise and so he had to shelve plans to publish this (in some ways, even more provocative) work. He continued to work on a number of other books, however, including a *Political Treatise* and a book on *Hebrew Grammar*, but both were left unfinished when Spinoza died on 21 February 1677. He was 44. It seems likely that his early death was caused by breathing in so much glass dust as he ground his lenses. Spinoza's friends collected his manuscripts and the *Ethics* was published later that year. The book caused a sensation at least as great as the *Theological-Political Treatise*. It became an (illegal) best-seller and numerous religious philosophers would write refutations in the ensuing years.

The book shocked European society because it was the first serious attempt to develop an alternative "naturalistic" worldview in contrast to the classical Christian worldview that had dominated European thinking since the fall of Rome. The book was understood at the time to be a defense of "atheism," although we should keep in mind that that term meant many different things in the seventeenth and eighteenth centuries. But it is certainly true that Spinoza's book went much further in this direction than had any other major thinker of his time. He called into question almost all of the most important beliefs that organized the lives of his contemporaries. He argued that there is no transcendent personal God, no free will, no moral responsibility, no afterlife, and that everything that happens is absolutely logically necessary—so much so that it's impossible even to conceive clearly and distinctly an alternative way that things could have been. Furthermore, Spinoza argued that accepting all these things is good for us because it brings us peace of mind and helps us to overcome harmful negative emotions. As such, the book is not only a defense of a radically naturalistic philosophy, but a form of philosophical psychotherapy as well.

Spinoza's arguments were nearly universally rejected—only the most radical of people at the time were willing to accept the nonexistence of a personal God or the daunting implications of a world that functioned via absolute necessity. But Spinoza's arguments were not ignored, in fact, they were widely debated. The seventeenth and eighteenth centuries in Europe were a time of major scientific advance and a new rational view of the natural world was beginning to take hold. Many feared that this new rational, naturalistic, and scientific approach to the world would eventually call into question the mysteries of revealed religion. Most of the leading thinkers of the day (e.g., Leibniz, Descartes, and Locke) argued against this fear, claiming that religion was one thing and science another. They dealt with two different subjects and did not contradict one another. (This view remains popular even today.) Spinoza's book directly challenged this moderate, conciliatory view and argued that the new rational approach to the universe entails a *total rejection* of not only traditional religion, but many other "common sense" beliefs as well. Spinoza did not believe that the "scientific revolution" could be confined to how we understand the natural world alone. Rather, it required us to rethink all aspects of our lives. If we are going to take this revolution seriously, Spinoza argues, then we have to face the question: how does one live in a world without a personal God, free will, robust moral agency, or the hope of an afterlife? The *Ethics* was written precisely to answer this series of pressing questions.

II. ETHICS FOR A RATIONAL UNIVERSE

It might strike the modern reader as curious, but Spinoza's core project in this book is not metaphysical, but ethical (in the broad sense of that term). To understand what this means, we have to be clear about what 'ethics' means in this context. Today we tend to think of ethics as a set of rules that we have to follow. We ask whether certain acts (abortion, say) are morally right or wrong. Does the act violate some important rule or does restricting it violate such a rule? These are not Spinoza's questions. He does not think of ethics as fundamentally about rules. Instead, Spinoza's question is deeper, and better accords with earlier historical predecessors. His question is: How do I live a happy life? What this book is supposed to teach the reader is how to live a truly happy human life given the assumption that we live in a rational universe. In this way, Spinoza means by "ethics" what we might today call "psychotherapy." He argues that accepting his form of naturalism gives one the mental tools needed to overcome negative emotions as well. When we see clearly how everything works, we are free not only of delusion, but of shame, fear, guilt, regret, and sadness.

The single deepest philosophical change that Spinoza introduces is the rejection of mystery. According to classical theism, God cannot in principle be understood. Augustine famously claimed that "if you understand it, then it's not God." Even Thomas Aquinas argued that his claims about God are more wrong than right. God, on this view, always remains infinitely beyond our grasp. He always remains a mystery. For this reason, our understanding of the natural world can only go so far before we run into a major conceptual brick wall: the mystery of God. God is the Absolute Mystery at the center of everything that exists. It is because God is such a mystery that faith becomes so important. The religious question can be phrased as: Do you trust this mystery or not? Spinoza rejects this foundational assumption of the medieval world and instead believes that the universe is totally rational and completely comprehensible. There is nothing that, in principle, cannot be understood.

The rejection of mystery and acceptance of a completely rational universe has two important consequences that will fundamentally shape Spinoza's arguments in the Ethics. The first is Spinoza's acceptance of the Principle of Sufficient Reason. Given that Spinoza conceives the universe as being fully rationally ordered, he is committed to PSR—though he does not use this precise terminology. Since Spinoza maintains that everything that happens in the universe can be fully understood, it follows that everything that happens has an intelligible explanation. If something comes into existence, then there must be a cause that brought it into existence; nothing "just happens." The second major effect that the assumption of a rational universe has on Spinoza's arguments is that it permits a kind of inference that we can call a "Conceptual-Metaphysical Inference." Since the universe is entirely rational, we know that the relationships that actually exist in reality will be exactly mirrored in our concepts of these things. Or, stated more simply, if one thing depends on another to exist, then it follows that the concept of that first thing would likewise be dependent on the other to be known. When one thing cannot exist without the other, the thing can also not be conceived without the other. So, if it is the case that some A is metaphysically dependent upon some B out there in reality, then Spinoza infers that the concept or idea of A must also be conceptually dependent upon the concept or idea of B. For example, a fist (A) is something that is metaphysically dependent upon a hand (B). A fist is a particular shape of the hand, and so if there were no hands, then there would be no fists. Spinoza infers that this metaphysical dependence (i.e., this dependence in being) is mirrored in a conceptual dependence: the idea of a fist requires and involves an idea of a hand. This example seems clearly right, but Spinoza goes further and argues that the causes that bring things into existence (e.g., my parents) are also included in the very ideas of the things themselves (e.g., the idea of me). So any sufficiently accurate idea of me must involve that I was born of certain parents. Similarly, any sufficiently accurate idea of my parents must involve that they were born of certain people, etc. This conclusion is universal and applies not only to people, but to everything that could ever exist.

But if the metaphysical dependence among things is exactly mirrored by the conceptual dependence of the ideas of those things, then we can investigate reality either with our senses (and physically see how things are related to one another) or with our minds (and mentally see how the ideas of things are related to one another). In this way, the universe is "rationally transparent" to us: things are exactly as we (philosophers) conceive of them to be. The assumption of rational transparency explains what can at first be a bewildering aspect of Spinoza's writing, namely, his going back and forth between claims about things and claims about concepts. For example, in Part I, Spinoza will define a substance as something that is "in itself and conceived through itself; in other words, that whose concept does not require the concept of any other thing from which it must be formed." The metaphysical independence of substance entails a conceptual independence as well. The two always go together because the universe is fully rational.

III. THE GEOMETRICAL METHOD

Spinoza's view that the universe is entirely rational also partly explains his choice of method. Perhaps the most distinctive aspect of Spinoza's *Ethics* is its "geometrical method." This is the same type of method used by Euclid in his *Elements of Geometry*. This same method will be used a few years after the publication of Spinoza's *Ethics* in 1687 in another hugely influential work, Newton's *Principia Mathematica*. The "geometrical method" begins with *definitions* of key terms and with a list of *axioms* (fundamental assumptions). The argument then proceeds by deducing logical consequences from these definitions and axioms. Each *proposition* is supposed to follow logically from the definitions, axioms, and prior propositions. The argument for the proposition is spelled out in the *proof* that follows it. Sometimes a proof is followed by a *corollary* (which proves a closely related point) or a *scholium* or *explanation* (where Spinoza comments or elaborates on the argument).

The "geometrical method" is a logical method. If the definitions and axioms are well chosen and the author is careful about the deductions, then accepting the definitions and axioms will logically commit the reader to everything that follows. Reading works written in this way is not like reading more literary philosophers (such as Plato, Augustine, Hume, or Berkeley). It is best to read Spinoza's work very slowly and to pause after each definition, axiom, or proof to consider what exactly it means before moving on. It is also necessary at times to look back at the prior definitions, axioms, and propositions in order to remind yourself what they were.

Of course, if all of the *Ethics* is meant to be a derivation from a relatively small set of definitions and axioms, then one might wonder about how Spinoza determines these original definitions and axioms. This is certainly an appropriate question to ask, since whatever is derived from these initial grounds can only be as strong as the grounds themselves. Though it is both reasonable and appropriate to wonder about these (particularly when, at first reading, many of the definitions and axioms may strike a contemporary reader as making rather dubious assertions), Spinoza does not himself attempt to justify these grounding points. Indeed, for Spinoza, to attempt to justify these grounds would be both impossible and foolish. Spinoza would deny that these initial grounds require their own justifications insofar as these points are (i) not controversial, as being starting points shared by all his contemporaries, and (ii) self-evident by the light of reason. This last point is particularly significant. Recall how Spinoza is very familiar with the work of Descartes, who encountered significant difficulty when he attempted to justify principles of rationality. The famous "Cartesian Circle" is the problem that Descartes encounters when he attempts to prove that what is evident by the light of nature (i.e., what is clearly and distinctly known) is reliable. Rather than get trapped in such a Gordian knot, Spinoza cuts the inquiry off at self-evidence. With a supreme faith in the power of rationality, Spinoza denies that one could ever have or need any greater ground than self-evidence. As long as his initial definitions and axioms are uncontroversial and/or self-evident, Spinoza believes that nothing more can or should be asked of them.

IV. SUBSTANCE, ATTRIBUTES, AND MODES

When reading Spinoza for the first time, it will be helpful to be familiar with the most important concepts in his philosophy: substance, attribute, and mode.

Let's begin with substance. Substance is defined by its total and complete independence from everything else. That is, a substance is something that does not rely on anything else for its existence. For this reason, Spinoza disagrees with almost all of his predecessors who argue that there are many substances (e.g., cats, tables, people, mountains, cups, etc.). Spinoza will argue that since by definition a substance must be totally independent, there can only be one substance. Spinoza infers that in the final analysis only one thing exists, which we can call 'God' or 'Nature.' Because this one substance needs nothing else in order to exist, the idea of this substance is an idea that requires no other ideas from which it is formed. So the idea of substance is not like the idea of a bachelor, because the idea of a bachelor is composed of two other ideas (being male and being unmarried). These ideas are then composed out of component ideas as well, etc. The idea of a substance is an idea so simple that it has no component parts in this way: it's a basic foundational concept or idea.

In defining substance through its independence, Spinoza's account of substance follows the view offered (though not as strictly maintained) in Descartes. Spinoza also follows Descartes in how he defines the *attributes* of substance. Descartes defines the attribute of a substance as the essence of that thing. The essence of a thing tells you *what* the thing is. The essence is contrasted with the existence of a thing which tells you *that* a thing is. According to Descartes, there are only two attributes: thought (consciousness) and extension (being spread out in space). Thus, according to Descartes, everything that exists is either a mind (if it has the attribute of thought) or a body (if it has the attribute of extension). Spinoza adopts all of this with a few small but significant changes. Instead of saying that an attribute is the essence of a substance, Spinoza claims (in the fourth definition of Part I) that it is what the "intellect perceives" as constituting the essence of substance. The difference is significant because Spinoza will go on to argue that there is in reality only one substance and that it has many attributes. In noting that the attribute is what the "intellect perceives" of the essence of substance, this does imply error in the perception. Rather, it leaves space for Spinoza's monism. In attributes being ways that substance is perceived, there can be a multiplicity of correct perceptions of substance without there being multiplicity in substance itself.

Since the one substance in Spinoza has both the attribute of thought and the attribute of extension, this means that the essence of that substance can be correctly conceived of as either thought itself (basic awareness or consciousness) or as extension itself (being spread out in space). So, according to Spinoza, there are two ideas in the mind, both of which perfectly represent the essence of substance. While there is no exact parallel to Spinoza's theory of attributes, we do have mundane cases where one thing can produce multiple adequate and correct ideas in the mind. This is possible because we can describe things in different ways. So sometimes we have two ideas in the mind only to discover later that they are one and the same. For example, my wife and I own a cat named Sergeant Peppurr. She is a large gray cat. We also know that someone has been urinating on our rug (but we think it is the dog). So we have two ideas in our mind. First, we have the idea of Sgt. Peppurr. Second, the idea of the animal that is urinating on our rug. Later we learned that the cat had been the naughty one and discovered that those two ideas actually pick out one and the same thing in reality. Though clearly an imperfect analogy, Spinoza is similarly pointing to the idea that two clear and conceptually distinct ideas can both pick out one and the same object. Spinoza argues that our ideas of thought (awareness or consciousness) and extension (space) both pick out the same thing. Both of these distinct ideas correctly and adequately represent the essence of the one substance.

Though the Sgt. Peppurr analogy is obviously imperfect, it is a helpful starting point when trying to grasp what Spinoza is saying about the attributes of substance. Spinoza argues that the idea of each attribute is primitive or conceptually basic (e.g., not composed of other ideas). The idea of raw consciousness (thought) cannot be broken down any further. It's a simple idea with no "parts." You either have the idea or you do not. The same applies to the idea of space or spread-out-ness (extension). So in the mind we have these two conceptually basic ideas (thought and extension). Spinoza's claim is that both of those ideas are ideas of the essence of the one substance. These are two ideas of the same thing (as in the cat example). The only difference between Spinoza's case and the cat case is that the ideas involved are themselves conceptually basic. Normally, when we have two ideas of one thing these two ideas are complex, but in the case of attributes, Spinoza is claiming that two absolutely primitive ideas are both of the same thing (the essence of substance), that both of these ideas are fully adequate representations of it.

So what is the essence of substance? It depends upon how you choose to think about substance. We can conceive of substance "under the attribute of thought" or "under the attribute of extension." That is, we can think of the one substance as an infinite mind or as an infinite body. "Okay," you might ask, "but what is the essence of substance in itself apart from how we think about it?" Spinoza would find this question incoherent. Whenever we think of something, we have to think of it under some description or other. A man can be described as a biological organism, a father, a husband, a taxpayer, a therapist, a disabled person, etc., but any time we think about him, we must think about him under some description or other. The same is true of substance. When we think of substance we must think of it under some basic concept or other—that is, under some attribute or other—we cannot just think about it somehow as it is in itself. Unlike the case of the man, however, we have to use primitive concepts to think about the essence of substance because as a substance it does not depend upon anything else in order to "be or be conceived." Accordingly, the idea of it cannot depend upon any other idea. (Don't worry, reader, if these ideas seem dense and confusing at this point. They are explored again and again in the text itself.)

This leads us to our last major concept: the concept of mode or modification. A mode is a *way* that something is. Modes depend upon substance in order to exist. Consider the example of a fat cat. Being fat is a way that the cat is. The cat could lose weight and then it would no longer be fat. Perhaps it would become a skinny cat. Similarly, the cat is furry, snuggly, smug, at times ferocious, etc. Each of these are different ways that cats are. Though the cat could lose any of these particular traits and still exist as a cat, there would be no traits without there being some being that possesses those traits. In this way, modes are dependent on substance but not vice versa.

We need to be careful not to be led astray by our analogy here. Though we may refer to furriness as a way that the cat is, for Spinoza there is only one substance ('God' or 'Nature'). This one substance (despite Sgt. Peppurr's occasional smugness) is not a cat. Indeed, we must conclude that cats are not themselves substances at all. Cats must be modes of the one infinite substance! In fact, everything that exists (other than substance) must be simply a mode of that one substance. What does that mean? That means that a cat is just a furry, fat, snuggly, smug region of space. A cat is not itself a thing that exists independently, but only a way in which a region of space is being. As "the cat moves," what is happening according to Spinoza is that different regions of space are becoming furry, snuggly, and smug, etc. This claim is a difficult one to grasp and takes a lot of reflection because we are so used to thinking of cats, tables, mountains, and ourselves(!) as being independent substances. If there is only one substance, however, then the ways we are used to thinking must be wrong. All of these "things" must merely be ways in which the one substance is.

V. OUTLINE OF THE *ETHICS*

Approaching the dense thicket of arguments that make up this book is easier once one sees the "big picture" that Spinoza is defending. So before jumping into the work itself, let's briefly examine the core claims of each of the five parts. Some of what follows will be repeated in the commentary inserted into the text, but the points made here are sufficiently difficult that they bear repeating.

In Part I, Spinoza presents and defends his core metaphysical picture. He argues (as briefly discussed in the previous section) that there exists only one absolutely infinite substance (which can be called either 'God' or 'Nature'), and that this one substance has an infinite number of attributes. Each attribute is what the intellect perceives as being the essence of the substance (see previous section). This one substance then "expresses" itself in an infinite number of modes. These modes are properties or *ways* that the substance is. Everything else that exists (the whole physical universe) is just a way in which the substance happens to be at a particular part. Furthermore, substance is absolutely logically necessary, which means that its non-existence is a contradiction. To think of substance not existing is like thinking of something perfectly round and perfectly square at the same time. Since substance is absolutely necessary and since everything else that exists follows logically from this one substance, Spinoza infers that everything that happens is absolutely necessary. Nothing could have been even the slightest bit different from the way it is. There is only one way that things could be and that is how they are.

In Part II, Spinoza focuses on the nature of the human mind. He argues here that the mind and the body are one and the same thing understood in two ways. That is, we are just a complex collection of modes that can be understood either under the attribute of thought or extension. Furthermore, he argues that everything that exists in the physical universe has a mind (a view called *panpsychism*). All of these little minds/bundles of ideas (the mind of the desk, chair, computer, phone, me, shirt, etc.) when taken together form one infinite mind. That is, we can think of the one substance as an infinite mind thinking every possible thought. Our minds are just little bits of that giant thought.

In Part III, Spinoza turns to the nature of the emotions (affects) and begins his "philosophical psychotherapy" project. Here he defines the fundamental emotions as desire, sadness, and joy. In this discussion, Spinoza tries to show how the emotions are just an extension of the overall metaphysical pictures described above. Essential to this account is Spinoza's discussion of the *conatus* (i.e., the internal striving of all things). All things strive to exist. This striving is the very essence of a thing. This striving is what explains "desire." Anything that supports this striving is a source of joy (i.e., the transition to greater power), whereas anything that thwarts this striving is a source of sadness (i.e., the transition to lesser power).

In Part IV, Spinoza focuses on the question of why emotions have so much power over us. In this part he develops his general moral and political theories. He seeks to explain why some emotions are better than others, despite the fact that his metaphysics denies all teleology and contingency, as such a system would exclude traditional grounds for an "ought." Spinoza explains how better and worse emotions can be evaluated in terms of how they enable or inhibit a person's ability to thrive. In identifying the good with affects that promote human flourishing, he both explains that he is focusing on human nature in general and explains how goods are always relative to kinds. What is good for persons is not good "in general." Indeed, though what is good for one person is good for any person (insofar as they share a common nature), what is good for persons is not good for other animals since they possess different natures. To whatever degree there is difference in kinds, there will be differences in what is good for that kind. Thus, differences in kinds lead to conflict over the differing (and often contrary) goods sought by each kind.

In Part V, Spinoza ends with the more practical question of *how* to live the best human life, given that all things are determined and there is no teleology. As the good for persons is their activity/striving, Spinoza argues that one lives well when one is most successfully striving. To succeed in striving, one must be able to resist those affects that act in opposition to this striving. Here Spinoza identifies the usefulness of having a mind well-trained to think on general rules that promote joyful affects. Likewise, to best succeed in striving is to maximally exist. Here Spinoza presents his controversial discussion on the eternal aspects of minds. The more adequate ideas one has, the more ably one (as conceived under the attribute of thought) succeeds in its function. Likewise, the more adequate ideas one has, the more the mind exists eternally. As the most adequate ideas are ideas about God, the more one thinks about God, the more one succeeds in striving. Thus, a person's greatest joy (i.e., the means by which they best strive) is through the intellectual love of God.

Through these five parts, Spinoza moves from questions of abstract metaphysics to issues of daily life. Though many readers focus on the earlier portions of the text, the later parts were clearly issues of pressing concern for Spinoza. The questions that concerned Spinoza are clearly ones that are relevant today: How should we live in a naturalistic universe? Why be virtuous? What is morality? How should I deal with my emotions? These and other related questions of practical concern are a central part of Spinoza's overall project. By clarifying some of the trickier aspects of this text, we hope Spinoza's unique insights might more easily be brought to bear on these difficult but perennial questions.

VI. SUGGESTED FURTHER READINGS

Allison, Henry. 1987. *Benedict de Spinoza: An Introduction*. New Haven: Yale University Press.

—. 2022. *An Introduction to the Philosophy of Spinoza*. Cambridge: Cambridge University Press.

Bennett, Jonathan. 1984. *A Study of Spinoza's Ethics*. Indianapolis: Hackett.

Curley, Edwin. 1969. *Spinoza's Metaphysics: An Essay in Interpretation*. Cambridge, MA: Harvard University Press.

—. 1988. *Behind the Geometric Method*. Princeton: Princeton University Press.

Della Rocca, Michael. 2008. *Spinoza*. New York: Routledge.

—, ed. 2018. *The Oxford Handbook of Spinoza*. New York: Oxford University Press.

Garrett, Don, ed. 1996. *The Cambridge Companion to Spinoza*. Cambridge: Cambridge University Press.

—. 2018. *Nature and Necessity in Spinoza's Philosophy*. New York: Oxford University Press.

Israel, Jonathan I. 2023. *Spinoza: Life and Legacy*. Oxford: Oxford University Press.

Koistinen, Olli, ed. 2009. *The Cambridge Companion to Spinoza's Ethics*. Cambridge: Cambridge University Press.

Lin, Martin. 2019. *Being and Reason: An Essay on Spinoza's Metaphysics*. Oxford: Oxford University Press.

Melamed, Yitzhak. 2013. *Spinoza's Metaphysics: Substance and Thought*. Oxford: Oxford University Press.

—, ed. 2021. *A Companion to Spinoza*. Hoboken, NJ: Wiley Blackwell.

Nadler, Steven. 2018. *Spinoza: A Life*. 2nd ed. Cambridge: Cambridge University Press.

Steinberg, Justin. 2018. *Spinoza's Political Psychology: The Taming of Fortune and Fear*. Cambridge: Cambridge University Press.

Youpa, Andrew. 2020. *The Ethics of Joy: Spinoza on the Empowered Life*. Oxford: Oxford University Press.

Yovel, Yirmiyahu. 1989. *Spinoza and Other Heretics*. 2 vols. Princeton: Princeton University Press.

—, ed. 1991. *God and Nature: Spinoza's Metaphysics*. Leiden: Brill.

—, ed. 1999. *Desire and Affect: Spinoza as Psychologist*. New York: Little Room Press.

VII. SELECTED HISTORICAL TIMELINE

1513	Copernicus first outlines heliocentric theory, *Commentariolus*
1519	Luther posts Ninety-Five Theses
1534	Henry VIII issues Act of Supremacy (rejects papal control)
1543	Establishment of the Roman Inquisition Copernicus's *The Revolution of Heavenly Bodies* published
1550	Council of Trent (Counter-Reformation)
1567	Birth of Galileo (1567–1642)
1587/8	Birth of Spinoza's father, Michael
1596	Birth of Descartes (1596–1650)
1618–48	Catholic church rejects Copernican Theory
1619	Beginning of Thirty Years' War
1622	Spinoza's father arrives in Amsterdam
1632	Birth of John Locke (1632–1704)
1632	**Birth of Spinoza (1632–77)**
1637	Descartes's *Discourse on Method* published
1638	Spinoza's mother dies. Spinoza begins study of Talmud
1641	Descartes's *Meditations on First Philosophy* published
1643	Birth of Newton (1642–1726/7)
1646	Birth of Leibniz (1646–1716)
1648	End of Thirty Years' War; Peace of Westphalia
1649	Charles I of England beheaded
1651	Hobbes's *Leviathan* published; Spinoza first reads Descartes
1652	Spinoza begins lens grinding
1654	Death of Spinoza's father
1655	Spinoza is accused of heresy
1656	Spinoza is excommunicated from Amsterdam

1660	Amsterdam Synagogue petitions to denounce Spinoza as a "menace to all piety and morals"
1663	Spinoza moves to Voorburg (outside The Hague)
1665	Beginning of Second Anglo-Dutch War
1669	Spinoza moves to The Hague
	Spinoza anonymously publishes the *Theological-Political Treatise*, which is denounced by the Calvinist Church Council of Amsterdam
1673	Spinoza offered professorship at University of Heidelberg (which he declines over concerns about religious freedom)
1675	Spinoza finishes the *Ethics* but does not publish it
	Leibniz visits Spinoza in The Hague several times
1677	**Spinoza dies of a lung ailment** (likely related to lens grinding)
	Spinoza's friends publish *Ethics*, *Political Treatise*, *Hebrew Grammar*, and *Letters* under initials B.D.S.
1678	Dutch translation of Spinoza's works published
	States of Holland and States General formally ban Spinoza's philosophy
	Theologico-Political Treatise published in French under clandestine titles
1685	Birth of Berkeley (1685–1753)
1687	Newton's *Principia* published
1689	*Theologico-Political Treatise* becomes first work of Spinoza published in English
1695	Locke's *Essays Concerning Human Understanding* published
1711	Birth of Hume (1711–76)
1713	Berkeley's *A Treatise Concerning the Principles of Human Knowledge* published
1724	Birth of Kant (1724–1804)

Translator's Note

Benedict de Spinoza's *Ethica* was published in the original Latin in December 1677—several months after the philosopher's death—alongside other works in a volume titled *Opera Posthuma* ("posthumous works"). At the same time, a Dutch translation of these works was published under the title *Nagelate Schriften* (same meaning). Unfortunately, the original/standard Latin edition is marred by several errors, so that despite being closer to the author's intention, it cannot be used without some textual criticism. As a consequence, there have been several critical editions of the *Ethics*.

Especially in the first three parts, Gebhard, whose edition we follow, adds in chevrons (< >) words and phrases not found in the standard Latin edition but present in the Dutch one. His research led him to conclude that the translator had followed an earlier version of the Latin text; thus, the inserted words were later deleted by Spinoza himself. Gebhard nonetheless thinks that they should be included in his edition so that the reader can better understand Spinoza's thinking. The *Nagelate Schriften* include the Latin terms written in the margins.

The present translation is a heavily revised version of that by R.H.M. Elwes. The footnotes carry their author's name: some are by Spinoza himself, some by me, Domingo Aviles ("D.A."), some by Lisa Shapiro ("L.S."), and some by Elwes.

ETHICS

DEMONSTRATED IN A
GEOMETRICAL MANNER

PART I
CONCERNING GOD

DEFINITIONS

I. By *self-caused* I mean that whose essence involves existence, that is, that whose nature is only conceivable as existent.

> The *essence* (or nature) of a thing is *what* a thing is whereas the *existence* of a thing is *that* a thing is. Most essences do not include existence and so we can conceive of what it is while at the same time supposing that it does not really exist (e.g., a unicorn). But if something is *self-caused*, then the very idea of *what* it is includes existence. So, it cannot even be conceived as not existing.

II. A thing is called *finite after its kind* when it can be limited by another thing of the same nature. For instance, a body is called 'finite' because we can always conceive another bigger body. Likewise, a thought is limited by another thought, but a body is not limited by a thought, nor a thought by a body.

> The language of "limitation" may be unclear in this context. Here Spinoza is discussing how one thing can causally determine another. Just as one body excludes another body from existing in the same place at the same time in the same respect, one thought can exclude another thought. For example, I cannot simultaneously conceive of something being a triangle and its having four sides. The content of the one thought excludes the other. In this way, Spinoza is explaining how these sorts of limitations only occur within kinds. Which is to say, bodies exclude bodies, and thoughts exclude thoughts, whereas bodies do not exclude thoughts and *vice versa*.

III. By *substance* I mean that which is in itself and is conceived through itself; in other words, that whose concept does not require the concept of any other thing from which it must be formed.

> Spinoza defines substance in terms of its *independence*. A substance is not *metaphysically dependent* upon anything else for its existence. That is, it requires nothing other than itself in order to exist. Likewise, one can form the idea of a substance without using or relying on any other ideas. Just as a substance is the foundation of reality upon which everything else depends, so the idea of a substance is *conceptually basic* or completely simple and not composed of any other ideas.

IV. By *attribute* I mean that which the intellect perceives about a substance as constituting its essence.

> Descartes defines an attribute as simply the essence of a substance. According to him there are two basic attributes (*extension* which is the

essence of a body and *thought* which is the essence of a mind). In this definition Spinoza modifies Descartes's definition in an interesting way by saying that an *attribute* is what the intellect perceives the essence of a substance to be. Because Spinoza refers to the perception of the intellect in this definition, we know that the perception is accurate or correct. The intellect is not mistaken to perceive the essence of a substance as a given attribute.

V. By *mode* I mean the modifications [*affectiones*] of a substance, that is, that which exists in, and is conceived through, something other than itself.

> Spinoza uses the term *mode* for what we would today call a *property*, i.e., a *way* that something is. A mode (or property) is a feature that something has. For example, if we suppose for a moment that cats are substances (as Descartes suggests), then *being furry* is a mode (or property) of the cat. Notice that the cat's *being furry* cannot exist apart from the cat, nor can we even conceive of this cat's furriness without at the same time thinking of this cat. Modes are dependent beings whereas substances are independent. In Part I Spinoza uses the term "mode" and "modification" interchangeably.

VI. By *God* I mean a being absolutely infinite, that is, a substance consisting of an infinite number of attributes, each of which expresses an eternal and infinite essence.

> *Explanation.* I say 'absolutely infinite', not 'infinite after its kind'; this is because, when a thing is infinite only after its kind, we can negate an infinite number of attributes <that is, one can conceive of an infinite number of attributes that do not belong to its nature>; but that which is absolutely infinite contains in its essence whatever expresses essence and involves no negation.

> By "absolutely infinite" Spinoza means *entirely unlimited.* So, Spinoza infers that the essence of God (if it exists) must be such that every *concept* that can be used to conceive of the essence of *any substance at all* can be used to conceive of the essence of God. Otherwise the essence of God would be limited in some way (e.g., God would be limited insofar as we could not conceive of God under the attribute x). To see Spinoza's point here, note that we use concepts to conceive of things outside of our own minds. Some of the concepts that we use are conceptually basic (e.g., the concepts of *thought* or *extension*) and others are constructed from more fundamental concepts (e.g., the concept of a *bachelor* is constructed from the more basic concepts *unmarried* and *male*). The concepts that we use to conceive of the

essence of a substance (e.g., attributes) are conceptually basic. But Spinoza is here leaving open the logical possibility that it might be possible to correctly conceive of a given essence *using more than one attribute*. In fact, if there exists a substance that is totally and completely unlimited (God), then its essence must be correctly conceived by all of the concepts that can be used to conceive of the essence of any substance. Otherwise this essence would have a limitation, which an unlimited essence does not have.

VII. A thing is called *free* if it exists solely by the necessity of its own nature and if it is determined to act by itself alone. On the other hand, a thing is necessary, or rather forced, if it is caused to exist and to act by something else in a fixed and determined way.

It is important to distinguish the idea of *freedom* in Spinoza from the idea of *free will* (in an incompatibilist sense, i.e., in the sense that freedom means having alternative possibilities). A thing is free when its own essence causes it to do something. That is not to say that the thing *freely chooses* to do it or *could have done otherwise than it did*. Spinoza will later reject the coherence of free will in the sense of choosing one thing rather than another (that is to say, a sense of free will that depends on the principle of alternative possibilities). But things can be free in Spinoza's sense without having this sort of free will. Things are free when they act from their own natures, unfree when other things force them to act.

VIII. By *eternity* I mean existence itself in so far as it is conceived to follow necessarily from the definition of an eternal thing alone.

Explanation. Existence of this kind is conceived of as an eternal truth like the essence of a thing; therefore, it cannot be explained by means of duration or time, even if we conceive duration as lacking a beginning and an end.

Spinoza is using the term 'eternity' in the sense of *timeless* or *atemporal*, not in the sense of *existing at all moments of time* (sometimes called *sempiternal*). Eternal things do not exist in time at all.

AXIOMS

I. Everything that exists, exists either in itself or in something else.

That is, everything that exists is either metaphysically dependent upon something else or it is not.

II. That which cannot be conceived through anything else must be conceived through itself.

III. From a given definite cause an effect necessarily follows; conversely, if no definite cause is given, it is impossible for an effect to follow.

> Here Spinoza is assuming that causation is not probabilistic. It is never the case that a cause produces an effect (say) only 50 percent of the time. Nor can it be the case that a cause sometimes produces one effect and at other times produces another. The same cause *always* results in the same effect—every single time.

IV. The idea of an effect depends on and involves the idea of a cause.

> The term translated here as 'idea' is '*cognitio*', which can have a wide range of meanings (including knowledge, conception, and acquaintance). But the claim being made here is reasonably straightforward. Because an effect is metaphysically dependent upon its cause, the idea of the effect must be conceptually dependent upon the idea of the cause. So, when we conceive of some effect, we must at the same time have some (usually very confused and incomplete) idea of the cause of that effect. Intuitively, to adequately understand the nature of the broken window, one would need to have knowledge of the baseball's having come into contact with a particular piece of glass.

V. Things that have nothing in common cannot be understood by means of one another; in other words, the concept of one does not involve the concept of the other.

VI. A true idea must correspond to its object [*ideatum*].[1]

> For an idea to be true it must represent things the way that they really are. Here Spinoza is assuming some kind of correspondence theory of truth. An idea is made true in virtue of corresponding to the way things are.

VII. If a thing can be conceived as non-existing, its essence does not involve existence.

---

1 See p. 115, n. 1.

PROPOSITIONS

PROP. I. *Substance is by nature prior to its modifications.*

Proof. This is clear from Def. 3 and 5.

> The kind of *priority* that Spinoza is referring to here must be both a metaphysical and conceptual priority. A substance cannot be in any way dependent upon its modes for its existence. Nor can the idea of a substance require the idea of any particular mode.

PROP. II. *Two substances whose attributes are different have nothing in common.*

Proof. Also evident from Def. 3. For each of them must exist in itself and be conceived through itself; in other words, the conception of one does not involve the conception of the other.

PROP. III. Things that have nothing in common cannot be the cause of one another.

> Here Spinoza directly addresses the interaction problem that had plagued Descartes. Rather than posit a mysterious means by way of which minds and bodies could interact, Spinoza just sees it as self-evident that such interaction is impossible and incoherent. Things that have nothing in common (i.e., things that are essentially different), have no common nature by means of which they can interact.

Proof. If they have nothing in common, it follows that they cannot be understood through each other, either (Ax. 5); therefore, one cannot be the cause of the other (Ax. 4). *Q.E.D.*

PROP. IV. Two or more distinct things are distinguished from one another either by the difference of the attributes of the substances or by the difference of their modifications.

> This claim maps the logical space of Spinoza's metaphysical framework. All that exists is substance, attributes, and modes. Because 'substance' refers to the simple concept of a thing as independent, there is no ground for a distinction possible in the nature of substance itself. As such, if there are to be any distinctions, they must be found in attributes or modes.

Proof. Everything that exists, exists either in itself or in something else (Ax. 1); that is, there is nothing outside the intellect except substances and their modifications (Def. 3 and 5). Consequently, outside the intellect there is nothing by which several things can be distinguished from one another except the substances or—which is the same (Def. 4)—their attributes and modifications. *Q.E.D.*

Everything that exists is either a substance, attribute, or a mode. As, however, attribute is just the essence of a substance (by means of which we can conceive of the substance), all that exists is substance or modes.

PROP. V. *There cannot exist in the universe two or more substances having the same nature or attribute.*

Proof. If several distinct substances existed, they would have to be distinguished from one another either by the difference of their attributes or by the difference of their modifications (previous Prop.). If only by the difference of their attributes, it will be granted that there cannot be more than one with the same attribute; and if by the difference of their modifications—as substance is naturally prior to its modifications (Prop. 1)—it follows that if we set the modifications aside and consider substance in itself, that is, truly (Def. 3 and 6), it cannot be conceived as different from another, that is, there cannot be several substances but one substance only (previous Prop.). *Q.E.D.*

If two substances are different from each other then there must be a reason why they are different. If there were no reason for their being different, then they would be the same. That reason cannot be found in the nature of *substance* itself since *substance* only includes the simple concept of independence. Likewise, two substances cannot be different only on account of their modes because this would make a substance metaphysically and conceptually dependent upon its mode (violating the absolute and total independence of a substance). Now suppose that we have two substances with the same nature or essence (i.e., of the same attribute). Why are there two substances rather than just one in this case? It cannot be because they have different essences (by hypothesis), so it must again be because they have different modes. However, the same problem arises. Modes cannot distinguish substances from each other without making the substance dependent on modes (an impossibility). One might intuitively conceive this via an analogy with two books: one red and one blue. When looking for a ground of the distinction between the two books, one might note that there must be two books because one and the same book cannot be both red all over and blue all over. In this way, one might suppose that a difference in mode might ground a difference in substance. Spinoza rejects this line of reasoning by noting that it is incorrect to say that there are two books *because* of their difference in color, since the very possibility of a difference in color required the prior metaphysical facts that there were two books that could bare these distinct properties. Since substances cannot be dependent on modes without violating the independence of substances, there cannot be multiple instances of one essence. Instead of there being many bodies and many minds, as Descartes supposed, Spinoza now infers that there can be at most one body and one mind.

PROP. VI. *One substance cannot be produced by another substance.*

Proof. It is impossible for there to be in the universe two substances with an identical attribute (previous Prop.), i.e., which have anything common to them both (Prop. 2). Therefore, they cannot be the cause of one another (Prop. 3); in other words, they cannot be produced by each other. *Q.E.D.*

Corollary. From this it follows that a substance cannot be produced by anything other than itself. For in the universe nothing exists except substances and their modifications (as appears from Ax. 1 and Def. 3 and 5); furthermore, a substance cannot be produced by another substance (Prop. 5). Therefore, it absolutely cannot be produced by anything other than itself. *Q.E.D.*

> If all that exists are substances and modes, and a mode cannot cause a substance (without violating the independence of substance), then a substance cannot be caused by anything but itself. It cannot be caused by another substance, because the only things that can causally interact are things of the same nature (essence/attribute), and there cannot be multiple things of the same attribute (Prop V).

Another proof. This is shown even more easily by the absurdity of the contrary Proposition. For if a substance could be produced by something else, the knowledge of it would depend on the knowledge of its cause (Ax. 4); consequently, it would not be a substance (Def. 3).

PROP. VII. *Existence belongs to the nature of a substance.*

Proof. A substance cannot be produced by anything else (Corollary to Prop. 6); it must therefore be its own cause, that is, its essence involves existence (Def. 1); in other words, existence belongs to its nature. *Q.E.D.*

> Spinoza is assuming, of course, that *something* exists. But if something exists, then at least one substance exists (a mode cannot exist on its own). But a substance cannot be brought into existence by another

substance, so either a substance exists for *no reason whatsoever* or it is *self-caused* (that is, exists necessarily). But Spinoza assumes that the universe is rational and so it obeys the *Principle of Sufficient Reason*. According to this principle, there must be an explanation for everything that exists. But if a substance came to be for no reason at all, then there would be no explanation as to why it exists. So, every substance that exists must be self-caused or have existence as part of its nature. In this way, there is a sufficient explanation for the substance's existence within its nature.

PROP. VIII. *Every substance is necessarily infinite.*

Proof. There can only be one substance with the same attribute (Prop. 5), and existence belongs to its nature (Prop. 7); its nature, therefore, involves existence, either as finite or infinite. It does not exist as finite, for it would then be limited by another substance of the same kind (Def. 2), which would also necessarily exist (Prop. 7), so that there would be two substances with the same attribute, which is absurd (Prop. 5). It therefore exists as infinite. *Q.E.D.*

Scholium I. As finiteness is, in fact, a partial negation and infinity is the absolute affirmation of the existence of a given nature, it follows from Prop. 7 alone that every substance is necessarily infinite, <because if one should posit substance as finite, one would be negating [*negare*] that part of its nature that is essential for its being [*existere*]; which is (*according to the previous Prop.*) absurd>.

One thing to note in this passage is that the idea of the infinite is conceptually prior to the idea of the finite. Infinite does not mean not-finite; rather, finite means not-infinite. This is evident insofar as Spinoza having already established that substance must have existence in its nature (in order for there to be a sufficient explanation for the existence of anything), he proposes that the "type" of existence contained in this nature would have to be either finite or infinite (given logical space). But, for the type of existence contained in substance to be finite, some additional fact would be required. There would need to be some limiting factor that established this existence as finite, whereas no additional factor is needed to explain existence as infinite. This priority is best understood by noting how Spinoza has distinguished finite and infinite in terms of limited versus unlimited. A limit requires an additional thing which *limits*, whereas nothing additional is required to explain unlimited.

Scholium II. I do not doubt that all those who think about things confusedly and are not accustomed to knowing them by their primary causes will find it difficult to comprehend the proof of Prop. 7—quite naturally, since they do not distinguish between the modifications of substances and the substances themselves and are ignorant of the way things are produced. Hence, they attribute to substances the principle they observe in natural objects: those who are ignorant of the true causes of things confuse everything and imagine without any embarrassment that trees might talk just as well as people, and imagine that people might be formed from stones as well as from seed or that any form might be changed into any other. Likewise, those who confuse divine and human nature readily attribute to God human feelings, especially so long as they do not know how feelings originate in the mind. On the other hand, if people would consider the nature of substance, they would have no doubt about the truth of Prop. 7; in fact, this Proposition would be a universal axiom and be considered a truism. For under 'substance' they would understand that which is in itself and is conceived through itself, that is, something the knowledge of which does not require the knowledge of anything else; under 'modifications',[1] on the other hand, they would understand things that exist in something else and whose concept is formed through the concept of the thing in which they exist. Thus, we can have true ideas of non-existent modifications; for although they may have no actual existence apart from the conceiving intellect, their essence is contained in something else in such a way that they can be conceived through it. Substances, on the other hand, have no truth outside the intellect except in themselves, because they are conceived through themselves. Consequently, if someone should claim to have a clear and distinct—that is, true—idea of a substance but nonetheless doubt whether such a substance exists, it would be the same as if one claimed to have a true idea but nonetheless not be sure whether it was false, as is plain to see with a little reflection; or if anyone affirmed that substance is created, it would be the same as saying that a false idea has become true, which is the most absurd notion possible. It must then necessarily be admitted that the existence of a substance as well as its essence is an eternal truth. And we can hence conclude, by another process of

---

1 *Modificationes*, whereas above S. calls them *affectiones*. (D.A.)

reasoning, that there is but one substance of a given nature, which I think it will be worthwhile for me to demonstrate at this point. To do this properly, I must first point out the following:

1. The true definition of each thing neither involves nor expresses anything beyond the nature of the thing defined. From this follows the next point:
2. No definition involves or expresses a particular number of individuals, since it expresses nothing beyond the nature of the thing defined. For instance, the definition of a triangle expresses nothing beyond the actual nature of a triangle; it does not imply any fixed number of triangles.
3. It should be noted that, for each individual existent thing, there must be a cause for its existence.
4. It should finally be noted that this cause for the existence of any given thing must either be contained in the very nature and definition of the thing defined (because its existence belongs to its nature) or exist outside of it.

These statements are the clearest passages concerning Spinoza's understanding of what a *definition* of a thing consists in. A definition of a thing consists in a statement of its essence only.

From these premises it follows that, if a given number of individual things exist in nature, there must be some cause for why exactly those individual things exist and not more or fewer. For example, if twenty people exist in the universe (for clarity's sake, I will suppose that they exist simultaneously and have had no predecessors), it will not be enough (that is, to explain why there are precisely twenty people) to show the cause of human nature in general, but we must also show why there are neither more nor fewer than twenty; for there must be a cause for the existence of each individual (Note 3). Now this cause cannot be contained in human nature itself (Notes 2 and 3), for the true definition of humanity does not involve the number twenty. Thus, the cause for the existence of these twenty people and, consequently, of each of them must necessarily be sought outside of each individual (Note 4). Therefore, we must draw the universal conclusion that everything of whose nature there can be several individuals must have an external cause for their existence. And since the nature of substance involves existence (as has already been shown in this Schol.), its definition must involve necessary existence; consequently, its existence must follow from its definition alone. But from its definition we cannot infer the existence of several substances (as we have shown in Notes 2 and 3); it follows necessarily that there is only one substance of the same nature, as we have posited.

Spinoza's reasoning here is fairly clear even if his terminology is somewhat confusing. The existence of a substance follows from its definition because the definition of a thing involves a statement of its essence and a substance's essence includes existence. But if substances were such that there could be many of a single kind, then the cause of their existence would have to be outside of them. But the cause of a substance's existence is internal to its essence, not external. For substance to have some additional limiting cause would require that there be something external to substance that could limit the existence given by the essence of substance. But nothing could limit substance without causally interacting with it, and there can be nothing to interact with substance unless there can be two things of one attribute (Prop V).

PROP. IX. *The more reality or being a thing has, the larger is the number of its attributes.*

Proof. This is evident from Def. 4.

This proof is extremely obscure. Definition IV reads: "By *attribute* I mean that which the intellect perceives about a substance as constituting its essence." Spinoza has not defined what it means to say that something has "more reality or being," but his reasoning here might be something like the following: The more being a thing has, the fewer limitations it has. A thing's essence can be correctly conceived according to some number of attributes. The fewer limitations a thing has, the greater the number of ideas can be used to correctly conceive of its essence. In this way, a substance that had an essence that could only be conceived of according to one attribute (e.g., an *extended* substance) would be more limited than a substance that had an essence that could be conceived of according to multiple attribute ideas (e.g., using both the idea of *extension* and the idea of *thought*).

PROP. X. *Each particular attribute of the one substance must be conceived through itself.*

Proof. An attribute is that which the intellect perceives of a substance as constituting its essence (Def. 4) and must therefore be conceived through itself (Def. 3). *Q.E.D.*

Scholium. It is thus evident that, though two attributes are in reality conceived as distinct—that is, without the help of each other—we still cannot conclude from it that they constitute two entities, that is, two different substances. For it is the nature of substance that each of its attributes is conceived through itself, as all the attributes it has have always existed simultaneously in it and none of them can have been produced by another, but each expresses the reality, or being, of a substance. It is, then, far from an absurdity to ascribe several attributes to one substance; on the contrary, nothing in nature is clearer than the fact that each and every entity must be conceived under some attribute and that the more reality or being it possesses, the more attributes it has expressing necessity—that is, eternity—and infinity. Consequently, there is also nothing clearer than that an absolutely infinite being must necessarily be defined as consisting of an infinite number of attributes each of which expresses a specific eternal and infinite essence (as we expounded in Def. 6). And should anyone ask by what sign we shall be able to distinguish different substances, let them read the following Propositions, which show that there is only one substance in the universe and that it is absolutely infinite, so that such a sign would be sought in vain.

This important proof is extremely dense. Spinoza's reasoning here may be something like the following: Each idea of an attribute in our minds (e.g., the idea of extension or the idea of thought) is conceived of as distinct from all of the other attributes. Each attribute idea is conceptually basic and so is not made up of any more basic ideas. But just because two ideas are distinct it does *not* follow that they must pick out two different things in the world. We can see this with many prosaic examples where things that we once thought were distinct (e.g., the morning star, the evening star, and Venus) turn out to be one and the same thing conceived in different ways. In the Venus case we have three conceptually distinct ideas, but all three ideas pick out just one object. We see the same phenomenon here except that in Spinoza's case the ideas that he is considering are each *conceptually basic* and each one is a different way of conceiving of one and the same external thing, namely, the essence of substance. But each of these different ways of conceiving of the essence of substance are equally correct. No attribute is better or worse than any other. Each one captures fully the essence of substance.

One may be tempted to ask what the essence of substance is like *in itself* apart from our different conceptions of it. But this question is nonsensical. In order to conceive of the essence of substance we must employ an attribute idea. We must conceive of substance using some basic or foundational idea. There is no way to conceive of the essence of substance without employing some basic concept.

PROP. XI. *God, that is, a substance consisting of an infinite number of attributes each of which expresses eternal and infinite essence, necessarily exists.*

Proof. If you deny this, conceive, if possible, that God does not exist. Consequently, his essence does not involve existence (Ax. 7). But this is absurd (Prop. 7). Therefore, God necessarily exists. *Q.E.D.*

As many commentators have pointed out there seems to be a rather significant problem with this proof. It is not clear how Spinoza rules out the option of an infinite number of distinct substances each having only one attribute (or other related options). God's existence excludes the existence of all one-attribute substances. But similarly, the existence of even a single one-attribute substance excludes the existence of God. It is unclear how we get from this claim to the conclusion that it must be God that is the substance that exists. It is perhaps to deal with this problem that Spinoza adds the following additional proofs.

Another proof. Each thing must have a cause (that is, a reason) assigned to it, either for its existence or for its non-existence. For instance, if the triangle exists, there must be a reason, or cause, for its existence; if, on the contrary, it does not exist, there must also be a reason, or cause, that prevents it from existing, in other words, removes its existence. This reason or cause must either be contained in the nature of the thing in question or be external to it. For instance, the reason for the non-existence of a square circle is indicated by its very nature: because it would involve a contradiction. On the other hand, the existence of a substance follows solely from its nature, too, namely because its nature involves existence (Prop. 7). The reason for the existence or non-existence of the triangle or the circle, however, does not follow from the nature of those figures but from the order of the entire material nature: from the latter it must follow either that the triangle necessarily exists or that it is impossible for it to exist. All of this is self-evident. It follows that a thing necessarily exists if there is no reason or cause that would prevent its existence. If, then, no cause or reason can be given that prevents the existence of God, in other words, removes his existence, we must certainly conclude that he necessarily does exist. If such a reason or cause existed, however, it would have to either be rooted in God's very nature or be external to it, that is, rooted in another substance of another nature. For if it were of the same nature, that very fact would be an admission that God exists; a substance of another nature <than the divine one>, on the other hand, could have nothing in common with God (Prop. 2), and therefore would be unable either to cause or to remove his existence. As, then, a reason, or cause, that would remove the divine existence cannot exist outside of the divine nature, this cause will necessarily, if God does not exist, have to be rooted in God's own nature, a nature that would therefore, <following our second example> involve a contradiction. Yet to make such a claim about a being absolutely infinite and supremely perfect is absurd; therefore, neither in the nature of God nor outside of it is there a cause, or reason, that would remove his existence; therefore, God necessarily exists. *Q.E.D.*

> In this proof Spinoza clearly accepts the Principle of Sufficient Reason in a very strong form. Not only must there be a reason for the *existence* of each thing that exists, but there must also be a reason for the *nonexistence* of each thing that fails to exist. Thus, Spinoza infers that "a thing necessarily exists if there is no reason or cause that would prevent its existence." The types of reasons that might prevent a thing's existence would either be internal or external to a thing. An external cause would need to block the existence of substance. Of course, a minimal feature of such a cause would be that it would be able to interact with substance to provide this block. As there can be no interaction without there being two things of the same attribute, nothing can exist outside of substance that would block its existence. An internal cause for a thing's nonexistence would be an impossible or contradictory nature; e.g., the fact that there are no square triangles in the world can be explained by looking at the concept itself. Spinoza claims, however, that there is nothing in principle that could prevent the existence of a "being absolutely infinite and supremely perfect." Thus, such a being must exist. Though this last claim is hasty, Spinoza seems to be offering an interesting variation of the classical *Ontological Argument* here. This argument may also resolve the significant problem noted above with the formal proof for Prop IX.

Another proof. Being able not to exist is lack of power and, conversely, the ability to exist is a power (which is self-evident). If, then, what necessarily exists is nothing but finite beings, finite beings are more powerful than a being absolutely infinite, and this is absurd (which is self-evident). Therefore, either nothing exists or a being absolutely infinite necessarily exists also. Now we exist either in ourselves or in something else that necessarily exists (Axiom. 1 and Prop. 7). Therefore, a being absolutely infinite—that is, God (Def. 6)—necessarily exists. *Q.E.D.*

Scholium. In this last proof I have purposely shown God's existence *a posteriori* in order that the proof might be more easily followed, not because, from the same premises, God's existence does not follow *a priori*. For since the ability to exist is power, it follows that the more reality the nature of a thing possesses, the greater the strength it has in virtue of itself for existence; consequently, a being absolutely infinite—that is, God—has in virtue of itself an absolutely infinite power of existence, and hence absolutely does exist. Perhaps many will be unable to see the force of this proof because they are accustomed to considering only those things that flow from external causes, and they see that those kinds of things quickly come to pass—that is, easily come into existence—easily disappear as well and, conversely, regard as more difficult to accomplish—that is, not so easy to bring into existence—those things that they conceive as being made up of more elements. To rid them of this misconception, however, I need not show in which respect the proverb 'What comes quickly, goes quickly' is true, nor need I discuss whether, from the point of view of universal nature, all things are equally easy or otherwise; it will suffice to point out that I am not speaking of things that come into existence through external causes but only of substances, which cannot be produced by any external cause (Prop. 6). For those things that are produced by external causes, whether they consist of many parts or few, owe whatever perfection, or reality, they possess solely to the efficacy of their external cause; therefore, their existence arises solely from the perfection of their external cause, not from their own. Conversely, whatever perfection a substance possesses is due to no external cause; thus, the existence of a substance must follow solely from its own nature, which is thus nothing but its essence. Consequently, the perfection of a ·thing does not remove its existence but, on the contrary, asserts (*ponit*) it; imperfection, on the other hand, does remove it; therefore, we cannot be more certain of the existence of anything than of the existence of a being absolutely infinite, that is, perfect, namely God. For since his essence excludes all imperfection and involves absolute perfection, it in and of itself removes all cause for doubt concerning his existence and provides the utmost certainty on the question. This, I think, will be evident to anyone who pays any attention to the matter.

> To understand Spinoza's claims about "perfection" in this argument, it is important to note that, according to Spinoza, being comes in degrees. Existing is not an *all-or-nothing* matter, but is a matter of *more-or-less*. Things can gain and lose *being* and some things have more *being* than others. The more a thing depends on something else for its being, the more limited it is. Conversely, the more being a thing has, the fewer limitations it has. A thing that is unlimited would thereby have the most possible being. This is offered as an *a posteriori* proof insofar as it begins with the evident fact that some (limited) things exist. Given that these finite/limited things obviously have sufficient being to exist, Spinoza argues that it is absurd to imagine a thing that is infinite/unlimited would somehow fail to exist.

PROP. XII. *No attribute of a substance can truthfully be conceived from which it would follow that that substance can be divided.*

Proof. The parts into which substance as thus conceived would be divided will either retain the nature of the substance or they will not. If the former, <namely that they maintain the nature of the substance,> then each part will necessarily be infinite (Prop. 8) and self-caused (Prop. 6) and will necessarily consist of a different attribute (Prop. 5), so that several substances could be formed out of one substance, which is absurd (Prop. 6). Moreover, the parts would have nothing in common with their whole (Prop. 2), and the whole could both exist and be conceived without its parts (Def. 4 and Prop. 10), which everyone will admit is absurd. If we adopt the second alternative, namely that the parts will not retain the nature of the substance, it will then follow that, if the whole substance were divided into equal parts, it would lose the nature of the substance and cease to exist, which is absurd (Prop. 7).

PROP. XIII. *An absolutely infinite substance is indivisible.*

Proof. If it could be divided, the parts into which it was divided would either retain the nature of the absolutely infinite substance or they would not. If the former, there will then be several substances of the same nature, which is absurd (Prop. 5). If the latter, an absolutely infinite substance could cease to exist (as demonstrated above), which is also absurd (Prop. 11).

Corollary. It follows that no substance, and consequently no material substance, in so far as it is a substance, is divisible.

> Spinoza's claim here is that the whole of substance is both conceptually and metaphysically prior to any of its parts. Any part of substance (e.g., a region of space) is always a mental breaking away in the mind from the whole (e.g., space). In this way there are only "potential parts" in Spinoza or parts that we choose to recognize in the one substance. Substance is not made up of an infinite number of small points that are then put together; rather there is the one substance first and we can choose to mentally divide it up later into various regions when we think about it. For more on this, see the *scholia* after Prop XV below. This priority is established via a *reductio*, whereby Spinoza imagines what would follow if an infinite thing could be divided. Spinoza argues that this is impossible because the thing would either remain or fail to remain infinite after such a definition, and that since both outcomes are impossible, dividing the infinite is impossible. (It's worth noting that Spinoza's understanding of infinite here described is not consistent with contemporary accounts—as further discussed in the note on Prop XV.)

Scholium. The indivisibility of a substance can be more easily understood from the mere fact that the nature of a substance can only be conceived as infinite and that by a part of a substance nothing can be understood other than finite substance, which involves an obvious contradiction (Prop. 8).

PROP. XIV. *Besides God no substance can exist or be conceived.*

Proof. Given that God is a being absolutely infinite of which no attribute can be negated that expresses the essence of substance (Def. 6) and he necessarily exists (Prop. 11), if there were any substance besides God, it would have to be explained by some attribute of God, and thus two substances with the same attribute would exist, which is absurd (Prop. 5). Therefore, there can be no substance besides God and, consequently, none can be conceived. For if it could be conceived, it would necessarily have to be conceived as existent; but this is absurd (first part of this proof). Therefore, besides God no substance can exist or be conceived. *Q.E.D.*

> This proposition differs from Prop 11 above in that here Spinoza infers not only the existence of God, but the existence of no other substance other than God. Spinoza is arguing not only that God exists, but that God is the *only thing* that exists.

Corollary I. From this it very clearly follows that (1) God is one, that is, only one substance can exist in the universe and that substance is absolutely infinite (Def. 6), as we have already indicated (Schol. Prop. 10).

Corollary II. It follows that (2) an extended thing and a thinking thing are either attributes of God or modifications of God's attributes (Ax. 1).

PROP. XV. *Whatever exists, exists in God, and without God nothing can exist or be conceived.*

Proof. Besides God no substance exists or can be conceived (Prop. 14), that is, nothing that is in itself and is conceived through itself (Def. 3). But modes can neither exist nor be conceived without substance (Def. 5); thus, they can only exist in the divine nature and can be conceived only through it. Now besides substances and modes there is nothing (Ax. 1); therefore, without God nothing can exist or be conceived. *Q.E.D.*

Scholium. Some portray God as consisting of body and mind, like a human being, and subject to passions; however, how far these people have strayed from the true knowledge of God is sufficiently evident from what has already been demonstrated. But these I shall pass over, for anyone who has in any way reflected on God's nature rejects the notion that he is material. They find excellent proof of this in the fact that under 'body' we understand some quantity—so long, so broad, so deep—limited by a certain shape, and there can be nothing more absurd than to represent God, that is, a being absolutely infinite, in such terms. At the same time, however, they show through the other reasons with which they try to prove this same point that they completely remove the material, that is, extended substance as such from God's nature and claim that it was created by God. Yet they have no idea what divine power it could have been created by, which clearly shows that they do not understand their own theory. I at least have, I think, proved sufficiently clearly that no substance can be produced or created by anything other than itself (Coroll. Prop. 6 and Schol. 2 Prop. 8). Furthermore, I have shown in Prop. 14 that besides God no substance can exist or be conceived. Hence, <in the second addition [*corollarium*] to the same

Proof in this part> we concluded that extended substance is one of the infinite attributes of God. However, in order to explain more fully, I will refute the arguments of my adversaries, which can all be reduced to the following points:

First, material substance, in so far as it is substance, consists, they think, of parts; hence they deny that it can be infinite and, consequently, that it can be part of God. This they illustrate with many examples, of which I will take one or two. If material substance, they say, is infinite, let us imagine that it is divided into two parts; each part will then be either finite or infinite. If the former is the case, something infinite is composed of two finite parts, which is absurd. If the latter, <to wit, that each part is infinite,> then one infinity will be twice as large as another infinity, which is also absurd. Further, if an infinite quantity is measured in parts equal to feet, it will have to consist of an infinite number of such parts, just as it will if it were measured in parts equal to inches; therefore, one infinity would be twelve times as big as the other, <which is no less absurd>.

> This argument concerning the absurdity of one "infinite" being larger than another infinite will strike the contemporary mathematician as naïve. Mathematical developments in set theory made in the nineteenth and twentieth centuries developed a more precise concept of "infinity" whereby infinite sets can have proper subsets that are equinumerous with the whole set. It is important to note here that Spinoza does not endorse this argument, but will reject it below.

Lastly, if we conceive two lines being drawn from a single point of some infinite quantity (let us say AB and AC), whose distance from each other is at the beginning well determined, but which are extended to infinity, no doubt the distance between the B and C will continually increase and eventually change from definite to indefinite. Since, they claim, such

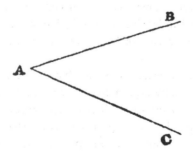

absurdities follow from positing an infinite quantity, they conclude that material substance must necessarily be finite and thus cannot be part of God's essence.

The second argument is also drawn from God's supreme perfection. God, they say, being a supremely perfect being, cannot be acted upon; material substance, however, being divisible, can; it follows that material substance is not part of the essence of God.

Such are the arguments I find on the subject in writers who try to prove that material substance is unworthy of the divine nature and cannot possibly be part of it. However, an attentive reader will see that I have already answered their objections, as these arguments are based entirely on the notion that material substance is composed of parts, a notion that I have shown to be absurd (Prop. 12 and Coroll. Prop. 13). Moreover, anyone who wants to look at the issue in the proper way will see that all these absurdities (assuming that they are all absurdities in the first place, which I am not going to discuss here) on whose grounds they want to prove that extended substance is finite by no means follow from positing an infinite quantity, but merely from the notion that an infinite quantity is measurable and composed of finite parts. Thus, from the absurdities that follow from it they can only conclude that infinite quantity is not measurable and cannot be composed of finite parts. But this is exactly what we have already proved (Prop. 12 etc.). So, in fact, they are hoist with their own petard. If, from this absurdity of theirs, they persist in drawing the conclusion that extended substance must be finite, they are doing nothing different from somebody who asserts that circles have the properties of squares and then concludes that circles have no center from which lines are drawn to the circumference that have the same length. For in order to prove that material substance, which can only be conceived as infinite, one, and indivisible (Prop. 8, 5, and 12), is finite, they conceive it as composed of finite parts as well as manifold and indivisible.

Likewise, others, after asserting that a line is composed of points, can find many arguments to prove that a line cannot be infinitely divided. And surely it is no less absurd to assert that material substance is made up of bodies, or parts, than it would be to assert that a body is made up of surfaces, the surfaces of lines, and the lines of points. This must be admitted by anybody who knows clear reason to be infallible, and most of all by those who deny the existence of a vacuum.

> Spinoza's reference here is to Descartes, who argues that a vacuum cannot exist because all of space is filled with a very fine substance called 'ether.' Descartes posited the existence of this substance at least in part to explain how planets could affect each other at a distance. His hypothesis was that they change the motion of the ether, which then affects the motion of the other planets.

For if material substance could be so divided that its parts were really separate, why would it not be possible for one part to be destroyed while the others remain joined together as before? And why should all parts be so fitted together as to leave no vacuum? No doubt, in the case of things that are really distinct from each other, one can exist without the other and remain in its original condition. As, then, there is no vacuum in nature (which I shall discuss elsewhere) but all parts are bound to come together to prevent it, it follows that the parts cannot really be distinguished, either; that is, material substance, in so far as it is substance, cannot be divided.

> Spinoza's arguments in this *scholium* concern paradoxes that arise from the infinite divisibility of space and bodies in space. The question is: Is there a smallest unit of space? Spinoza's answer is "no, because the whole of space exists prior to any divisions. Space is not made up of some small bits that are then put together." The same holds true for the divisibility of bodies.

If anyone asks me the further question, Why are we naturally so prone to divide quantity?, I answer that quantity is conceived by us in two ways: in the abstract, or superficially, as we <commonly> imagine it; or as substance, which is done solely by the intellect <without the help of the imagination [*imaginatio*]>. If, then, we regard quantity as it is represented in our imagination, which we often and more easily do, we shall find that it is finite, divisible, and made up of parts; but if we regard it as it is represented in our intellect and conceive it to the extent that it is substance, which is very difficult to do, we shall then, as I have sufficiently proved, find that it is infinite, one, and indivisible. This will be plain enough to all who have learned to distinguish between the imagination and the intellect, especially if they pay attention to the fact that matter is the same everywhere and in it no parts can be distinguished, except in so far as we conceive matter as diversely modified (*affecta*), so that its parts are distinguished, not really, but modally. Water, for instance, in so far as it is water, we conceive as divided, and its parts as separated from one another, but not in so far as it is material substance; from this point of view it is neither separated nor divisible. Further, water, in so far as it is water, is produced and corrupted; but in so far as it is substance, it is neither produced nor corrupted. And by this I think I have now answered the second argument as well; it is, in fact, founded on the same assumption as the first, namely that matter, in so far as it is substance, is divisible and made up of parts.

But even if this were not the case, I do not know why material substance should be considered unworthy of the divine nature, as besides God there can be no substance that could act upon it (Prop. 14). All things, I affirm, are in God and all that happens, happens solely through the laws of God's infinite nature and follows from the necessity of his essence (as I will shortly show). Thus, it cannot in any way be said that God is acted upon by something else or that extended substance is unworthy of the divine nature, even if it is assumed to be divisible, so long as it is granted to be infinite and eternal. But enough of this for the present.

PROP. XVI. *From the necessity of the divine nature must follow an infinite number of things in infinite modes (that is, everything that can fall within the domain of an infinite intellect).*

Proof. This Proposition will be obvious to anyone who pays attention to the fact that from the given definition of anything the intellect infers several properties that, as a matter of fact, must follow from it (in other words, from the very essence of the thing defined)—the more reality the definition of that things expresses, that is, the more reality the essence of the thing defined involves, the more properties. Now as the divine nature has an absolutely infinite number of attributes (Def. 6), each of which expresses infinite essence after its kind, it follows that from the necessity of such nature an infinite number of things (that is, everything that can fall within the domain of an infinite intellect) must necessarily follow. *Q.E.D.*

It may be instructive to compare this reasoning to the (reconstructed) reasoning behind Prop IX above. The more reality or being a substance has, the fewer are its limitations. Not having an attribute or a mode would be a limitation. Thus, God has an infinite number of attributes and an infinite number of modes. That is, every attribute that a substance can have is had by God and every mode (and combination of modes) that a substance can have is had by God as well.

Corollary I. It follows that God is the efficient cause of all that can fall within the domain of an infinite intellect.

An *efficient cause* is the cause that initiates or brings about a given change. God is the efficient cause of all of its modes or properties insofar as all of these properties follow directly from the essence of God and are not given to God by some external cause. As modes of thought are individual ideas, an *infinite intellect* is an intellect that has every idea that an intellect can have, i.e., a mind that is thinking every possible thought.

Corollary II. It also follows that God is a cause in himself, not through an accident of his nature.

Corollary III. It follows, thirdly, that God is the absolute first cause.

By *first cause* here Spinoza cannot mean temporally first. Instead, he means metaphysically first or the most fundamental.

PROP. XVII. *God acts solely by the laws of his own nature and under no coercion by anyone.*

Proof. We have just shown that solely from the necessity of the divine nature, or—what is the same thing—solely from the laws of the same, an absolutely infinite number of things follow in an infinite number of ways (Prop. 16); and we have proven that without God nothing can be or be conceived, but all things are in God (Prop. 15). Therefore, nothing can exist outside God himself by which he can be determined or forced to act; consequently, God acts solely by the laws of his own nature and without being forced by anyone. *Q.E.D.*

Spinoza identifies here God's *necessity* with the *laws* that follow from God's nature. Insofar as Spinoza uses the terms 'God' and 'Nature' interchangeably, he here identifies the Laws of Nature with the necessity of God's essence. In this way, every particular thing that exists, which might otherwise be conceived as externally caused by Laws of Nature, is appropriately conceived as following from God's essence. Thus, every property that God has follows from the nature of God and nothing has a cause external to this nature. For God to be obedient to the natural laws is simply for God to be self-determined according to its own nature.

Corollary I. It follows (1) that there is no cause that, either from the outside or from the inside, moves God to act besides the perfection of his own nature, <but that he is an efficient cause [*causa efficiens*] by virtue of his perfection alone>.

Corollary II. It follows (2) that God is the sole free cause. For only God exists solely out of the necessity of his nature (Prop. 11 and Coroll. 1 to Prop. 14) and acts by the sole necessity of his own nature (preceding Prop.). Therefore, God is the sole free cause (Def. 7). *Q.E.D.*

Scholium. Others think that God is a free cause because he can, as they think, make it so that those things that we have said follow from his nature, that is, the things that are in his power, do not happen or are not produced by him.

Spinoza is here distinguishing between *freedom* in the sense of doing what one naturally does or wants to do from *free will* in the sense of being able to do otherwise than one actually does.

This, however, is the same as if they were to say that God can make it so that it does not follow from the nature of a triangle that its three interior angles are equal to two right angles,[1] or that from a given cause no effect should follow, which is absurd. Moreover, I will show below, without the aid of this Proposition, that neither the intellect nor the will are part of God's nature.

According to Spinoza, the essence of God can be identified with the attributes (each attribute being an equally correct way to conceive of this essence) whereas God has neither intellect nor will insofar as each is conceived as a faculty of deciding or choosing among alternatives. The reference seems to be to Prop XXXI.

I am well aware that there are many who think they can show that supreme intellect and free will are indeed part of his nature, since—they say—they know of nothing more perfect that they can attribute to God than that which is the highest perfection in ourselves. Also, although they conceive God as actually[2] supremely

---

1 A right-angle measures 90 degrees, and it can be geometrically proven that the sum of the internal angles of a triangle always amounts to 180 degrees. (D.A.)
2 Cf. Schol. Prop. 31. (D.A.)

intelligent, they do not believe that he can bring into existence everything he actually understands, for they think that they would thus destroy God's power. If, they contend, God had created everything which is in his intellect, he would not be able to create anything more, and this, they think, would clash with God's omnipotence; therefore, they prefer to assert that God is indifferent to all things and that he creates nothing except what, by some absolute exercise of will, he has decided to create. However, I think I have shown sufficiently clearly that from God's supreme power, or infinite nature, an infinite number of things—in other words, all existing things—have necessarily flowed forth in an infinite number of ways or always follow from the same necessity in the same way as from the nature of a triangle it follows, from eternity and for eternity, that its three interior angles are equal to two right ones (Prop. 16). Thus, God's omnipotence has actually been there from all eternity and will for all eternity remain in the same state of actuality.

> It is important to note that *eternity* here does not mean existing at all times, but rather as existing non-temporally or entirely outside of time. The nature of time in Spinoza is difficult to determine. He clearly claims that substance is not temporal and so time has to do only with the nature of modes.

This manner of treating the question affirms God's omnipotence, in my opinion, as far more perfect—or rather, my opponents (if I may speak openly) seem to outright deny God's omnipotence, for they are compelled to admit that God understands an infinite number of creatable things without ever being able to create them, since if he created all that he understands, he would in their view exhaust his omnipotence and render himself imperfect. Thus, in order to affirm God's perfection, they are led to a position where they must at the same time claim that he cannot bring into existence everything over which his power extends—a claim than which I do not see one more absurd and more blatantly at odds with God's omnipotence. Further (to say a word here concerning the intellect and the will that we commonly attribute to God), if intellect and will are part of the eternal essence of God, we must understand these words in quite a different way from that in which people usually understand them. For an intellect and a will that should constitute the essence of God would have to be completely and utterly different from the human intellect and will and have nothing in common with them but the name; there would be about as much correspondence between the two as there is between the Dog, the heavenly constellation, and a dog, an animal that barks. This I will prove as follows. If intellect belongs to the divine nature, it cannot be in nature—as most take ours to be—posterior to or simultaneous with the things understood, because God is prior to all things by virtue of being their cause (Coroll. 1 Prop. 16); on the contrary, the truth and formal essence of things is as it is because it exists objectively in that way in the intellect of God. Consequently, God's intellect, in so far as it is conceived as constituting God's essence, is in truth the cause of things, both of their essence and of their existence, which seems to have also been recognized by those who have asserted that God's intellect, God's will, and God's power are one and the same.

> Spinoza is *not* here claiming that God has an intellect or a will. In fact, he seems to reject this claim in Prop XVII *scholium* and in Prop XXXI. Instead he is arguing here from within his imaginary opponent's point of view. His claim is that if God did have an intellect, then this intellect would have to be very different from ours. In our case, something first exists and then we come to know it. In God's case, the knowledge of a thing would be prior to the existence of the thing. To some degree, this resembles the priority given to the God of classical theism: the God of classical theism first knows a thing and then brings it into existence. Spinoza's point here may be to imply that his own view is less radical than it might first seem since even classical theists have to accept something similar. Spinoza's own view is that everything that exists can be understood to be part of one giant mind or infinite intellect. But he takes pains to point out that his view is quite different from classical theism.
>
> The *formal essence* of a thing is what it would be to be that kind of thing. The formal essence can be distinguished from the *actual essence*, which is the essence of a really existing thing. In other words, the formal essence comprises the features that characterize a thing to be one of a specific kind, whereas the actual essence would provide criteria to pick out one particular entity (e.g., a particular member of a larger kind). For example, the formal essence of a cat would be the features that determine a cat to be a cat, whereas there are a distinct set of criteria needed to be the particular cat Sgt. Peppurr.

Thus, as God's intellect is the sole cause of things—namely, as we have shown, both of their essence and of their existence—it must necessarily differ from them in respect to its essence as well as its existence. For the thing caused differs from its cause precisely in that which it receives from it, <which is why it is referred

to as a product [*effectus*] of such a cause>. For example, a person is the cause of another person's existence but not of their essence, for the latter is an eternal truth; consequently, the two may be entirely similar in essence but must be different in existence; hence, if the existence of one of them ceases, the existence of the other will not necessarily cease because of that; but if the essence of one could be destroyed and made false, the essence of the other would be destroyed as well. Thus, a thing that is the cause both of the essence and of the existence of a given effect must differ from such an effect both in respect to its essence and in respect to its existence. Now God's intellect is the cause both of the essence and the existence of our intellect; therefore, God's intellect, in so far as it is conceived as constituting the divine essence, differs from our intellect both in respect to essence and in respect to existence and cannot have anything to do with it except in name only, as we have argued. The reasoning is identical in the case of the will, as anyone can easily see.

> The metaphysical intuition behind this argument seems to be something like the following. Insofar as X is an effect of Y, X is necessarily distinct from Y insofar as it is an effect. This distinction may not be absolute in the case of persons, however. Since, even though the existence of one is necessarily distinct from the other (given that X is an effect of Y), it does not follow that they must be distinct in every way. Indeed, they are not essentially different: they both share the essence of personhood. When describing how God is the cause of all things, however, the distinction is absolute. God is the cause of both a thing's essence and its existence. As such, there cannot be an essential identity between God's intellect (cause) and the intellect of a finite thing (effect).

PROP. XVIII. *God is the immanent and not the transient cause of all things.*

Proof. All things that exist are in God and must be conceived through God (Prop. 15); therefore, God is the cause of those things that are in him (Coroll. 1 Prop. 16), which is our first point. Further, besides God there can be no substance (Prop. 14), that is, a thing that is in itself outside of God (Def. 3)—which is our second point. God, therefore, is the immanent cause of all things, but not the transient. *Q.E.D.*

> An *imminent cause* is a cause that comes from inside a thing. A *transient cause* is a cause that comes from outside a thing. Every mode in

Spinoza will be imminently caused by the essence of substance, but transiently caused by other modes. We can visualize this as two orders of causation: vertical (imminent) and horizontal (transient). The vertical causation refers to the way in which nothing could exist without substance, whereas the horizontal causation picks out the series of cause and effect relations required to explain the particular things that exist at a point in the series. Though the existence of the entire series is explained by substance, the thing that exists at the particular point in the series is explained by the causal circumstances surrounding that point.

PROP. XIX. *God—that is, all of God's attributes—is eternal.*

Proof. God is substance (Def. 6), which necessarily exists (Prop. 11), in other words, of whose nature existence is a part (Prop. 7) or (what is the same thing) from whose definition follows its very existence; therefore, God is eternal (Def. 8). Further, under God's attributes we must understand that which expresses the essence of the divine substance (Def. 4), in other words, that which is part of his substance; this very thing, I say, must be involved by the attributes themselves. Now eternity is part of the nature of substance (as I have already shown based on Prop. 7); therefore, each of the attributes must involve eternity, and thus all are eternal. *Q.E.D.*

This proof is revealing because here Spinoza identifies God with his attributes only. Furthermore, this proof seems to shed some light on his theory of attributes. The essence of substance includes both eternity and infinity. Thus, when we conceive of the essence of substance under a given attribute, we must conceive of it as some eternal and infinite thing. That is, the essence of God can be correctly conceived as an *eternal and infinite space* (employing the attribute of extension) or as an *eternal and infinite mind* (employing the attribute of thought). These are two equally good ways to conceive of it. Each attribute idea "expresses" the essence of substance in a different way.

Scholium. This Proposition is also evident from the manner in which I demonstrated the existence of God (Prop. 11); I affirm that from that proof it is evident that the existence of God, as well as his essence, is an eternal truth. Further, I have proved God's eternity in another manner (Prop. 19 of my *Principles of the Cartesian Philosophy*), which I need not repeat here.

PROP. XX. *The existence of God and his essence are one and the same.*

Proof. God and all his attributes are eternal (previous Prop.), that is, each of his attributes expresses existence (Def. 8). Therefore, the same attributes of God that explain his eternal essence (Def. 4) explain at the same time his eternal existence; in other words, the very thing that constitutes God's essence constitutes at the same time his existence. Therefore, God's existence and God's essence are one and the same. *Q.E.D.*

This claim goes beyond what Spinoza argues in the proof of Prop VII, namely, that existence belonged to the essence of substance. Now he infers that nothing else belongs to the essence of substance other than existence (eternal and infinite existence). It may, therefore, be helpful to think of substance as just pure *being itself*.

Coroll. I. It follows that (1) God's existence, as well as his essence, is an eternal truth.

Coroll. II. It also follows that (2) God—that is, all the attributes of God—is unchangeable. For if these attributes were to change with respect to existence, they would also have to change with respect to essence (previous Prop.), that is, be changed from true to false (as is self-evident), which is absurd.

The claim that the attribute would be changed "from true to false" can seem far from clear since attributes do not have truth-values. The core idea here seems to be that if God gained or lost an attribute, then God's essence would change. But since God's essence is necessary, for God's essence to change would mean that what is necessary would fail to be, and thus, the necessary truth of this thing's existence would become false.

PROP. XXI. *All things that follow from the absolute nature of any attribute of God must always exist and be infinite; in other words, they are eternal and infinite through that attribute.*

Proof. If you deny this Proposition, conceive, if possible, that something in some attribute of God follows from the absolute nature of that attribute, and that at the same time it is finite, and has a determined existence, that is, duration; for instance, the idea of God in thought. Now thought, in so far as it is supposed to be an attribute of God, is by its own nature necessarily infinite (Prop. 11). However, in so far as it possesses the idea of God, it is posited as finite. It cannot, however, be conceived as finite unless it is limited by thought itself (Def. 2)—but not by thought itself in so far as it constitutes the idea of God (for to this extent it is posited as finite); therefore, it is limited by thought in so far as it does not constitute the idea of God, which nevertheless must necessarily exist (Prop. 11). There is, therefore, such a thing as thought not constituting the idea of God; accordingly, the idea of God does not naturally follow from its nature in so far as it is absolute thought (for it is conceived as both constituting and not constituting the idea of God), which contradicts our premise. Thus, if the idea of God in thought—or anything else in any attribute of God (the same applies to any example we may choose, as this proof is of universal application)—follows from the necessity of the absolute nature of the attribute itself, that thing must necessarily be infinite, which was our first point. Further, a thing that thus follows from the necessity of the nature of any attribute cannot have a limited existence, that is, duration. If you deny it, let us posit that a thing that follows from the necessity of the nature of some attribute exists in some attribute of God, for instance, the idea of God in thought, and let us also posit that at some point it did not exist or will not exist. But since thought is posited as being an attribute of God, it must exist both by necessity and unchanged (Prop. 11 and Coroll. 2 Prop. 20). Consequently, beyond the limits of the duration of the idea of God (which we posit at some point did not or will not exist) thought must exist without the idea of God; but this is contrary to our hypothesis, for we have posited that from a given thought the idea of God necessarily follows. Therefore, the idea of God in thought, or anything that necessarily follows from the absolute nature of some attribute of God, cannot have a limited duration, but through the same attribute is eternal, which is our second point <that was being argued>. Bear in mind that the same Proposition must be affirmed of anything that in any attribute of God necessarily follows from God's absolute nature.

This proof is extremely obscure and raises a number of interpretive puzzles. Spinoza has nowhere defined the "absolute nature" of an attribute, so we have to infer the meaning from the proof itself. The *absolute nature* of an attribute seems to be an *attribute of substance* as it is in itself abstracted from all of the modes that substance has. But given the nature of God, an attribute cannot just be as it is in itself. Instead an attribute must "express" itself (see Prop XVI). For example, *thought* is an attribute of God. But pure thought or simple raw consciousness cannot exist empty of content. Instead thought must be "expressed": consciousness must be consciousness *of something*. This something is the "idea of God." So, the idea of God follows immediately from thought. Spinoza's argument here may be that the idea of God exhausts the whole attribute of thought. The whole attribute is *expressed* in the idea of God. Or, to put it another way, the infinite intellect (God's mind) is thinking only one huge thought: the idea of God. Every finite thought is just a part of this one infinite thought. The same can be said concerning extension. There cannot just exist empty space with nothing in it. Instead space has to "express" itself in bodies, that is, as the whole physical universe without any spaces/limits.

PROP. XXII. *Whatever follows from any attribute of God, in so far as it is modified by such a modification as exists necessarily and as infinite through the same attribute, must also exist necessarily and as infinite.*

Proof. The proof of this Proposition proceeds in the same way as that of the preceding one.

Since each attribute expresses infinite essence, it follows that each attribute must express itself in every possible way. Thus, each mode that exists had to exist, i.e., is necessary. The necessity of the finite modes identifiable within this infinite expression requires a further explanation, however. The finite modes are explained by how some parts of this infinite expression relate to other parts. As an expression of an infinite attribute, we only know that every possible mode will exist, but what modes are possible is determined by the particular order of modes.

The general picture here described might be clarified by an analogy. Imagine a computer screen showing a still picture of Paris and the Eiffel Tower. Now let's consider this picture in different ways from the most metaphysically foundational to the least. First, what exists most foundationally is just a collection of colored dots. That's all a picture on a screen is: just a collection of small colored dots in a given arrangement. All of the work we do on a computer just changes the arrangement of those little colored dots. Second, from the arrangement of these colored dots a picture of Paris follows at a higher level. These colored dots come together to form a whole. Third, since we have a picture of Paris we can now identify the object in the center of the picture as the Eiffel Tower. We can now note the many small finite parts of the one picture. The progression here is not temporal, but logical. Similarly, under the attribute of extension, what exists most fundamentally is an infinite number of small bodies moving around. This fact is metaphysically grounded in the immediate causal efficacy of God. This infinite whole can, however, be organized and understood in smaller "parts." Just as the Eiffel Tower is explained by facts about how a particular bunch of dots relates to the surrounding dots, various small parts of the physical universe, like you and me, can be identified within the mass of the infinite essence. To apply classical terminology, God's essence causes the *immediate infinite modes* (e.g., the infinite number of moving bodies/complete screen of lights), whereas the *mediate infinite modes* are things like the Eiffel Tower/you and I, which are determinations within the whole grounded on relationships within the whole.

PROP. XXIII. *Every mode that exists both necessarily and as infinite must necessarily follow either from the absolute nature of some attribute of God or from an attribute modified by a modification that exists necessarily and as infinite.*

Proof. A mode exists in something else through which it must be conceived (Def. 5), that is, it exists solely in God and can be conceived solely through God (Prop. 15). Thus, if a mode is conceived as necessarily existing and infinite, both of these things must necessarily be inferred or perceived through some attribute of God in so far as that attribute is conceived as expressing infinity and necessity of existence, in other words, eternity (on these two things being the same see Def. 8)—that is, in so far as it is considered absolutely (Def. 6 and Prop. 19). A mode, therefore, which exists both necessarily and as infinite, must follow from the absolute nature of some attribute of God, either immediately (see Prop. 21) or by means of some modification that follows from its absolute nature, that is, which exists necessarily and as infinite (Prop. 22). *Q.E.D.*

The purpose of this proof is simply to claim that all modes are all necessary, though this necessity is either explained immediately or mediately from the infinite essence. A mode is either conceived to be necessary insofar as it is a determinate expression of the infinite attribute (immediately), or it is necessary because of the limiting external facts posed by the series of surrounding modes (mediately).

PROP. XXIV. *The essence of things produced by God does not involve existence.*

Proof. This Proposition is evident from Def. 1. For that whose nature (if considered in itself) involves existence is self-caused and exists solely by the necessity of its own nature.

Corollary. It follows that God is not only the cause of things coming into existence, but also of their continuing to exist, that is (to use a Scholastic term), God is the cause of the being of things (*essendi rerum*). For whether things do or do not exist, whenever we contemplate their essence, we find that it involves neither existence nor duration; consequently, their essence cannot be the cause of either its existence or its duration, but God alone can be the only being for which existence is an integral part of its own nature (Coroll. 1 Prop. 14). *Q.E.D.*

Here Spinoza clarifies that though every mode is necessary, for modes, the necessity is not found in the essence of the mode in the way that God's necessity is found in its essence. The necessity of a mode exists external to its own essence; namely, in the external facts which define the limits of possibility.

PROP. XXV. *God is the efficient cause not only of the existence of things but also of their essence.*

Proof. If you deny this, then God is not the cause of the essence of things; therefore, the essence of things can be conceived without God (Ax. 4). This, however, is absurd (Prop. 15). Therefore, God is the cause of the essence of things as well. *Q.E.D.*

Scholium. This Proposition follows more clearly from Prop. 16. For from it follows that from the divine nature it must necessarily be deduced both the essence of things and their existence; in short, God must be called the cause of all things in the same sense as he is called the cause of himself, which will be made still clearer by the following corollary.

Corollary. Individual things are nothing but modifications of God's attributes, that is, modes by which the attributes of God are expressed in a fixed and definite manner. The proof is evident from Prop. 15 and Def. 5.

If we consider substance under the attribute of extension, then we can imagine substance as an infinite space. Everything else that exists is a bundle of properties had by this space. So, when an orange, fluffy cat walks from one place to another what happens, on Spinoza's view, is that different regions of space become orange and fluffy in succession. The cat is not a substance that moves on this view, but only a *way* that different regions of space express themselves successively.

PROP. XXVI. *A thing that is determined to act in a particular manner has necessarily been so determined by God; and one that has not been determined by God cannot determine itself to act.*

Proof. That by which things are said to be determined to act in a particular manner is necessarily something positive (as is self-evident); consequently, God is by the necessity of his own nature the efficient cause both of its essence and of its existence (Prop. 25 and 16); this is our first point. Our second point follows from it in a most clear fashion. For if a thing that has not been determined by God could determine itself, the first part of our proof would be false, and this, as we have shown, is absurd.

> Spinoza now turns to the two different kinds of causation that jointly determine each mode. Since modes are simply *ways* that substance is, each mode metaphysically depends upon substance for its existence and nature. Each mode depends upon its substance in the way that any property needs substance in order to exist at all. Properties cannot exist apart from a substance in which to inhere. But what follows from the essence of the one infinite substance is the infinite totality of all modes (that is, the whole physical universe or the "idea of God"). These modes interact with one another and form a complex infinite chain of events or changes. In this proposition and the next Spinoza is talking about the "vertical" relationship between modes and substance. In Prop XVIII Spinoza turns to the "horizontal" causal relationships that modes have to one another.

PROP. XXVII. *A thing that has been determined by God to act in a particular manner cannot render itself undetermined.*

Proof. This Proposition is evident from Ax. 3.

PROP. XXVIII. *Every individual thing, that is, everything that is finite and has a determined existence, cannot exist or be determined to act unless it is determined to exist and act by a cause other than itself that is also finite and has a determined existence. This cause, in turn, cannot exist or be determined to act unless it is determined to exist and act by another cause that is also finite and has a determined existence, and so on to infinity.*

Proof. Whatever is determined to exist and act has been so conditioned by God (Prop. 26 and Coroll. Prop. 24). Now what is finite and has a determined existence cannot have been produced by the absolute nature of any attribute of God, for whatever follows from the absolute nature of any attribute of God is infinite and eternal (Prop. 21). It must, therefore, have followed from some attribute of God in so far as it is considered as in some way modified; for besides substance and modes nothing exists (Ax. 1 and Def. 3 and 5), and modes are nothing but modifications of the attributes of God (Coroll. Prop. 25). But a determined thing cannot follow from God or from any of his attributes, either, in so far as the latter is modified by a modification that is infinite and eternal (Prop. 22). Therefore, it must have followed from or have been determined to exist and act by God or one of his attributes in so far as it is modified by some modification that is finite and has a determined existence. This is our first point. Further, this cause or mode must in turn have been determined by another cause that is also finite and has a determined existence (by the same reasoning by which we established the first part of this proof), and this last, in turn, by another (by the same reasoning); and so on (by the same reasoning) to infinity. *Q.E.D.*

> Spinoza here is defending a view here that is called *determinism*. On this view, everything that happens is causally determined by what has happened before. Nothing that happens is either random or uncaused.

Scholium. As certain things must have been produced immediately by God—namely those that necessarily follow from his absolute nature as well as others by means of these first ones, which nonetheless can neither exist nor be conceived without God—it follows

(1) that God is the absolutely nearest cause of the things immediately produced by him; <I say absolutely the nearest cause and> not after his kind, as is usually stated. For the effects of God can neither exist nor be conceived without their cause (Prop. 15 and Coroll. Prop. 24).

(2) It also follows that God cannot properly be said to be the remote cause of individual things, except, perhaps, for the sake of distinguishing them from those he immediately produced, or rather follow from his absolute nature. For under 'remote cause' we understand one that is in no way connected to the effect. But all things that exist are in God and depend on God in such a way that without him they can neither exist nor be conceived.

PROP. XXIX. *In the universe nothing is contingent, but all things are determined to exist and act in a particular manner by the necessity of God's nature.*

Proof. Whatever exists is in God (Prop. 15); God, however, cannot be called a contingent thing. For he exists necessarily, not contingently (Prop. 11). Further, the modes of God's nature have followed necessarily from that nature, not contingently (Prop. 16), either in so far as God's nature is considered absolutely (Prop. 21) or in so far as it is considered as having been determined to act in a particular way (Prop. 27). Further, God is the cause of these modes not only in so far as they simply exist (Coroll. Prop. 24), but also in so far as they are considered as determined to act in a particular manner (Prop. 26). For if they are not determined by God, it is impossible, not contingent, for them to determine themselves (Prop. 26); conversely, if they are determined by God, it is impossible, not contingent, for them to render themselves undetermined (Prop. 27). Thus, all things are determined by the necessity of the divine nature not only to exist, but also to exist and act in a particular manner, and there is nothing that is contingent. *Q.E.D.*

> Whereas in Prop XVIII Spinoza is concerned with the "horizontal" determinism of modes, that is, that each mode is causally determined by prior modes to exist and act in a given way, now he is concerned with "vertical" determinism: substance could not have expressed itself differently than it in fact did. Spinoza will take one more step in Prop XXXIII by noting that God's essence is necessary and then infer that everything else that exists is as necessary as the existence of God.

Scholium. Before going any further, I want here to explain what we should understand by 'nature viewed as active' (*natura naturans*) and 'nature viewed as passive' (*natura naturata*)—or rather call attention to it. For I think that, from what has been said, it is already sufficiently clear that by *natura naturans* we should understand that which is in itself and is conceived through itself, that is, those attributes of substance that express eternal and infinite essence—in other words, God, in so far as he is considered a free cause (Coroll. 1 Prop. 14 and Coroll. 2 Prop. 17). By *natura naturata* I understand all that follows from the necessity of God's nature or of each one of God's attributes—that is, all the modes of God's attributes in so far as they are considered as things that are in God and which cannot exist or be conceived without God.

This distinction is helpful because it helps to clarify the two aspects of reality on Spinoza's view. First, there is the *active* part of reality, namely, substance or being itself. What substance is doing is *expressing itself* in modes. These modes are the *passive* part of reality.

To use an analogy, suppose that we pour some water out of a cup onto the floor and watch it in slow motion. The water is like substance and the different shapes that the water takes are like modes. (The analogy is imperfect since the water is being affected by external causes, but set that aside for a moment.) But water cannot just be: it must take some shape or other. In just this way, substance must fully express itself in modes. There cannot be just raw existence. So, at the risk of stretching the analogy too far, suppose that the water was the only thing that existed and given its own nature it had to take on every possible shape in order to fully express itself. The water is the active part and the complex shape that it takes on is the passive part of reality. Sometimes Spinoza seems to restrict the term 'God' to the active part of substance and 'Nature' to the passive part. But, of course, these are just two ways of looking at the same thing.

PROP. XXX. *The intellect, whether actually finite or actually infinite, must comprehend God's attributes and God's modifications, and nothing else.*

Proof. A true idea must agree with its object (*ideatum*) (Ax. 6); in other words, what is contained in the intellect objectively must necessarily exist in nature (as is self-evident). Now in nature there is no substance except God (Coroll. 1 to Prop. 14), nor any modifications except those that are in God (Prop. 15) and can neither exist or be conceived without God (ibid.). Therefore, the intellect, be it actually finite or actually infinite, must comprehend God's attributes and God's modifications, and nothing else. *Q.E.D.*

PROP. XXXI. *The intellect, whether actually finite or infinite, as well as will, desire, love, etc., must be referred to* natura naturata *and not to* natura naturans.

Proof. By 'intellect' we do not mean absolute thought (as is self-evident), but only a certain mode of thinking that differs from other modes such as love, desire, etc., thus requiring to be conceived through absolute thought (Def. 5), namely through some attribute of God that expresses the eternal and infinite essence of thought (Prop. 15 and Def. 6), and must be conceived in such a way that without that attribute it could neither exist nor be conceived. Therefore, it must be referred to *natura naturata* rather than to *natura naturans* (Schol. Prop. 29), as must the other modes of thinking. *Q.E.D.*

> The claim that intellect and will relate to the passive part of reality is interesting because it shows that we should not think of intellect and will as capacities that something has. Normally, we would think of a will as a capacity that something has to do something. But on Spinoza's view such capacities do not exist. Instead there are only individual or particular willings and acts of understanding. Your mind does not consist of a certain capacity for thought that you sometimes exercise to think about things. Instead there is only the "bundle" of actual thoughts, willings, desires, etc. While Spinoza continues to use capacity language and talk about "the will" and "the intellect," it is important to keep in mind here that he is only referring to particular acts of willing or understanding.

Scholium. The reason I speak of 'actual' intellect is not that I admit that there is such a thing as 'potential' intellect, but, wishing to avoid all confusion, I decided to speak only of what is most clearly perceived by us, namely the very act of understanding, than which nothing is more clearly perceived. For we cannot understand anything that does not lead to a more perfect knowledge of the act of understanding.

> Since substance is fully expressed in its modes, there is no such thing as *potentiality* in Aristotle's sense of something that might be actualized and come to be. Instead, there is only full *actuality*—everything that can exist at this moment of time does exist at this moment of time. For this reason, there can be no such thing as the *potential* to understand something. There exists only individual acts of understanding. For Spinoza, to say that one has the "potential" to (say) understand French, one can only be predicting that one may possess understanding of French at some future time if an appropriate causal process exists to manifest it. One does not now have potential French knowledge. To *now have* such a "potentiality" would mean that there is a way the infinite attribute of thought could be which it is not—an impossibility.

PROP. XXXII. *The will cannot be called a free cause, but only a necessary one.*

Proof. The will is only a particular mode of thinking, like the intellect; therefore, no volition can exist or be determined to act unless it is determined by some cause other than itself, which in turn is conditioned by a third cause, and so on to infinity (Prop. 28). But if the will is posited as infinite, it would also have to be determined to exist and act by God, not in so far as he is a substance absolutely infinite, but in so far as he possesses an attribute that expresses the infinite and eternal essence of thought (Prop. 23). Thus, however it is conceived—whether as finite or as infinite—it requires a cause by which it is determined to exist and act; consequently, it cannot be called a free cause, but only a necessary or constrained one (Def. 7). *Q.E.D.*

Coroll. I. It follows (1) that God does not act out of freedom of the will.

Coroll. II. It follows (2) that the will and the intellect stand in the same relation to God's nature as do motion, rest, and absolutely all natural phenomena, which must be determined by God to exist and act in a particular manner (Prop. 29). For the will, like the rest, needs a cause by which it is determined to exist and act in a particular manner. And although an infinite number of things follow from a given will or intellect, God cannot on that account be said to act out of freedom of the will any more than, on account of what follows from motion and rest (as from these too an infinite number of things follow), he can be said to act out of the freedom of motion and rest. Therefore, will is no more a part of God's nature than anything else in the universe but stands in the same relation to it as motion, rest, and everything else, which we have shown to follow from the necessity of the divine nature and to be determined by it to exist and act in a particular manner.

PROP. XXXIII. *Things could not have been produced by God in any manner or in any order other than that in which they have in fact been produced.*

Proof. All things have necessarily followed from the given nature of God (Prop. 16) and have been determined by the necessity of God's nature to exist and act in a particular way (Prop. 29). Thus, if things could have been of a different nature or have been determined to act in a different way, so that the order of nature would have been different, it follows that God's nature could also have been different from what it now is; therefore, that different nature would have to exist, too (Prop. 11); consequently, there could exist two or more Gods, which is absurd (Coroll. 1 Prop.14). Therefore, things could not have been produced in any other manner, order etc. *Q.E.D.*

This claim goes quite a bit beyond mere determinism. According to the determinist, the whole physical universal is causally determined and so given the past there is only one possible future. But intuitively there were other possible universes that could have existed but do not. So, while everything is determined, it is not strictly necessary because the whole universe could have been different. Spinoza rejects this view and embraces a view called *necessitarianism*. On this view, everything that happens is not only causally determined, but it is *logically incoherent* to imagine anything being different from the way that it actually is. Given the Principle of Sufficient Reason, the argument here is straightforward: God's existence is necessary. The idea that God does not exist is logically incoherent (God is being itself). Similarly, the nature of God is necessary and so it makes no sense to suppose that God could have been a different kind of thing. But everything else that exists follows logically from God's nature and so everything else that occurs must likewise be necessary. To imagine things to be different from the way that they are is to imagine God being different from the way it is, which is incoherent.

Scholium I. Given that with these arguments I have shown more clearly than bright daylight that there is absolutely nothing in things that justifies calling them contingent, I now want to explain briefly what we will have to understand by the word 'contingent'; but first I will explain the words 'necessary' and 'impossible'.

A thing is called 'necessary' either with respect to its essence or with respect to its cause; for the existence of a thing necessarily follows either from its essence and definition or from a given efficient cause. Further, a thing is said to be impossible for these same reasons, namely because its essence or definition involves a contradiction or because there is no external cause that has been determined to produce such a thing. However, a thing can in no respect be called contingent save in relation to the imperfection of our knowledge; for when we do not know whether the essence of a thing involves a contradiction or when we positively know that it does not but are still unable to say with certainty whether it exists as the order of causes escapes us, such a thing cannot appear to us either as necessary or as impossible. This is why we call it contingent or possible.

Spinoza rejects *metaphysical contingency*. That is, he rejects the claim that facts about our daily lives are contingent and so could have been different. Instead, everything that happens is as necessarily true as mathematics. Nevertheless, Spinoza does admit to *epistemological contingency* or uncertainty about the truth of something. For example, at the moment we do not know whether various mathematical claims (e.g., the Riemann Hypothesis) are true or not. Nevertheless, it is generally believed that if such a claim is true, then it is true necessarily. So, when we say that this mathematical truth is *possible*, we mean only that it is possibly true given our current state of knowledge. Similarly, whether I will die today in a car accident is determined by the chain of causes and so must either happen or cannot happen. Thus, for Spinoza, although I can say that it is possible that I may die in a car accident today, all I can truthfully be saying is that I do not now know enough about the chain of causes to know whether or not I will be in a car accident today.

Scholium II. It clearly follows from what we have said that things have been produced by God in the highest perfection, as they have necessarily followed from the given most perfect nature. Nor does this prove any imperfection in God, for his very perfection has compelled us to affirm it. If anything, it is from the contrary Proposition that it would clearly follow (as I have just shown) that God is not supremely perfect; for if things had been produced in any other way, we should have to attribute to God another nature, different from the one that we had to attribute to him through the consideration of an absolutely perfect being.

By *supremely perfect* here Spinoza cannot mean consistent with some transcendent or ideal moral standard, for as we will see, no such standard exists. Instead, Spinoza can only mean that it follows from the absolute and unlimited being that is God.

I do not doubt, however, that many will dismiss this Proposition as absurd and refuse to devote themselves to contemplating it, simply because they are accustomed to attributing to God a freedom very different from that which we have put forward (Def. 7), namely, absolute free will. On the other hand, I am also convinced that if these people were to reflect on the matter and duly weigh in their minds our series of demonstrations, they would reject such freedom as they now attribute to God, not only as inconsequential, but also as a great impediment to the pursuit of knowledge. There is no need for me to repeat what I have said in Schol. Prop. 17; for the sake of my opponents, however, I will further show that even if we accept the notion that the will pertains to the essence of God, it nevertheless follows from his perfection that things could not have been created by him in any other way or order. This is easily proved if we reflect, to begin with, on what they themselves concede, namely that it depends solely on God's decree and will that each thing is what it is; for otherwise God would not be the cause of all things; further, that all of God's decrees have been ratified from all eternity by God himself, for if it were otherwise, God would be convicted of imperfection or change. But since in eternity there is no such thing as *when*, *before*, or *after*, it follows—from God's perfection alone—that God can never decree, nor could ever have decreed, anything but what is; in other words, that God did not exist before his decrees and could not exist without them.

> In this interesting argument Spinoza adopts the perspective of his opponents and argues that even if God had an incompatibilist free will, He could not have made things any differently than He did. Suppose that the God of classical theism exists and chose to create this particular universe rather than some other possible universe. Since God exists *eternally* and does not exist in time, then God's choice to create this universe rather than another has existed eternally. There could have been no time at which this choice was different. Thus, Spinoza infers, this sort of "free" choice would still be as necessarily determined as the nature of God himself.

They will say, however, that even if we posited God to have made a different universe or had from all eternity decreed otherwise concerning nature and its order, there still would follow no imperfection in God. But if they make this claim, they will be admitting that God can change his decrees, for if God had issued different decrees concerning nature and its order from those he has in fact issued—in other words, if he had willed and conceived something different concerning nature—he would necessarily have had a different intellect and a different will from those he in fact has. But if it is permissible to attribute to God a different intellect and a different will without any change in his essence and his perfection—What reason is there why he cannot change his decrees concerning the things created and nevertheless remain perfect? For his intellect and will concerning the things created and their order with respect to his essence and perfection are the same however they may be conceived.

> Spinoza is arguing here that those who believe that the God of classical theism exists, and could have done otherwise than He did without

becoming any less perfect, contradict themselves. Spinoza claims that if God had chosen differently than He did, then He would have had to have had a different intellect. This follows from the assumption that our reasons, beliefs, and desires determine our choices. It makes no sense, Spinoza thinks, to suppose that one had the *exact same reasons, beliefs, and desires* and yet chose differently. In such a case there could be no explanation for why one choice was made rather than another. To see why, imagine a person trying to choose between chocolate ice cream and vanilla. Suppose that this person choses vanilla. Spinoza thinks that it is incoherent to imagine this person choosing chocolate with the exact same mental states (beliefs, desires, and reasons) as he did when he chose vanilla.

Further, all the philosophers I have read admit that there is no intellect in God potentially but only actually; and since both his intellect and his will are not distinguished from his essence (as they also admit), it follows that, if God had actually had a different intellect and a different will, his essence would also have been different, too; thus, as I concluded at first, if things had been produced by God differently from how they are, God's intellect and will, that is (as is admitted) his essence, would necessarily have been different, which is absurd.

In the classical theistic tradition, God is maximally simple and has no parts. (The reasoning for this conclusion is that God is dependent upon nothing else for his existence, and if He had parts then he would be metaphysically dependent upon Him. Thus, God has no parts). For this reason God's will, intellect, being, etc. must all be one and the same. From this claim, Spinoza infers that—even for classical theists— one has to accept that the only way for God to have been able to do differently is for God to have had a different essence than He in fact has. These arguments are designed to show that those who believe in the God of classical theism must also accept necessitarianism and so should have no objection to Spinoza on this point.

So, as these things could not have been produced by God in any other way and order, and as the truth of this Proposition follows from the supreme perfection of God, certainly no sound reasoning can possibly persuade us that God did not wish to create all the things that were in his intellect with the same perfection as he understands them. They will say, however, that there is in things no perfection nor imperfection, but whatever is in them that makes it so that they are perfect or imperfect and are called good or bad depends solely on God's will. Thus, if God had so willed, he could have made it so that what is now perfection should be extreme imperfection and conversely <that what is now an imperfection in things would have been the most perfect>. What is such an assertion, however, if not an open declaration that God, who necessarily understands the things he wants, could through his will cause himself to understand things differently from the way in which he in fact does? This, as I have just shown, is the height of absurdity.

Therefore, I can turn the argument against my opponents as follows: All things depend on the power of God. So, in order that things could be different from what they are, God's will would necessarily have to be different, too; but God's will cannot be different (as we have just most clearly demonstrated from God's perfection). Therefore, things cannot be different, either. I will admit, however, that the view that subjects all things to some indifferent will of God and asserts that they are all dependent on his fiat is less far from the truth than the view of those who maintain that God acts in all things with a view to what is good. For these latter people seem to posit something outside of God that does not depend on God but which God in acting looks to as a model or which he aims at as a definite goal. This, to be sure, is nothing other than subjecting God to destiny, an utter absurdity with respect to God, whom we have shown to be the first and only free cause of the essence of all things as well as of their existence. Therefore, I need not spend any time refuting such an absurdity.

Spinoza's objection here (as he will develop in the Appendix) is to what Aristotelians call *final causes*. A final cause is the goal or end towards which something changes. For example, an acorn has the final cause of becoming an oak tree and so when it changes naturally it changes towards this goal. Spinoza rejects the notion that changes have a natural end in themselves and instead will try to explain everything in terms of *efficient causes*. That is, an acorn becomes an oak tree because its own essence when interacting with the outside world causes it to become one. Acorns themselves have no "natural end" instead they simply change in predictable ways when they interact with external objects. Though Spinoza rejects the Aristotelian notion of final causes generally, he particularly rejects them as being applied to God. For God to act for the sake of some other end goal is to make God subject to this goal.

PROP. XXXIV. *God's power is identical with his essence.*

Proof. From the mere necessity of the essence of God it follows that God is the cause of himself (Prop. 11) and of all things (Prop. 16 and Coroll.). Consequently, the power of God, by which he and all things are and act, is identical with his essence. *Q.E.D.*

Remember that the term 'power' must be read in a Spinozistic way. We sometimes use the term power (and *potentia*) to mean the *potential* for bringing something into being. On this usage, I currently have the power to walk across the room. Although I am not now walking but am sitting at my desk, nevertheless, I currently have the power to perform this activity. This cannot be the sense in which Spinoza is using the term. On Spinoza's view there are no potentialities or metaphysical possibilities. Everything that is, is actual.

PROP. XXXV. *Whatever we conceive to be in the power of God necessarily exists.*

Proof. Whatever is in God's power must be comprehended in his essence (previous Prop.) in such a manner that it necessarily follows from it, and therefore necessarily exists. *Q.E.D.*

PROP. XXXVI. *There is nothing from whose nature some effect does not follow.*

Proof. Whatever exists expresses God's nature, or essence, in a definite and determined manner (Coroll. Prop. 25); that is, whatever exists expresses in a definite and determined manner God's power (Prop. 34), which is the cause of all things; therefore, an effect must necessarily follow from it (Prop. 16). *Q.E.D.*

Spinoza is arguing here that no finite thing is causally isolated. Every finite thing that exists is both caused to exist *and* is itself a cause of other things. The argument here is quite curious and seems to be something like the following: God's essence is power. Power just is the active bringing into being of some effect. All finite modes are little bits of God's power expressed in "a definite and determinate manner." So, all finite modes must bring into being some effect.

APPENDIX

With these arguments I have explained God's nature and his properties, such as that he necessarily exists; that he is one; that he is and acts solely by the necessity of his own nature; that he is the free cause of all things, and how he is so; that all things are in God and so depend on him that without him they can neither exist nor be conceived; lastly, that all things have been predetermined by God, not through his free will, or absolute fiat, but through his absolute nature, or infinite power.

Further, I have taken care to remove the prejudices that might impede the comprehension of my demonstrations wherever I have had the opportunity to do so. Yet, as there still remain quite a few prejudices that might then and may now equally, if not maximally hinder people's grasping the whole of the arguments in the way that I have laid it out, I have thought it worthwhile here to bring these misconceptions before the bar of reason. All the prejudices that I here undertake to point out spring from a single one, which is commonly entertained, namely that all things in nature act with an end in view, as people do; more yet, God himself is thought, as a matter of course, to direct all things to a definite goal, for they say that God made all things for man, and made man so that he might worship him. I will therefore begin by looking into this conception, seeking *firstly* the reason why most accept this prejudice and why everybody is naturally so prone to adopt it; *then*, I will point out its falsity; *lastly*, I will show how it has given rise to prejudices about *good and bad, right and wrong, praise and blame, order and confusion, beauty and ugliness,* and the like. However, this is not the place to deduce these misconceptions from the nature of the human mind; it will be sufficient here if I assume as a starting point what ought to be universally admitted, namely that all people are born ignorant of the causes of things and that they all have the desire to pursue their own benefit and are conscious of this fact. For from this it follows, *first*, that people think themselves free because they are conscious of their volitions and desires but never even dream of the causes that make them hold such wishes and desires, since they are totally oblivious to them. *Secondly*, it follows that people do everything for an end, namely for the benefit they desire. As a consequence, they look only for a knowledge of the final causes of events, and when they have learned them, they are content, since they have no reason to ask any further questions. And if they cannot learn such causes from someone else, they are left with nothing but turning to themselves and reflecting on the goals by which they themselves are usually prompted to do something similar, and thus they necessarily judge other natures by their own. Further, as they find both in and outside themselves many means that assist them not a little in the search for their benefit, for instance, eyes for seeing, teeth for chewing, herbs and animals for food, the sun for giving light, the sea for breeding fish, <and so with almost all other things, whose natural causes they have no reason to doubt,> hence they come to look at all natural things as means toward their own benefit; and as they are aware that they have merely happened upon such means but have not created them, they think they have reason to believe that someone else exists who has made them for their use.

Spinoza contends that a central error in human thinking is that natural causes have a goal, end, or purpose. He thinks that we make this error because we are aware of our own purposes and the effects of our actions, but are not aware of the causes of our actions. We thus infer that what we are not aware of does not exist and so we suppose that we do things uncaused or freely. Despite these strong claims, there appears to be a tension in Spinoza's view. He seems committed to the claim that there are no final causes or ends, that humans are perfectly natural and just like everything else that exists, and yet also to suggest that humans act for an end. Whether humans act for an end on Spinoza's view or merely appear to act for an end is a difficult question

For once they started looking upon things as means, they could not believe them to be self-created but, judging from the means they are used to preparing for themselves, they have been led to conclude that there is some ruler or rulers of the universe, endowed with human freedom, who have taken care of everything on their behalf and created all things for their use. And they have been led to judge the mind of such rulers (having never received any information about it) in accordance with their own; consequently, they assert that the gods ordained everything for the use of humanity in order to bind people to themselves and obtain from him the highest honour. Therefore, they each thought out for themselves, following their own mindset, a different way of worshiping God so that God might love them more than others and direct all of nature toward the satisfaction of their blind cupidity and insatiable greed. Thus, the prejudice developed into superstition and took deep root in their minds; and for this reason everyone strove most zealously to understand and explain the final causes of things; but in their endeavour to show that nature does nothing in vain, to wit, nothing that is useless to man, they only seem to have demonstrated that nature and the gods are just as insane as people. Consider, I pray you, where all this has led! Among the many amenities of nature, they were bound to find some inconveniences, such as storms, earthquakes, diseases and the like; so they declared that such things happen because the gods, <whom they deem to be of the same kind as they are,> are angry at some wrong done to them by humans or at some fault committed in their worship. However loudly experience would protest day by day and show through countless examples that good and bad fortunes fall indiscriminately to the pious and impious alike, they did not abandon their inveterate prejudice, for they found it easier to class this state of affairs among other unknown things of whose use they were ignorant, and thus to retain their present and innate state of ignorance, than to destroy the whole fabric of their reasoning and come up with a new one. They therefore laid down as an axiom that the gods' judgments far transcend human understanding. Such a doctrine might well have sufficed to conceal the truth from humankind for all eternity if mathematics, which deals not with final causes but solely with the essence and properties of figures, had not shown humanity another standard of truth; as well, even outside of mathematics it is possible to establish other causes (it would be entirely superfluous to list them here), which have prompted people <(albeit very few compared to the entirety of the human race)> to become aware of these common misconceptions and led them to the true knowledge of things.

> The belief that the universe is ordered to some end (or set of ends) leads people to conclude that the reasoning of God (or the gods) is a great mystery. The classical theistic worldview of the Medieval philosophers places the mystery of God at the center of all that exists. All reasoning about the nature of the world then ends up eventually encountering this Mystery and these thinkers conclude therefore that the deep answers are unknowable. Mathematics, on the other hand, posits no unknowable mysteries but works with ideas that are entirely conceptually transparent (e.g., line, point, plane, set, etc.). One of Spinoza's core convictions is that the universe is entirely rational and so is entirely open to human reason. There is nothing that cannot in principle be known. There is no Mystery.

I have now sufficiently explained what I announced as my first point. To show that nature has no particular goal in view and that all final causes are nothing more than figments of the human imagination, I do not need to argue at length, for I think that this is already evident enough both from the causes and foundations from which I have shown this prejudice to originate and from Prop. 16 and Coroll. 1 and 2 Prop. 32 and, besides, from all those passages in which I have shown that everything in nature proceeds from some eternal necessity and with the greatest possible perfection. However, I will still add the following: This doctrine of finality turns nature completely on its head, for what is really a cause it regards as an effect and conversely <as a cause what is an effect>. Additionally, it paints as last what by nature is first; finally, it turns what is highest and most perfect into what is most imperfect. I shall pass over the first two points because they are self-evident; now it results from Prop. 21, 22, and 23 that the most perfect effect is the one that is produced immediately by God, and that the more intermediate causes an effect requires, the more imperfect it is. On the other hand, if those things that were produced immediately by God had been made with the goal of enabling him to attain his end, then the things last produced, for whose sake the first ones were made, would necessarily have to be the most excellent of all. Further, this doctrine does away with God's perfection, for if God acts toward a goal, he necessarily desires something that he lacks. Certainly, theologians and metaphysicians draw a distinction between goal of want (*finis indigentiae*) and goal of assimilation (*finis assimilationis*);[1] still, they admit that God made all things for his own sake, not for the sake of the things to be created, for they are unable to point to anything prior to creation, except God himself, for whose sake God should act; so they are inevitably forced to admit that God lacked those things for the sake of which he created means and—as is self-evident—that he desired them. And we must not omit to note that the followers of this doctrine, anxious to show off their wits in assigning ends to things, have come up with a new kind of argument to prove their theory, namely a reduction, not to the impossible, but to ignorance, thereby showing that there is no other way of arguing

---

1 That is, God made things not out of selfish desire but in order to share his perfection with the things created. (D.A.)

this doctrine. For example, if a stone falls from a roof onto someone's head and kills them, they will demonstrate by their new method that the stone fell in order to kill that person; for if it did not fall to that end, by God's will, how could so many circumstances (and there are often many concurrent circumstances) have all happened together by chance? You may answer that it happened because the wind was blowing and the person was walking that way. 'But why,' they will insist, 'was the wind blowing at that moment? And why was that person walking that way at that same time?' If you again answer that the wind had then started to blow because the sea had begun to be agitated the day before, when the weather was still calm, and that the person had been invited by a friend, they will again insist (as there is no end to the questions): 'But why was the sea agitated? Why was the man invited at that time?' And so they will continue to ask about the causes of the causes, till at last you take refuge in the will of God—in other words, the sanctuary of ignorance.

Spinoza's argument here is that the classical theist cannot ultimately explain anything because the central being in their metaphysics is a total mystery. The unknowable thing at the center of every feature of reality is God's will, and as God is unknowable, deep knowledge of everything else is impossible too. Nothing can be really explained because the chain of "why" questions will inevitably lead back to the mystery of God. The only way to make everything rational and comprehensible is to make God fully comprehensible.

Likewise, when they survey the build of the human body, they are amazed and, being ignorant of the causes of so great a work of art, conclude that it has been fashioned, not mechanically, but by divine or supernatural skill, and has been put together in such a way that one part does not hurt another. Hence anyone who seeks for the true causes of miracles and strives to understand natural phenomena, like a scholar, instead of gazing at them in wonder, like a fool, is everywhere regarded as a heretic and as impious and declared to be such by those whom the masses revere as the interpreters of nature and the gods. For these people know that, if ignorance, <or rather dullness,> were to be removed, wonder, that is, their only means of arguing and preserving their authority, would be removed; <but I leave it to them to judge what power there is in such reasoning [*argumen-*

tari].> Now, however, I quit this subject and pass on to my third point.

After people persuaded themselves that everything that comes to pass does so for their sake, they were bound to consider as the chief quality in everything what is most useful to them and to regard those things that have the most beneficial effect on them as the best of all. Hence they were bound to form notions with which to explain the nature of things, namely *good, bad, order, confusion, warm, cold, beauty, ugliness*; and from the belief that they were free agents arose the notions of *praise* and *blame, wrong* and *right*; but I will speak of the latter below, when I deal with human nature; the former I will briefly explain here.

Everything that conduces to health and the worship of God they have called *good*, and everything that is contrary to these things they have called *bad*; and as those who do not understand the nature of things but merely imagine them do not verify anything about things and mistake their imagination for understanding, they firmly believe that there is an order in things, being ignorant both of the nature of things and their own. For when things are ordered in such a way that when they are represented by our senses, we can easily imagine them and, consequently, easily remember them, we say that they are <in good order [*ordo*] or> well-ordered; if the contrary, we say that they are ill-ordered or confused. And since what is easily imagined is more pleasing to us, people prefer order to confusion— as though there were any order in nature except in relation to our imagination—and say that God has created all things in order, thus unknowingly attributing imagination to God out of their own fancy—unless perhaps they would have it that God provided for human imagination and arranged everything in such a way that they could most easily imagine it; and maybe they would not be daunted by the fact that we find an infinite number of phenomena that greatly surpass our imagination and very many others that confound it because of its weakness. But enough on this subject.

Everything that exists is absolutely necessary and could not have been different. There is no "objective" sense in which what exists is either good or bad, beautiful or ugly. Everything just is. These value terms only have meaning from different *perspectives*. There are things that are good-for-humans or bad-for-humans, but nothing that is good-in-itself. Cancer is bad *for humans*, but may be good *for worms and flowers* (who use the corpses for food). Similarly, nothing is in itself beautiful or ugly except from different perspectives. Something is beautiful-to-humans when it is easy for humans to imagine or understand. There are no objective transcendent standards of beauty or ugliness.

The other notions are nothing but modes of imagining by which the imagination is diversely affected, yet they are considered by the ignorant as the main attributes of things, as they believe that everything was created for their benefit and call the nature of any given thing 'good' or 'bad', 'healthy' or 'rotten' and 'corrupt' depending on how they are affected by it. For instance, if the movement our nerves receive from the objects represented by our eyes is conducive to health, the objects causing it are called 'beautiful', whereas the objects that cause the opposite movement are called 'ugly'. Further, the things that are perceived through our sense of smell are referred to as 'fragrant' or 'fetid'; those perceived through our taste, 'sweet' or 'bitter', 'full-flavored' or 'insipid', and so on; those perceived through our touch, 'hard' or 'soft', 'rough' or 'smooth', and the like; finally, what affects our ears is said to give rise to noise, sound, or harmony; this last thing has made people so foolish as to believe that God himself takes pleasure in harmony. There are even philosophers who have persuaded themselves that the motion of the heavenly bodies gives rise to harmony. All of these instances sufficiently show that everyone has judged things according to the state of their brain, or rather mistaken for things the modifications of their imagination.

The absurdity, Spinoza thinks, is to infer that something is good-for-God or good-in-itself just because it has a positive effect on human brains.

Thus, it is no surprise (let me point this out in passing) that as many controversies as we witness among people should have arisen at all, controversies that finally birthed Skepticism. For while human bodies are similar in many respects, they differ in very many others, so that what seems good to one seems bad to another; what seems well-ordered to one seems confused to another; what is pleasing to one displeases another; and so on with all the rest, which I will not delve into here, first, because this is not the place to deal with this subject at length, and also because everybody has experienced it abundantly. It is commonly said: 'So many heads, so many minds;'[1] 'everyone is full of their own wisdom;' 'brains differ no less than palates.' All of these proverbs show that people judge things according to their mental disposition and imagine things rather than understand them; for if they had understood things, the aforementioned truths would, if not attract them, at least convince them, as the case of mathematics shows.

Thus, we see that all the notions by which most people are wont to explain nature are mere modes of imagining and do not indicate the true nature of anything but only the constitution of the imagination; and since they have names as though of entities existing outside the imagination, I call them entities not of reason but of imagination; therefore, all the arguments that are drawn against us from such notions are easily refuted. Many usually argue in this way: If all things have followed from the necessity of the absolutely perfect nature of God, why have so many imperfections come about in nature, such as the corruption of things to the point of putridity, nauseating ugliness, confusion, evil, wrong, and so on. As I have just said, however, these people are easily refuted, for the perfection of things must be judged only from their own nature and power; consequently, things are not more or less perfect depending on whether they delight or offend human senses or whether they are serviceable or repugnant to human nature. To those who ask why God did not create all people to be amenable to being governed by reason alone, I give no answer but this: because he did not lack matter for creating everything, that is, every degree of perfection from highest to lowest; or to put it more correctly, because the laws of his nature were so vast as to suffice to produce everything conceivable by an infinite intellect, as I have shown in Prop. 16.

This passage is extremely interesting because here Spinoza attempts to translate one of his own proofs into the language that his theistic opponents would understand.

---

1 '*Quot capita, tot sensûs*'; the most popular version of this saying is probably *Quot capita, tot sententiae* ('so many heads, so many opinions'). It harkens back to the Roman playwright Terence's *quot homines tot sententiae* (*Phormio* v. 454). (D.A.)

Such are the prejudices I have undertaken to note here. If there are any more of the same sort, they can easily be corrected by anyone with the aid of a little reflection; <therefore, I see no reason to dwell on those things any longer, etc.>.

End of Part I.

PART II
ON THE NATURE AND ORIGIN OF THE MIND

I now go on to explain what must necessarily follow from the essence of God, that is, an eternal and infinite being; not, however, all of it (for we proved in Prop. 16 Pt. 1 that an infinite number of things must follow from it in an infinite number of ways), but only what can lead us, as if by the hand, to the knowledge of the human mind and its highest blessedness.

It is important to note that Spinoza here reminds us that this text is meant to be a work in "Ethics." The goal of this book is not to provide a naturalistic or scientific account of everything, but instead to help humans attain the "highest blessedness."

DEFINITIONS

I. By *body* I mean a mode that expresses in a definite and determinate manner the essence of God in so far as he is considered as an extended thing (see Coroll. Prop. 25 Pt. 1).

II. I consider something as belonging to the *essence* of a thing if, when it is present, the thing in question is necessarily there[1] and, if it is removed, that same thing is necessarily removed as well; in other words, if without it the thing can neither exist nor be conceived, nor can it itself be or be conceived without the thing.

III. By *idea* I mean a conception of the mind that the mind forms because it is a thinking thing.

Explanation. *I say 'conception' rather than 'perception' because the word 'perception' seems to imply that the mind is acted upon by the object, whereas 'conception' seems to express an activity of the mind.*

---

1 *Ponitur.* This Latin word conveys a weaker meaning than *esse* but a stronger one than the English 'is posited.' In the present work it is used to refer to conditional existence, that is, the fact that the existence or non-existence of a thing is dependent on some other thing, without committing to an affirmation or negation of the actual existence of the same. In Duns Scotus's metaphysics, *ponere* designates the lowest possible kind of existence. (D.A.)

IV. By *adequate idea* I mean an idea that, in so far as it is considered in itself without relation to the object (*objectum*), has all the properties or intrinsic marks of a true idea.

Explanation. *I say 'intrinsic' in order to exclude that mark which is extrinsic, namely the agreement of the idea with its object* (ideatum).

> This claim is interesting insofar as Spinoza here claims that true ideas have two different features. First, they correspond to the way the world is. Second, they have the quality of adequacy which is something that we can know about an idea without knowing anything about its correspondence. Spinoza's conception of *adequacy* allows him to avoid skepticism because one can know whether an idea corresponds to reality just by considering its internal phenomenal characteristics. For example, to consider the adequacy of an idea we can ask about the coherence and completeness of the idea.

V. *Duration* is the indefinite continuance of existence.

Explanation. *I say 'indefinite' because it cannot in any way be determined through the nature of the existing thing itself nor by its efficient cause, for the latter necessarily causes* (ponit[1]) *the existence of the thing but does not remove it.*

VI. By *reality* and *perfection* I mean the same thing.

> According to Spinoza, all of the following terms seem to mean the same thing: *power, being, reality,* and *perfection.* A few others will be added to this list later in the work. Note that for Spinoza, these identities show how "perfection" does not include a moral component.

VII. By *particular things* I mean things that are finite and have a determined existence. If, however, several individual <or singular [*singularia*]> things should concur in one action in such a way as to be all simultaneously the cause of one effect, I consider them all—to this extent—as one particular thing.

> Spinoza here addresses the *mereological question* of what causes a collection of finite modes to compose a larger, complex individual. His definition here may seem deceptively straightforward. As given, a group of modes come together to compose a whole complex individual A insofar as the bundle of modes jointly bring about effect B. The complexity to this account follows from the apparent presupposition that effects always come into being by means of a *single* cause. If any bundle of modes brings about a particular effect, then it seems that

---

1 See previous n.

when air, water, sunlight, seeds, etc. come together to bring about a flower, they all are to be conceived as a single individual or particular thing. Of course, this complex individual thing only exists when it is considered in relation to the flower. This individual may be broken into other component parts when considering different particular effects related to the active components of this larger sum.

AXIOMS

I. The essence of man does not involve necessary existence; that is, out of the order of nature this or that man might just as well exist as not exist.

> It is important to note that the claim that a man has an equal chance of existing or not existing given the order of nature is an epistemic claim (a claim about our knowledge) and not a metaphysical one (a claim about the nature of reality).

II. Man thinks, <or, to put it differently, we know that we think>.

III. Modes of thinking, such as love, desire, or whatever other passions of the psyche are distinguished by a name, do not exist unless in the same individual there is an idea of the thing loved, desired, and the like. An idea, on the other hand, can exist even if no other mode of thinking is there.

IV. We perceive that a certain body is affected in many ways.

V. We feel and perceive no particular things, <that is, nothing of the natured nature [*natura naturata*],> except for bodies and modes of thought.

The Postulates are given after Prop. 13.

> After Prop XIII in this Part, there is a "Short Treatise on the Nature of Bodies" where Spinoza explains the fundamental laws that he believes govern the physical world.

PROPOSITIONS

I. *Thought is an attribute of God, that is, God is a thinking thing.*

Proof. Particular thoughts, that is, this and that thought, are modes that express the nature of God in a definite and determined manner (Coroll. Prop. 25 Pt. 1). God, therefore, possesses the attribute (Def. 5 Pt. 1) whose conception is involved by all particular thoughts and through which these are conceived. Thus, thought is one of the infinite attributes of God, which expresses God's eternal and infinite essence (Def. 6 Pt. 1); in other words, God is a thinking thing. *Q.E.D.*

> It is important to note an ambiguity in Spinoza's use of the term 'God.' He sometimes uses this term to refer *only to substance* apart from its modes and at other times he uses the term to refer to both substance and its modes together. Here he is using it in the broader sense, not the narrow one.

Scholium. This Proposition is also evident from the fact that we are able to conceive an infinite thinking being. For the more thoughts a thinking being can think, the more reality, or perfection, we conceive it as possessing; therefore, a being that can think an infinite number of things in an infinite number of ways is necessarily infinite in its ability to think. Thus, since from the consideration of thought alone we conceive of an infinite being, thought is necessarily one of God's infinite attributes (Def. 4 and 6 Pt. 1), as we have claimed.

> Spinoza infers from our ability to conceive of an infinite thinking being that one must exist. While parts of this proof remain quite obscure, the core inference may be that if the idea of an infinite intellect is coherent, then we must attribute such an intellect to the one unlimited or absolutely infinite substance.

PROP. II. *Extension is an attribute of God; that is, God is an extended thing.*

Proof. The proof of this Proposition is similar to that of the previous one.

> Similarly, from the internal coherence of the idea of an infinite physical universe we can infer that such a physical universe must be attributed to the unlimited or absolutely infinite substance. This follows the same reasoning as above: what is coherent is conceivable. What is conceivable is not logically impossible. Substance will express itself in every way possible. What is conceivable is actual.

PROP. III. *In God there is necessarily the idea both of his essence and of all things that necessarily follow from it.*

> In other words, God necessarily understands both the cause and the effect. God knows that its own nature is infinite. To understand this is to understand the infinite things that must and do follow from it.

Proof. God can think an infinite number of things in infinite ways (Prop. 1 of this part) or (what is the same thing: see Prop. 16 Pt. 1) can form the idea of his essence and of all things that necessarily follow from it. Now all that is in the power of God necessarily exist (Prop. 35 Pt. 1); therefore, such an idea necessarily exists and cannot be except in God alone (Prop. 15 Pt. 1). *Q.E.D.*

Scholium. By 'God's power' most understand God's free will and his authority over everything that exists and, accordingly, is generally considered as contingent. For they say that God has the power to destroy everything and to reduce it to nothing; also, they very often liken the power of God to the power of kings. However, we have refuted this idea in Coroll. 1 and 2 Prop. 32 Pt. 1 and have shown in Prop. 16 Pt. 1 that God acts by the same necessity by which he understands himself; that is, just as it follows from the necessity of the divine nature that God understands himself (as all proclaim in unison), it also follows from the same necessity that God performs infinite acts in infinite ways. We also showed in Prop. 34 Pt. 1 that God's power is identical with God's essence as acting; therefore, it is as impossible for us to conceive God as not acting as it is to conceive him as non-existent. Additionally, if I wanted to pursue the subject further, I could also point out here that the power commonly attributed to God is not only human (which shows that God is conceived by most as a human being, or in the likeness of a human being), but also involves powerlessness. However, I am unwilling to go over the same ground so many times. I would only beg readers again and again to turn over frequently in their mind what I have said in Part 1 from Prop. 16 to the end on this subject. For nobody will be able to correctly understand what I mean unless they are very careful not to confuse the power of God with the human power and authority of kings.

PROP. IV. *The idea of God, from which an infinite number of things follow in infinite ways, can only be one.*

Proof. An infinite intellect comprehends nothing but God's attributes and modifications (Prop. 30 Pt. 1). Now God is one (Coroll. 1 Prop. 14 Pt. 1). Thus, the idea of God, from which an infinite number of things follow in infinite ways, can only be one. *Q.E.D.*

PROP. V. *The formal being of ideas acknowledges God as its cause only in so far as he is considered as a thinking thing, not in so far as he is explained by any other attribute; that is, the ideas both of the attributes of God and of particular things do not acknowledge their objects (ideata), that is, the things perceived, as their efficient cause, but God himself in so far as he is a thinking thing.*

Proof. This Proposition is evident from Prop. 3 of this Part. There we drew the conclusion that God can form the idea of his essence and of all things that follow necessarily from it solely because he is a thinking thing, not because he is the object of his own idea. Therefore, the formal being of ideas acknowledges God as its cause in so far as he is a thinking thing. It may also be proved in a different way: The formal being of ideas is a mode of thought (as is self-evident), which expresses in a certain manner the nature of God (Coroll. Prop. 25 Pt. 1) in so far as he is a thinking thing; therefore, it does not involve the conception of any other attribute of God (Prop. 10 Pt. 1); consequently, it is not the effect of any attribute save thought (Ax. 4 Pt. 1). Thus, the formal being of ideas regards God as its cause only in so far as he is considered as a thinking thing. *Q.E.D.*

The *formal being* (or reality) of an idea is the being the *idea itself* has as opposed to the *objective being* of an idea which is the *content of the idea.* To see the distinction Spinoza is making here, imagine a photo of a dog. The formal being of this photograph is the "amount" of being the actual physical photo itself has, as just ink on paper; the objective being of this photograph corresponds to the amount of formal being that a dog has.

It is also important to note here that our *ideas* of the bodies in the world do not come from the bodies themselves. Intuitively, we would explain the fact that I see a book right now in the following "common sense" way: *there is a book in reality, then this book somehow affects my eyes (light bounces off of it and hits my eyes, etc.) which affects my brain. Then my brain affects my mind and I have an idea or experience of seeing a book.* The problem with this common-sense story is that it seems impossible for the mind and the body to interact with one another. Minds are not located in space and so there is nowhere for the body (brain) to "touch" the mind. How can the brain cause an idea in the mind without interacting with it? Spinoza replies that it can't. Instead, Spinoza will develop a very different theory of sense perception.

PROP. VI. *The modes of any given attribute are caused by God in so far as he is considered under the attribute of which they are modes, and not in so far as he is considered under any other attribute.*

Proof. Each attribute is conceived through itself, without any other (Prop. 10 Pt. 1). Therefore, the modes of each attribute involve the conception of their own attribute, but not of any other. Thus, they regard as their cause God only in so far as he is considered under the attribute of which they are modes, and not in so far as he is considered under any other (Ax. 4 Pt. 1). *Q.E.D.*

Corollary. It follows that the formal being of things that are not modes of thought does not follow from the divine nature because that nature has prior knowledge of the things, but things represented in ideas follow and are deduced from their attributes in the same manner and with the same necessity as we have shown ideas to follow from the attribute of thought.

> Here we start to see how Spinoza will explain sense-perception. Substance must fully "express" itself in an infinite number of modes. Because substance can be correctly conceived according to an infinite number of attributes, these modes can be understood correctly in an infinite number of different ways. One way to understand the modes of substance is as an *infinite physical universe*. Another way is as an *infinite mind*. Both are equally good ways to understand substance and its modes. But then it follows that all of the bodies that exist in the infinite physical universe exist not because they were first thought up by God and then created, but rather simply because they follow from the nature of substance considered under the attribute of extension. Similarly, all of the ideas that exist (including the sense-perceptions) are not caused by external bodies, but rather follow from substance alone considered under the attribute of thought.

PROP. VII. *The order and connection of ideas is the same as the order and connection of things.*

Proof. This Proposition is evident from Ax. 4 Pt. 1. For the idea of everything that is caused depends on the knowledge of the cause of which it is an effect.

> The fourth axiom of Part I is: "The idea of the effect requires and involves the idea of the cause." It is hard to see how it follows from this claim alone that the order and connection of ideas must be the same as the order and connection of bodies. Instead, a more intuitive argument for this proposition would seem to follow from the nature of the attributes. Because substance considered under the attribute of extension is the same substance as the substance considered under the attribute of thought, then the modes of extension are identical to the modes of thought. These are the same modes considered in two different ways. For this reason, the order and connection of ideas will be

the same as the order and connection of bodies. This argument is made in the *Scholium* below.

Corollary. It follows that God's power of thinking is equal to his actual power of action; that is, whatever follows from God's infinite nature formally (*formaliter*) follows in the same order and connection from God's idea in God objectively (*objectivē*).

Scholium. Before going any further, we must recall what we have pointed out above, namely that whatever can be perceived by an infinite intellect as constituting the essence of a substance belongs only to one substance; consequently, thinking substance and extended substance are one and the same substance, comprehended now under one attribute, now under the other. Similarly, a mode of extension and the idea of that mode are one and the same, albeit expressed in two different ways—something that seems to have been dimly recognized by some Jews, namely those who maintain that God, God's intellect, and the things understood by God are one and the same. For instance, a circle existing in nature and the idea of a circle existing, which is also in God, are one and the same thing explained through different attributes. Thus, whether we conceive nature under the attribute of extension, under the attribute of thought, or under any other attribute, we will find the same order, in other words, one and the same connection of causes—that is, the same things following from one another. And if I said <before> that God is the cause of an idea—for instance, that of the circle—only in so far as he is a thinking thing, and of the circle only in so far as he is an extended thing, it is for no other reason than because the formal being of the idea of a circle can only be perceived as a proximate cause through another mode of thinking, and that again through another, and so on to infinity. It follows that, so long as we consider things as modes of thinking, we must explain the order of the whole of nature, in other words, the whole chain of causes, through the attribute of thought only; and in so far as we consider things as modes of extension, we must explain the order of the whole of nature solely through the attribute of extension as well; and the same I maintain must apply to the other attributes. Therefore, God is really the cause of things as they are in themselves in so far as he consists of infinite attributes. I cannot for the time being explain these things more clearly.

So, to repeat the key ideas here, there is the one substance which is fully expressed in an infinite number of modes. These modes causally interact with one another. Because the substance has no limitations it can be conceived in an infinite number of different ways. So, the idea of the infinite physical universe and the idea of the infinite mind are two different ways of thinking about the same thing (substance and its modes). From these claims two interesting conclusions follow (as we will see). First, minds and bodies are the same thing conceived in two ways. Second, every physical body has a mind.

PROP. VIII. *The ideas of particular things—in other words, modes— that do not exist must be comprehended in the infinite idea of God in the same way that the formal essences of particular things (that is, modes) are contained in the attributes of God.*

Proof. This Proposition is evident from the previous one; it is however more clearly understood from the preceding Scholium.

Corollary. It follows that, so long as particular things do not exist except in so far as they are comprehended in God's attributes, their objective being (that is, their ideas) does not exist except in so far as the infinite idea of God exists; and when particular things are said to exist, not only in so far as they are contained in God's attributes, but also in so far as they are said to last (*durare*), their ideas will also involve existence, through which they are said to last.

> It rightly seems very problematic for Spinoza to talk about "ideas of things that do not exist," since there cannot be an idea that does not correspond to some actual bodily fact without violating Spinoza's claim that "The order and connection of ideas is the same as the order and connection of things." As such, Spinoza's claim here requires some explanation. This puzzle might be explained in this way. At the moment, there are sadly no penguins in my office. Given the order and connection of causes it is, in fact, impossible that there could have been a penguin in my office right now. But the *epistemological possibility* of a penguin existing in my office right now does exist. Given the nature of space we know *what it would be* for a penguin to be in my office right now (e.g., it would be black and white, cute, smell like fish, etc.), and given the laws that govern bodies there is no internal contradiction in the idea of there being a penguin in my office (e.g., a penguin would fit in my office) and so the ideal essence of such a penguin must exist even if the actual penguin does not.

Scholium. If anyone desires an example to explain this point more extensively, I will not be able to give them any that adequately explains the thing I am addressing here, since it is unique; however, I will endeavour to illustrate it as far as possible <with an example>. The circle is of such nature that, with any of the straight lines that intersect within it, the rectangles[1] under their segments will be equal to one another; thus, the circle contains infinite rectangles equal to each other. Yet none of these rectangles can be said to exist except in so far as the circle exists, nor can the idea of any of these rectangles be said to exist except in so far as they are comprehended in the idea of the circle. Let us now imagine that, out of this infinite number of rectangles, only two, E and D, exist. Certainly, their ideas too now exist not only in so far as they are contained in the idea of the circle, but also in so far as they involve the existence of those rectangles; as a consequence, they are distinguished from the remaining ideas of the remaining rectangles.

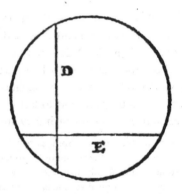

PROP. IX. *The idea of a particular thing actually existing is caused by God, not in so far as he is infinite, but in so far as he is considered as affected by another idea of a particular thing actually existing, of which too he is the cause in so far as he is affected by a third idea, and so on to infinity.*

Proof. The idea of an individual thing actually existing is an individual mode of thinking, which is distinct from other modes (Coroll. and Schol. Prop. 8 of this part); thus, it is caused by God only in so far as he is a thinking thing (Prop. 6 of this part); not, however, in so far as he is a thinking thing absolutely (Prop. 28 of

---

1 Here the word obviously refers to a figure with at least one straight angle, not one with four. (D.A.)

Pt. 1), but in so far as he is considered as affected by another <definite> mode of thinking; and of this latter too God is the cause in so far as he is affected by yet another <definite mode of thinking>, and so on to infinity. Now the order and connection of ideas is the same as the order and connection of causes (Prop. 7 of this part); therefore, the cause of a given individual idea is another idea, that is, God in so far as he is considered as modified by another idea; and so is he of this one too, in so far as he is affected by another idea, and so on to infinity. *Q.E.D.*

From God (conceived under the attribute of thought) an infinite number of ideas follow. That is, raw consciousness (thought) is expressed in an infinite number of particular thoughts (modes of consciousness). So, when we consider *God insofar as he is infinite* we are considering God understood through a particular attribute. When we consider *God insofar as he is affected by another thing* we are considering a particular mode of substance. The idea of a mode includes the idea of God because it includes the idea of the relevant attribute which is the essence of God. So when I think about the coffee cup on my desk, I am thinking of a particular body in space and so the idea of extension considered in a definite and determinate way.

Corollary. The knowledge of anything that takes place in the particular object of any idea exists in God only in so far as he has the idea of the object.

Proof. The knowledge of anything that takes place in the particular object of any idea exists in God (Prop. 3 of this part), not in so far as he is infinite, but in so far as he is considered as affected by another idea of an individual thing (previous Prop.). Now the order and connection of ideas is the same as the order and connection of things (Prop. 7 of this part); therefore, the knowledge of what takes place in any particular object will be in God only in so far as he has the idea of that object. *Q.E.D.*

PROP. X. *The being of substance is not a part of the essence of man; in other words, substance does not constitute the form of man.*

Proof. The being of substance involves necessary existence (Prop. 7 Pt. 1). If, therefore, the being of substance were a part of the essence of man, it would follow that, substance being given, man would necessarily exist (Def. 2 of this part); consequently, man would necessarily exist, which is absurd (Ax. 1 of this part). Therefore, etc. *Q.E.D.*

By *form* here Spinoza seems to be referring to the Aristotelian distinction between matter and form whereby everything that exists is some material arranged according to some particular form that defines and directs its nature. In this context, Spinoza is only asserting that substance is not part of the essence of man. Which is simply to say, a person does not qualify as a substance for Spinoza.

Scholium. This Proposition may also be proved from Prop. 5 Pt. 1, in which it is shown that there cannot be two substances of the same nature. Since, on the other hand, there can be more than one person, it is not the being of substance that constitutes the form of man. Also, the Proposition is evident from all the other properties of substance, namely that substance is by its own nature infinite, immutable, indivisible, and so on, as anyone can easily understand.

Corollary. It follows that the essence of man is constituted by certain modifications of God's attributes.

Proof. The being of substance does not belong to the essence of man (previous Prop.). Therefore, it is something that is in God and can neither exist nor be conceived without God (Prop. 15 Pt. 1), that is, a modification—in other words, a mode—that expresses God's nature in a certain and determined manner (Coroll. Prop. 25 Pt. 1).

Scholium. Everyone must surely admit that nothing can exist or be conceived without God, for everybody agrees that God is the one and only cause of all things, both of their essence and of their existence; that is, God is not only the cause of things with respect to their being made (*secundum fieri*), as is generally granted, but also with respect to their being (*secundum esse*). At the same time, most claim that that without which a thing can neither exist nor be conceived belongs to the essence of that thing; consequently, they believe either that God's nature is a part of the essence of the things created or that the things created can exist or be conceived without God; or—what is more accurate—they hold inconsistent beliefs.

The problem Spinoza is addressing here is that we traditionally think of the essence of something as the necessary and jointly sufficient conditions for the existence of that thing. That is, all the properties that something must have such that when it has them all it is guaranteed to be a thing of that kind. So for a book (as historically conceived) to be a copy of Spinoza's *Ethics* it must be made of paper, have covers, have individual pages with particular ink marks on them, etc. Each of these features is necessary if something is to count as being a copy of Spinoza's *Ethics*. Now if we were careful in listing these necessary conditions, then we could get a jointly sufficient list of conditions such that having them all would guarantee that the book was a copy of the *Ethics*. But Spinoza identifies a problem with this traditional way of thinking about essences. Since substance is necessary for the existence of anything, this definition of essence would make God an essential part of everything that exists! Of course, since God is necessary and infinite, if God were a part of everything that exists, then all modes would be necessary and infinite by their own nature (a clear contradiction for Spinoza: see Prop V Part I). To avoid this consequence, Spinoza changes the definition of essence in the following way after diagnosing what he takes to be the root cause of the error.

I think the cause for such confusion is mainly that they have not kept to the proper order of philosophical thinking. For God's nature, on which they should have reflected first since it is prior both in the order of knowledge and the order of nature, they have taken to be last in the order of knowledge and have thought that what is called 'the objects of sensation' come before everything else; hence in considering natural phenomena they paid nothing less attention than God's nature, and when afterwards they applied their mind to the study of the divine nature, they paid nothing less attention than the first figments with which they had overlaid the knowledge of natural phenomena, all things that could not at all help in understanding the divine nature. It is hardly surprising, then, that these people have contradicted themselves all the time. But I will pass over this point. My intention here was <not so much to contradict them but> merely to explain the reason why I did not claim that that without which a thing cannot exist or be conceived belongs to the essence of that thing. In fact, individual things cannot exist or be conceived without God, yet God is not part of their essence. I said instead[1] that something necessarily constitutes the essence of a thing if, when it is given, the thing is necessarily given (*ponitur*) also, and when it is removed, the thing is necessarily removed (*tollitur*) also; in other words, that without which the thing can neither exist nor be conceived and which itself, in turn, can neither exist nor be conceived without the thing.

---

1 In Def. 2 of this part. (D.A.)

So the essence of a mode is not the necessary and jointly sufficient conditions for it, but rather that which when posited to exist guarantees the existence of the mode. It is not immediately obvious how this definition is different from the problematic one except to say that by "posit" to exist Spinoza seems to be implicitly restricting himself to modes. So his new definition is something like: The essence of a mode is defined by the relation the mode bears to surrounding modes. This relative position guarantees the existence of the mode when the surrounding modes are posited to exist. One interesting consequence of this definition is that it gives modes essential historical properties. That is, since it is impossible that I could have been the child of other parents than I was, being the child of A and B is part of my essence.

PROP. XI. *The first element that constitutes the actual being of the human mind is nothing other than the idea of some particular thing actually existing.*

Proof. The essence of man is constituted by certain modes of God's attributes (Coroll. previous Prop.), namely by the modes of thinking (Ax. 2 of this part), the idea of all of which is prior in nature (Ax. 3 of this part); and once the idea is given, the other modes (those to which the idea is prior in nature) must be in the same individual (same Ax.). Therefore, an idea is the first element that constitutes the being of the human mind. Not, however, the idea of a non-existent thing; for in that case the idea itself cannot be said to exist (Coroll. Prop. 8 of this part); it must therefore be the idea of a thing that actually exists. Not, however, of an infinite thing; for an infinite thing must necessarily always exist (Prop. 21 and 22 Pt. 1); this, however, is absurd (Ax. 1 of this part). Therefore, the first element that constitutes the actual being of the human mind is the idea of an individual thing actually existing. *Q.E.D.*

Corollary. It follows that the human mind is part of God's infinite intellect; thus, when we say that the human mind perceives this or that, we are saying nothing other than that God has this or that idea, not in so far as he is infinite, but in so far as he is explained through the nature of the human mind, that is, in so far as he constitutes the essence of the human mind; and when we say that God has this or that idea not only in so far as he constitutes the essence of the human mind, but also in so far as he also has the idea of another thing together with the human mind, we are saying that the human mind perceives a thing in part, that is, inadequately.

Scholium. At this point my readers will no doubt get stuck and call to mind many things that will cause them to hesitate; so I beg them to accompany me step by step and refrain from judging until they have read the entire argument.

Spinoza has now explicitly drawn two important consequences of his view. Namely, that every human mind is part of the infinite intellect of God and that every physical body that exists must have a mind. That is, everything that exists can be understood under the attribute of thought.

PROP. XII. *Whatever occurs in the object of the idea that constitutes the human mind must be perceived by the human mind, that is, there will necessarily be in the human mind an idea of that occurrence. In other words, if the object of the idea constituting the human mind is a body, nothing can take place in that body without being perceived by the mind, <that is, without there being an idea in the mind>.*

Proof. Whatever occurs in the object of any idea, there is necessarily a knowledge of it in God (Coroll. Prop. 9 of this part) in so far as he is considered as affected by the idea of said object, that is, in so far as he constitutes the mind of anything (Prop. 11 of this part). Therefore, whatever occurs in the object of the idea constituting the human mind, there is necessarily knowledge of it in God in so far as he constitutes the nature of the human mind; that is, the knowledge of said thing will necessarily be in the mind (Coroll. Prop. 11); in other words, the mind perceives it. *Q.E.D.*

Scholium. This Proposition is also evident and more clearly to be understood from Schol. Prop. 7 of this part, to which I here refer.

Since ideas (modes of thought) and bodies (modes of extension) are the same thing, a change in one necessitates a change in the other because there is only one thing here that we are just thinking about in two ways.

PROP. XIII. *The object of the idea that constitutes the human mind is the body, that is, a certain mode of extension that actually exists, and nothing else.*

Proof. If the body were not the object of the human mind, the ideas of the modifications of the body would not be in God in so far as it constitutes our mind, but in so far as it constitutes the mind of something else (Coroll. Prop. 9 of this part); that is, the ideas of the modifications of the body would not be in our mind (Coroll. Prop. 11). Now we do possess the idea of the modifications of the body (Ax. 4); therefore, the object of the idea constituting the human mind is the body, and it actually exists (Prop. 11). Further, if besides the body there were some other object of the idea constituting the mind, then, as nothing can exist from which some effect does not follow (Prop. 36 Pt. 1), there would necessarily have to be in our mind the idea of some effect of that other object (Prop. 12 of this part); there is, however, no idea of it (Ax. 5). Therefore, the object of our mind is the body that exists and nothing else. *Q.E.D.*

> So we know that the mind and body are one and the same thing conceived in two ways. But we get in these passages another key idea that the mind is only thinking about one thing, that is, the body. So the representational content of a human mind is one's body. The only thing you are thinking about is your body and different changes that your body is undergoing. In this way we don't perceive external bodies directly; instead we just perceive the changes that external bodies make to our body.
>
> But to go one step deeper. The mind and the body are the same thing. So every idea is just an idea *of itself* under a different attribute.

Corollary. It follows that a human being is composed of mind and body and that the human body exists exactly in the way that we perceive it.

Scholium. We thus understand not only that the human mind is united to the body, but also what is to be understood by the union of mind and body. However, no one will be able to grasp this adequately, that is, distinctly, unless they first have adequate knowledge of the nature of our body.

> Spinoza here references "adequate" knowledge. Just as an adequate idea is complete, adequate knowledge is here described as the sort of knowledge which allows one to recognize that one thing is distinct from another. Such knowledge requires an adequate idea of the body since if you were not sure about the nature of a particular body, then you could not be certain that one body is distinct from the other bodies with which it is immediately conjoined. A principled ground for distinguishing objects requires that a complete and coherent "internal" account of the thing can be conceived independently from the things surrounding it.

For the Propositions we have put forward thus far have been entirely general and apply no more to human beings than to all other individual things, all of which are animated, albeit to different degrees. For of each and any thing there is necessarily an idea in God, of which God is the cause in the same way as he is the cause of the idea of the human body; thus, whatever we have asserted of the idea of the human body must necessarily also be asserted of the idea of everything else. Yet neither can we deny that ideas—just like the objects themselves—differ from each other, one being more excellent than another and containing more reality, just as the object of one idea is more excellent than the object of another and contains more reality. Thus, in order to determine wherein the human mind differs from other things and wherein it surpasses them, we need to know the nature of its object, that is, of the human body. However, I cannot explain on said nature here, nor is it necessary to do so for the purpose of proving my Propositions. I will only say, in general terms, that the more capable any given body is of doing many things or receiving many impressions at once compared to others, the more capable its mind will be of forming many simultaneous perceptions compared to others; and the more the actions of one body depend on itself alone and the less other bodies concur with it in action, the more capable its mind will be of distinct comprehension. From this we can recognize the superiority of one mind over others and can further see the reason why we have only a very confused knowledge of our body, and many other things that I will deduce from it in the following. Thus, I think it will be worth while to explain and more strictly prove my present statements. In order to do so, I must premise a few Propositions concerning the nature of bodies.

> Here begins a temporary break in Part II. Spinoza is inserting into his text a "Short Treatise on the Nature of Bodies." Since the format of this short treatise differs from the rest of the book, it is reasonable to believe that Spinoza wrote it separately and inserted it here.

AXIOM I. All bodies are either in motion or at rest.

AXIOM II. Every body moves sometimes more slowly, sometimes more quickly.

LEMMA I. *Bodies are distinguished from one another with respect to motion and rest, quickness and slowness, and not with respect to substance.*

Proof. The first part of this Proposition is, I take it, self-evident. That bodies are not distinguished with respect to substance is clear both from Prop. 5 Pt. 1 and Prop. 8 Pt. 1, but is made even clearer by what I have said in the Schol. Prop. 15 Pt. 1.

LEMMA II. *All bodies agree in certain respects.*

Proof. All bodies agree in the fact that they involve the conception of one and the same attribute (Def. 1 of this part); further, in the fact that they can move now more slowly, now faster, and that they can be at all (*absolutè*) in motion or at rest.

LEMMA III. *A body in motion or at rest must have been determined to move or rest by another body, which was in turn determined to move or rest by another one, and this last one again by another one, and so on to infinity.*

Proof. Bodies are individual things (Def. 1 of this part), which are distinguished from one another with respect to motion and rest (Lemma 1); thus, each must necessarily have been determined to move or rest by another individual thing (Prop 28 Pt. 1), namely by another body (Prop. 6 of this part), which too is either in motion or at rest (Ax. 1). And this body could, in turn, not be moving or resting had it not been determined to move or rest by another body (same reasoning), and the latter again by another (same reasoning), and so on to infinity. *Q.E.D.*

Corollary. It follows that a body in motion stays in motion until it is determined to rest by some other body; and a body at rest remains so until it is determined to move by some other body. This is also self-evident: when I suppose that a body, say A, is at rest and do not take into consideration other bodies in motion, I cannot affirm anything concerning body A except that it is at rest. If it afterwards comes to pass that A is in motion, this cannot have resulted from its having been at rest, for no other consequence could have been involved than its remaining at rest. If, on the other hand, A is posited to be moving, we will, so long as we only consider A, be unable to affirm anything concerning it except that it is in motion. If A is subsequently found to be at rest, this rest cannot be the result of A's previous motion, for from its motion there could have followed nothing but that A should move; the state of rest must therefore have resulted from something that was not in A, namely from an external cause by which <the moving body A> was determined to rest.

Axiom I. All modes by which one body is affected by another follow from the nature of the body affected and, at the same time, from that of the body affecting, so that one and the same body may move in different modes according to the difference in the nature of the bodies moving it and, on the other hand, different bodies may be moved in different modes by one and the same body.

Axiom II. When a body in motion impinges on another one that is at rest without being able to move, it is reflected in order to continue its motion, and the angle formed by the line of motion in the reflection and the plane of the body at rest that the moving body has impinged on will be equal to the angle formed by the line of motion of incidence and the same plane.

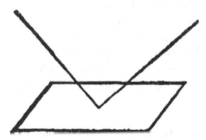

So far we have been speaking only of the simplest bodies, which are distinguished from each other solely by motion and rest, quickness and slowness. We now pass on to compound bodies.

Definition. *When a number of bodies the same or different sizes are compelled by other bodies to remain in contact or if they are moving at the same or different rates of speed in such a way as to share their movements among themselves in a certain fixed way, we will say that such bodies are united to each other and that together they compose one body, or individual thing, which is distinguished from all other bodies by the fact of this union.*

Axiom III. The greater or smaller the surface over which the parts of an individual thing, namely a compound body, are in contact, the harder or easier it will be to force them to move from their position and, consequently, the harder or easier it will be to cause the individual thing in question to assume another form. Thus, I will call the bodies whose parts are in contact over large surfaces *hard*; those whose parts are in contact over small surfaces, *soft*; and those whose parts are in motion relative to one another, *fluid*.

LEMMA IV. *If from a body, that is, an individual thing made up of several bodies, some bodies are separated and, at the same time, an equal number of other bodies of the same nature take their place, the individual thing will preserve its nature as before, without any change to its form.*

Proof. Bodies are not distinguished in respect of substance (Lemma 1); what constitutes the form of an individual thing consists <merely> in a union of bodies (previous Def.); but this union, although there is a continual change of bodies, will be maintained (according to our hypothesis); the individual thing, therefore, will retain its nature as before, both with respect to substance and with respect to mode. *Q.E.D.*

LEMMA V. *If the parts composing an individual thing become greater or smaller, but in such proportion that they all preserve the same mutual relations of motion and rest, the individual thing will likewise preserve its original nature as before, without any change to its form.*

Proof. The same as for the previous Lemma.

LEMMA VI. *If certain bodies composing an individual are compelled to change the motion that they have in one direction for motion in another direction, but in such a manner that they can continue their motions and keep sharing them in the same relation as before, the individual thing will likewise retain its own nature without any change to its form.*

Proof. This Proposition is self-evident, for the individual thing is posited to retain everything we spoke of in its definition as its actual nature <(see the Definition before the fourth Lemma)>.

LEMMA VII. *In addition, the individual thing thus composed preserves its nature, regardless of whether it is in motion or at rest as a whole or whether it moves in this or that direction, as long as each part retains its motion and shares it with the others as before.*

Proof. This Proposition is \<also\> evident from the definition of an individual thing, which you can find before Lemma 4.

Scholium. We thus see how a composite individual thing can be affected in many different ways (*modi*) and nevertheless preserve its nature. Thus far we have conceived an individual thing as composed of nothing but bodies that are distinguished from each other solely by motion and rest, speed and slowness—in other words, of bodies of the simplest character. If, however, we now conceive another thing, composed of several individual things of diverse natures, we will find that it can be affected in many more ways, all while preserving its nature. For as each of its parts consists of several bodies, each part will admit, without change to its nature, of quicker or slower motion and, consequently, be able to share its motions more quickly or more slowly with the remaining parts (Lemma 6). If we further conceive a third kind of individual thing composed of individual things of this second kind, we will find that it can be affected in yet many other ways without changing its form at all. We could easily proceed in this way to infinity and conceive the whole of nature as one individual thing whose parts—that is, all bodies—vary in infinite ways without any change to the individual thing as a whole. I would have to explain and demonstrate this point at greater length if I were writing explicitly \<and specifically on matter or\> on the body; but I have already said that this is not my goal and that I will only touch on the question because it enables me to deduce easily what I have set out to prove.

> So Spinoza has now given us two criteria for distinguishing complicated bodies from one another (that is, for determining what constitutes a part of a whole and what does not). First, he has told us that individuals form a whole insofar as they come together to produce one effect. Second, here he tells us that insofar as the different bodies share the same relatively stable pattern of interactions they form one body. It is possible to reconcile these two views if we see the stable complex pattern of interactions among various bodies as itself an effect. Then those bodies are all parts of one whole *in regard to that stable pattern of motions* by the first principle. But these principles for the individuation of complex bodies work at all levels of complexity and so Spinoza infers that the whole physical universe considered as one whole maintains a given complex pattern of interactions and so must be considered as a single complicated individual for that reason.

POSTULATES

I. The human body is composed of very many individual parts (of diverse natures), each one of which is in itself extremely complex.

II. Of the individual parts composing the human body, some are fluid, some soft, and finally some are hard.

III. The individual parts composing the human body and, consequently, the human body itself are affected by external bodies in very many ways.

IV. The human body needs for its preservation a number of other bodies by which it is continually regenerated, as it were.

V. When the fluid part of the human body is determined by an external body to impinge on another soft part many times, it changes the surface of the latter and leaves on it the impression, as it were, of the external body that pushes it.

VI. The human body can move and arrange external bodies in very many ways.

PROP. XIV. *The human mind is capable of perceiving a large number of things, the more so the more are the ways in which its body can be disposed.*

Proof. The human body is affected by external bodies in very many ways and is so disposed as to affect external bodies in very many ways as well (Post. 3 and 6). Now the human mind must perceive all that takes place in the human body (Prop. 12 of this part); the human mind is, therefore, capable of perceiving a large number of things, the more so <the more the human body [*Corpus humanum*] is capable>. Q.E.D.

PROP. XV. *The idea that constitutes the formal being of the human mind is not simple but composed of a large number of ideas.*

Proof. The idea that constitutes the formal being of the human mind is the idea of the body (Prop. 13 of this part), which is composed of a large number of complex individual parts (Post. 1). Now there is necessarily in God the idea of each individual part of which the body is composed (Coroll. Prop. 8); therefore, the idea of the human body is composed of these numerous ideas of its component parts (Prop. 7). *Q.E.D.*

PROP. XVI. *The idea of every mode in which the human body is affected by external bodies must involve the nature of the human body and at the same time the nature of the external body at hand.*

Proof. All the modes in which any given body is affected follow from the nature of the body affected as well as from the nature of the affecting body (Ax. 1 after Coroll. Lemma 3); therefore, their idea will also necessarily involve the nature of both bodies (Ax. 4 Pt. 1). Consequently, the idea of every mode in which the human body is affected by an external body involves the nature of the human body and of the external body at hand. *Q.E.D.*

> Spinoza's reasoning here is relatively straightforward. The human mind (and every other mind for that matter) is simply a bundle of ideas of physical bodies. But those bodies are impacted by external bodies. When they are impacted, the external bodies "leave a mark" on them (E1a4: "The idea of an effect depends on and involves the idea of a cause"). So the more complex the bundle of bodies is, the more complex the mind corresponding to it is. And the ideas of that complex body will also include many ideas of those impacts or indentations to different parts of it—and so some vague, confused, mutilated idea of the cause of those impacts.

Corollary I. It follows, first, that the human mind perceives the nature of innumerable bodies along with the nature of its own.

Corollary II. It follows, secondly, that the ideas we have of external bodies point to the constitution of our own body rather than the nature of external bodies. I have amply illustrated this in the Appendix to Part 1.

PROP. XVII. *If the human body is affected in a manner that involves the nature of any external body, the human mind will regard the same external body as actually existing or as present to itself until the human body is affected by a modification that excludes the existence or the presence of said external body.*

Proof. This Proposition is self-evident; for as long as the human body continues to be thus affected, so long will the human mind contemplate this modification of the body (Prop. 12 of this part); that is, it will have an idea of the mode that involves the nature of the actually existing external body (previous Prop.). In other words, it will have an idea that does not exclude but posits (*ponit*) the existence or presence of the nature of the external body; therefore, the mind will regard the external body as actually existing or present (Coroll. 1 previous Prop.), until it is affected, etc. *Q.E.D.*

> This proposition is very interesting because it tells us that the default way in which ideas are had in the mind is as presently existing. That is, to think of X is to think of X as presently existing unless one has another idea that excludes the present existence of X. But every idea in itself not only is about something, but affirms the present existence of that thing.

Corollary. The mind will be able to regard external bodies by which the human body has once been affected as if they were present, even though they may no longer exist or be present.

Proof. When external bodies determine the fluid parts of the human body to impinge on the softer parts many times, they change the surface of the latter (Post. 5); hence they are reflected from them in a different manner from before (Ax. 2 after the Coroll. Lemma 3); also, when afterwards they run into the same new surfaces by their own spontaneous movement, they will be reflected in the same manner as when they were impelled towards those surfaces by external bodies. Consequently, while they continue to move after being thus reflected, they will affect the human body in the same manner, which the mind will reflect upon again (Prop. 12 of this part); that is, the mind will again regard the external body as present (Prop. 17 of this part), and will do so as often as the fluid parts of the human body run into the same surfaces by their own spontaneous motion. Therefore, although the external bodies by which the human body was once affected no longer exist, the mind will nevertheless regard them as present as often as this action of the body is repeated. *Q.E.D.*

> Spinoza's biology here is obviously lacking and should probably be best interpreted as a placeholder for a more developed biology in the future.

Scholium. We thus see how it is possible for us to regard as present things that are not, as we often do. It is possible that the same result may be brought about by other causes; here, however, it is enough for me to have indicated one cause by which I can explain this fact just as well as if I had pointed out the true one. Indeed, I do not think I am very far from the truth, as all the postulates I have posited hardly contain anything not backed up by experience, which we may not doubt since we have shown that the human body exists as we feel it (see Coroll. after Prop. 13 of this part). Furthermore, we clearly understand the difference between the idea, say, of Peter that constitutes the essence of Peter's mind and the idea of said Peter that is in another person, for instance, Paul (previous Coroll. and Coroll. 2 Prop. 16 of this part): the former directly explains the essence of Peter's own body and does not involve existence except so long as Peter exists; the latter indicates the constitution of Paul's body rather than Peter's nature <(see the second addition [*Corollarium*] of the sixteenth presentation [*Propositio*] in this part)>; therefore, as long as this constitution of Paul's body lasts, Paul's mind will regard Peter as present to itself even if he does not exist. Further—to retain the usual terminology—we will call the modifications of the human body whose ideas represent external bodies as present to us 'the images of things' although they do not relate the figures of things. And when the mind regards bodies in this fashion, we say that it imagines. At this point, in order to indicate where error lies, I would like you to note that the imaginations of the mind, looked at in themselves, do not contain an error; in other words, the mind does not err in the mere act of imagining, but only in so far as it is regarded as being without the idea that excludes the existence of the things it imagines to be present to it. For if the mind, while imagining non-existent things as present to it, were at the same time conscious that they do not really exist, it would certainly ascribe this power of imagination to a virtue of its nature, not to a fault, especially if this faculty of imagination depended solely on its own nature, that is, if this faculty of imagination of the mind were free (Def. 7 Pt. 1).

Spinoza here is saying that all ideas considered in themselves are true. The only difference between a true idea and a false one is that a false idea is a fragment of a true idea. By analogy, if we consider a painting, we may see that a certain patch of color represents a hat. But if most of the painting were covered up then we would see only a brown splotch. But the brown splotch does exist. The falsity only comes when the mind affirms that it is only a brown splotch.

PROP. XVIII. *If the human body has once been affected by two or more bodies at the same time, when the mind afterwards imagines any of them, it will immediately remember the others too.*

Proof. The mind imagines any given body (Coroll. previous Prop.) because the human body is affected and disposed by the impressions from an external body in the same manner as it was affected when some of its parts were pushed by said external body; but (in our hypothesis) the body was then so disposed that the mind imagined two bodies at once; therefore, it will again imagine two bodies at once and, when it imagines either, will immediately remember the other too. *Q.E.D.*

> This argument is slightly harder to see. So the claim is that if two objects impacted your body at the same time, then the two impacts will be understood to be one complex impact. Thus, whenever one of those impacts is again recalled the other will be recalled as well.

Scholium. We now clearly see what memory is: it is simply a certain concatenation of ideas involving the nature of things outside the human body, a concatenation that arises in the mind according to the order and concatenation of the modifications (*affectiones*) of the human body. I say, *firstly*, that it is a concatenation only of those ideas that involve the nature of things outside the human body, but not of ideas that explain the nature of these things; for ideas of the modifications of the human body are in truth those that involve the nature both of the human body and of external bodies (Prop. 16 of this part). I say, *secondly*, that this concatenation arises according to the order and concatenation of the modifications of the human body, in order to distinguish it from that concatenation of ideas that arises from the order of the intellect, by which the mind perceives things through their primary causes and which is the same in everybody. And from this we can further clearly understand why the mind immediately moves from the thought of one thing to the thought of another thing that has no similarity to the first; for instance, from the thought of the word *pomum* ('apple') a Roman would immediately fall into the thought of the fruit, which has no similitude with the articulate sound in question nor anything in common with it except for the fact that the body of that person has often been affected by these two things: they have often heard the word *pomum* while seeing the fruit. Likewise, everyone will go on from one thought to another according to how the habit of each has ordered the images of things in their body. A soldier, for instance, upon seeing the tracks of a horse in sand, will at once pass from the thought of a horse to the thought of a horseman, and from there to the thought of war, etc.; a farmer, on the other hand, will pass from the thought of a horse to the thought of a plough, a field, etc. Thus, everybody will pass from one thought to this or that other one depending on how they have accustomed themselves to connecting and associating the mental images of things in this or that manner.

> Spinoza is here talking about bodies as if they are substances which have modifications and it will be easier for the remainder of the *Ethics* to think of them in this way. But, of course, a body is just a collection of properties had by a region of space and external bodies alter that bundle of properties in various ways. So we are dealing here with modes of modes. Spinoza is saying in this section that memories are just ideas of physical changes in the body. So the physical patterns of changes in the body determine (are the same thing as) the order of memories in the mind.

PROP. XIX. *The human mind has no knowledge of the human body itself and does not know it exists except through the ideas of the modifications by which the body is affected.*

Proof. The human mind is the very idea, or knowledge, of the human body (Prop. 13 of this part), which is in God in so far as he is regarded as affected by another idea of a particular thing (Prop. 9 of this part). Or so: The human body needs very many bodies by which to be, as it were, continually regenerated (Post. 4); and the order and connection of ideas is the same as the order and connection of causes (Prop. 7 of this part); this idea will be in God in so far as he is regarded as affected by the ideas of very many particular things. Thus, God has the idea of the human body—that is, knows the human body—in so far as he is affected by very many other ideas, and not in so far as he constitutes the nature of the human mind; that is, the human mind does not know the human body (Coroll. Prop. 11 of this part). Now the ideas of the modifications of the body are in God in so far as he constitutes the nature of the human mind, that is, the human mind perceives the same modifications (Prop. 12 of this part) and, consequently, the human body itself (Prop. 16), and as actually existing (Prop. 17). Therefore, the mind perceives the human body itself only to this extent. *Q.E.D.*

> The argument here is extremely difficult, but Spinoza needs it to solve an obvious problem with his view. If my mind is just a bundle of ideas of each part of my body, then why don't I know my own body in perfect detail? Why don't I directly perceive how my own kidneys are functioning? His answer is that the human mind is not all of the ideas of the human body, but only the ideas of interactions with the human body. That is, the human mind is the complicated bundle of ideas only of all the interactions that are taking place between the body and the external world. This conclusion resolves the rather obvious objection to Spinoza's views and it leads to some interesting consequences. Because ideas are modes considered under the attribute of thought, there is in God an idea of my kidneys down to the smallest detail. Here we seem to come close to the idea of something like an "unconscious" mind. Because I am aware of only a small number the ideas of my body, most of the ideas of my body are not conscious to me. But unlike in most theories of the unconscious, these ideas are conscious—they are just had by someone else. "Your" mind is only one of probably many minds that are related directly to your body. Also see Prop XXIV below.

PROP. XX. *In God too there is an idea, or knowledge, of the human mind which follows in God in the same manner and relates to God in the same manner as the idea, or knowledge, of the human body.*

Proof. Thought is an attribute of God (Prop. 1 of this part); therefore, there must necessarily be in God the idea both of thought itself and of all its modifications (Prop. 3) and, consequently, also of the human mind (Prop. 11). Also, that this idea, or knowledge, of the mind is in God does not follow in so far as he is infinite, but in so far as he is affected by another idea of an individual thing (Prop. 9). Now the order and connection of ideas is the same as the order and connection of causes (Prop. 7); therefore, this idea, or knowledge, of the mind is in God and relates to God in the same manner as the idea, or knowledge, of the body. *Q.E.D.*

> Spinoza is arguing here that not only are there ideas of the body, but there are also ideas of the ideas of the body. Furthermore, these ideas of the ideas of the body are just different ways of conceiving of the ideas of the body. My idea of X and my idea of my idea of X are the same idea considered in two ways. It is, admittedly, very hard to see how this could be true. Spinoza will compare his idea here to Descartes's idea of the "formal reality" of an idea (see next proof).

The formal reality of the idea is just the idea considered without regard to its representational content, like considering an oil painting as just "paint on a canvas" without reference to what it is trying to represent. But this analogy is imperfect because by definition the Cartesian formal reality of an idea has no representational content. It is not about anything at all. But the idea of the idea of X in Spinoza is about something, namely, the idea of X. It somehow represents the idea of X.

PROP. XXI. *This idea of the mind is united with the mind in the same way that the mind is united with the body.*

Proof. That the mind is united with the body we have shown from the fact that the body is the object of the mind (Prop. 12 and 13 of this part). Consequently, the idea of the mind must, by the same reasoning, be united with its object, that is, with the mind itself in the same manner that the mind is united with the body. *Q.E.D.*

Scholium. This Proposition is comprehended much more clearly from what we have said in Schol. Prop. 7 of this part. There we showed that the idea of the body and the body—that is, mind and body (Prop. 13 of this part)—are one and the same individual thing conceived now under the attribute of thought, now under the attribute of extension; therefore, the idea of the mind and the mind itself are one and the same thing, which is conceived under one and the same attribute, namely thought. I therefore claim that the existence in God of the idea of the mind and that of the mind itself follow by the same necessity from the same power of thinking. For in truth the idea of the mind, that is, the idea of an idea, is nothing but the form of an idea in so far as it is conceived as a mode of thought without reference to an object. For at the same time that someone knows something, they know by that very fact that they know it, and at the same time know that they know that they know it, and so on to infinity. But I will deal with this matter later.

PROP. XXII. *The human mind perceives not only the modifications of the body, but also the ideas of such modifications.*

Proof. The ideas of the ideas of modifications follow in God in the same manner and relate to God in the same manner as the ideas of the modifications themselves. This is proved in the same way as Prop. 20 of this part. Now the ideas of the modifications of the body are in the human mind (Prop. 12), that is, in God in so far as he constitutes the essence of the human mind (Prop. 11); therefore, the ideas of these ideas will be in God in so far as he has the knowledge, or idea, of the human mind; that is, they will be in the human mind itself (previous Prop.). Therefore, the human mind perceives not only the modifications of the body but also the ideas of those modifications. *Q.E.D.*

PROP. XXIII. *The mind does not know itself except in so far as it perceives the ideas of the modifications of the body.*

Proof. The idea or knowledge of the mind follows in God in the same manner and relates to God in the same manner as the idea, or knowledge, of the body (Prop. 20 of this part). But since the human mind does not know the human body itself (Prop. 19), that is, since the knowledge of the human body does not relate to God in so far as he constitutes the nature of the human mind (Coroll. Prop. 11), neither does the knowledge of the mind relate to God in so far as he constitutes the essence of the human mind; therefore, the human mind has to this extent no knowledge of itself (same Coroll.). Also, the ideas of the modifications by which the body is affected involve the nature of the human body itself (Prop. 16), that is, they agree with the nature of the mind (Prop. 13), which is why the knowledge of these ideas will necessarily involve knowledge of the mind. Now the knowledge of these ideas is in the human mind itself (previous Prop.); it follows that the human mind has knowledge of itself only to this extent. *Q.E.D.*

PROP. XXIV. *The human mind does not involve an adequate knowledge of the parts composing the human body.*

Proof. The parts that compose the human body do not belong to the essence of that body, except in so far as they share their motions with one another in a certain fixed relation (see Def. after Coroll. Lemma 3), but not in so far as they can be regarded as individual things independent of their relation to the human body. For the parts of the human body are highly complex individual things (Post. 1), whose parts can be separated from the human body all while its nature and form are fully maintained

(Lemma 4) and can share their motions with other bodies in another relation (Ax. 1 after Lemma 3). Therefore, the idea, or knowledge, of each part will be in God (Prop. 3 of this part), and this in so far as he is regarded as affected by another idea of a particular thing (Prop. 9), a particular thing that is prior in the order of nature to the part itself (Prop. 7). The same thing must also be said of any part of the very individual thing that composes the human body; therefore, the knowledge of each part that composes the human body is in God in so far as he is affected by very many ideas of things, and not in so far as he has the idea of the human body only, in other words, the idea that constitutes the nature of the human mind (Prop. 13). Consequently, the human mind does not involve an adequate knowledge of the human body (Coroll. Prop. 11). *Q.E.D.*

> Here Spinoza gives an interestingly different argument for why the human mind only consists of the ideas of interactions and not the ideas of the bodies themselves. The reason is that the essence of the human body is just a complicated pattern of movements or motions. So to have an idea of the essence of the human body does not involve having some particular idea, but instead consists in having a collection of ideas concerning a particular pattern of interactions. To have an adequate understanding of any pattern of actions (an effect) requires an understanding of the causal facts that result in that pattern. As the causal explanation for any particular pattern of interactions is explained by way of the infinite causal series, by focusing on some portion of this series apart from the whole requires that the idea be thereby inadequate.

PROP. XXV. *The idea of any modification of the human body does not involve an adequate knowledge of the external body.*

Proof. We have shown that the idea of a modification of the human body involves the nature of an external body in so far as that external body conditions the human body in a given manner (Prop. 16 of this part). Now in so far as the external body is an individual thing that does not relate to the human body, the knowledge, or idea, thereof is in God in so far as God is regarded as affected by the idea of a further thing (Prop. 9), which is by nature prior to said external body (Prop. 7). Therefore, an adequate knowledge of the external body is not in God in so far as he has the idea of the modification of the human body; in other words, the idea of the modification of the human body does not involve an adequate knowledge of the external body. *Q.E.D.*

PROP. XXVI. *The human mind does not perceive any external body as actually existing except through the ideas of the modifications of its own body.*

Proof. If the human body is in no way affected by a given external body, then neither is the idea of the human body—that is, the human mind (Prop. 13 of this part)—affected in any way by the idea of the existence of said external body; in other words, it does not perceive its existence in any way (Prop. 7 of this part). On the other hand, to the extent that the human body is in any way affected by some external body, it does perceive that external body (Prop. 16 with Coroll. 1). *Q.E.D.*

Corollary. To the extent that the human mind imagines an external body, it lacks an adequate knowledge thereof.

Proof. When the human mind regards external bodies through the ideas of the modifications of its own body, we say that it imagines (see Schol. Prop. 17 of this part); nor can the mind imagine external bodies as actually existing in any other manner (previous Prop.). Consequently, in so far as the mind imagines external bodies, it lacks an adequate knowledge of them (Prop. 25). *Q.E.D.*

So an imagined idea in Spinoza is just the idea of a modification of a part of the body. Because the idea is not directly of the cause, but only of the way in which the cause modified the body, the imagined idea will be inadequate. Remember that one of Spinoza's most important assumptions is that the idea of the effect requires and involves the idea of the cause. So if an external body bumps into me and (let's just say) creates a square shaped indentation on my skin, then the idea of that indentation will include the idea of the cause only insofar as the cause is square. The cause may be blue or expensive, but those properties didn't leave an impression. Only the shape did. Thus, the idea will be inadequate, that is, partial or incomplete.

PROP. XXVII. *The idea of any modification of the human body does not involve an adequate knowledge of the human body itself.*

Proof. Any idea of a modification of the human body involves the nature of the human body to the extent that the human body itself is regarded as affected in a certain definite manner (Prop. 16 of this part). Now as the human body is an individual thing that can be affected in many other ways, its idea, etc. (See the Proof of Prop. 25 of this part.) *Q.E.D.*

PROP. XXVIII. *The ideas of the modifications of the human body, in so far as they relate only to the human mind, are not clear and distinct but confused.*

Proof. The ideas of the modifications of the human body involve both the nature of external bodies and that of the human body itself (Prop. 16 of this part), and they must involve the nature not only of the human body but also of its parts. For the modifications are modes by which the parts of the human body and, consequently, the human body as a whole is affected (Post. 3). Now the adequate knowledge of external bodies as well as of the parts that compose the human body is not in God in so far as he is regarded as affected by the human mind but in so far as he is regarded as affected by other ideas (Prop. 24 and 25), <that is (following the thirteenth Proposition of this part), this knowledge is not in God in so far as he constitutes the nature of the human mind [*Mens humana*]>. Thus, these ideas of modifications, in so far as they relate to the human mind alone, are like consequences without premises—in other words, confused ideas (as is self-evident). *Q.E.D.*

Scholium. The idea that constitutes the nature of the human mind can in the same manner be proved not to be clear and distinct when considered in itself alone; so can the idea of the human mind and the ideas of the ideas of the modifications of the human body, <to wit, [it can be proven] that they are confused [*Confusae*]> in so far as they relate to the mind only, as anyone can easily see.

PROP. XXIX. *The idea of the idea of any modification of the human body does not involve an adequate knowledge of the human mind.*

Proof. The idea of a modification of the human body does not involve an adequate knowledge of said body (Prop. 27 of this part); in other words, it does not adequately express its nature. This means that it does not agree with the nature of the mind adequately (Prop. 13). Therefore, the idea of this idea does not adequately express the nature of the human mind, that is, does not involve an adequate knowledge thereof (Ax. 6 Pt. 1). *Q.E.D.*

Corollary. It follows that the human mind, any time it perceives things after the common order of nature, has not an adequate but only a confused and fragmentary knowledge of itself, its own body, and external bodies. For the mind does not know itself except in so far as it perceives the ideas of the modifications of body (Prop. 23 of this part). It does not perceive its own body except through the ideas of the modifications themselves (Prop. 19), and only perceives external bodies by the same means (Prop. 26). Thus, in so far as it has these ideas, it lacks an adequate knowledge of itself (Prop. 29), of its own body (Prop. 27), and of external bodies (Prop. 25), but has only a fragmentary and confused one (Prop. 28 with Schol.). *Q.E.D.*

Scholium. I say expressly that the mind has not an adequate but only a confused <and fragmentary> knowledge of itself, its own body, and of external bodies whenever it perceives things after the common order of nature, that is, whenever it is determined from without, by the fortuitous play of circumstance, to reflect on this or that; not, however, whenever it is determined from within, by its own reflecting on several things at once, to understand their points of agreement, difference, and contrast. In fact, whenever it is determined from within in one way or another, it regards things clearly and distinctly, as I will show below.

PROP. XXX. *We can have no knowledge of the duration of our body except a very inadequate one.*

Proof. The duration of our body does not depend on its essence (Ax. 1 of this part) nor on the absolute nature of God (Prop. 21 Pt. 1) but it is determined to exist and act by such <other> causes as are, in turn, determined by other causes to exist and act in a definite and determinate matter, these last again being determined by others, and so on to infinity (Prop. 28 Pt. 1). Thus, the duration of our body depends on the common order of nature and the constitution of things. As for the way these are constituted, an adequate knowledge of this is in God in so far as he has the ideas of all things, but not in so far as he has the idea of the human body only (Coroll. Prop. 9 of this part). Consequently, the knowledge in God of the duration of our body is very inadequate in so far as he is only regarded as constituting the nature of the human mind; that is, this knowledge in our mind is very inadequate (Coroll. Prop. 11). *Q.E.D.*

Spinoza makes an interesting point in this proof which he will develop in Part III. Things can only be destroyed by external causes: nothing can destroy itself. Insofar as we cannot know the duration of a body by knowing the essence of the body, we know that the duration is not determined by internal facts found in that essence.

PROP. XXXI. *We can have no knowledge of the duration of particular things external to ourselves except a very inadequate one.*

Proof. Every particular thing, such as the human body, must be determined by another particular thing to exist and act in a definite and determinate manner; this other particular thing must likewise be conditioned by a third, and so on to infinity (Prop. 28 Pt. 1). Now in the previous Prop. we have shown, based on this common property of particular things, that we have only a very inadequate knowledge of the duration of our body; hence we must draw a similar conclusion with regard to the duration of particular things, namely that we can only have a very inadequate knowledge of their duration. *Q.E.D.*

Corollary. It follows that all particular things are contingent and corruptible. For we can have no adequate idea of their duration (previous Prop.), and this is what we must understand by the contingency and corruptibleness of things (see Schol. 1 Prop. 33 Pt. 1). For nothing is contingent except in this sense (Prop. 29 Pt. 1).

By contingent here, Spinoza means only that we do not know when it will cease to exist. He does not mean that it is metaphysically contingent in that it could have failed to exist or could have been destroyed at a time other than when it was in fact destroyed.

PROP. XXXII. *All ideas are true in so far as they relate to God.*

Proof. All ideas that are in God agree in every respect with their <metaphysical and> epistemic objects[1] (Coroll. Prop. 7 of this part); therefore, they are all true (Ax. 6 Pt. 1). *Q.E.D.*

---

1 *Cum suis ideatis* in the original edition. Gebhardt changes the received text into *cum suis <Objectis et> ideatis* on the basis of the Dutch text, which reads: *met hun Voorwerpen / Objecta / en gedachte zaken / Ideatum /* ("with their objects [*Objecta*] and things thought [*Ideatum*]"). *Objectum* designates the metaphysical object, whereas *Ideatum* refers *(continued)*

PROP. XXXIII. *There is in ideas nothing positive on account of which they are called false.*

Proof. If you deny this, conceive, if possible, a positive mode of thinking that constitutes the form of error, that is, falsehood. This mode of thinking cannot be in God (previous Prop.); on the other hand, outside of God it cannot exist or be conceived (Prop. 15 Pt. 1). Therefore, there can be nothing positive in ideas on account of which they are called false. *Q.E.D.*

> Here is a very clear statement of Spinoza's views that falsity only comes from fragmentation. If an idea is not fragmented—that is, if the idea is adequate—then it must be true.

PROP. XXXIV. *Every idea that in us is absolute, that is, adequate and perfect, is true.*

Proof. When we say that there is an idea in us that is adequate and perfect, we say nothing other than that there is in God an idea that is adequate and perfect in so far as he constitutes the essence of our mind (Coroll. Prop. 11 of this part); consequently, we say nothing other than that such an idea is true (Prop. 32). *Q.E.D.*

> So we can know whether an idea corresponds to the way the external world is by considering only the nature of the idea itself. This claim undercuts the assumptions of radical Cartesian skepticism because Spinoza is saying here that if an idea is not fragmentary but whole and complete, then it must be true and we can know it is true just by considering it and recognizing that it is adequate. To understand what Spinoza means by the internal adequacy of an idea, it may be helpful to consider specific examples. The idea of a point is perhaps an idea of this type. Or, one can think of how Descartes presents his idea of a supremely perfect being. Descartes, like Spinoza, claims that the idea of God is wholly self-evident and complete. There is nothing about the idea that is obscure or less than clear and distinct. And just as Descartes trusts the veracity of clear and distinct ideas, Spinoza maintains that an idea's being wholly adequate guarantees the truth of the idea irrespective of an appeal to some external truthmaker.

---

to the epistemic one. Here as well as in Schol. Prop. 43, the earlier version of the *Ethics* on which the Dutch translation is based must have coupled the two terms, separated by *sive* ('or', which in S. more often than not simply means 'that is' or 'in other words'), whereas the later, published version of the Latin text drops *objectum* in these contexts. (D.A.)

PROP. XXXV. *Falsity consists in the privation of knowledge involved by inadequate, that is, fragmentary and confused ideas.*

Proof. There is in ideas nothing positive that constitutes the form of falsity (Prop. 33 of this part). Now falsity cannot consist in absolute privation <of knowledge> (for minds, not bodies, are said to err and be fooled), nor can it consist in absolute ignorance, for not knowing and being wrong are different things. Therefore, it consists in the privation of knowledge involved by inadequate knowledge of things, that is, fragmentary and confused ideas. *Q.E.D.*

Scholium. In Schol. Prop. 17 of this part I explained in what sense error consists in the privation of knowledge; however, in order to explain this subject more extensively I will give an example. People are mistaken when they think themselves free, <that is, think that they can do or refrain from doing something out of their own free will>; this opinion is made up solely of awareness of their own actions and ignorance of the causes by which they are determined. Their idea of freedom, therefore, is simply their ignorance of any cause for their actions. For when they say that human actions depend on the will, these are words about whose meanings they have no clue, since what the will is and how it moves the body none of them know; those who bring up other things and make up dwellings and habitations for the soul are wont to provoke either laughter or disgust. So when we look at the sun, we imagine that it is about two hundred feet away from us, an error that does not lie in this imagining alone but in the fact that, while we thus imagine, we do not know the sun's true distance or the cause of the imagining. For although we afterwards learn that it is more than six hundred of the earth's diameters away from us, we will nonetheless imagine it to be near; for we do not imagine the sun as near us because we are ignorant of its true distance, but because the modification of our body involves the essence of the sun in so far as the body itself is affected by it.

PROP. XXXVI. *Inadequate and confused ideas follow from the same necessity as adequate, that is, clear and distinct ones.*

Proof. All ideas are in God (Prop. 15 Pt. 1) and, in so far as they relate to God, they are true (Prop. 32 of this part) and adequate

(Coroll. Prop. 7). Therefore, no ideas are confused or inadequate except in so far as they relate to someone's particular mind (on this subject see Prop. 24 and 28 of this part); therefore, all ideas, whether adequate or inadequate, follow from the same necessity (Coroll. Prop. 6). *Q.E.D.*

> The core idea here is pretty intuitive. There is only one infinite mind and all of the ideas in it follow with logical necessity. All false ideas are just parts of these ideas considered out of context. Thus, the inadequate ideas follow with the same necessity as the adequate ones.

PROP. XXXVII. *That which is common to all things* (cf. Lemma 2 above) *and which is equally in a part and in the whole does not constitute the essence of any particular thing.*

Proof. If you deny this, conceive, if possible, that it constitutes the essence of some particular thing, for instance, the essence B. Thus, it can neither exist nor be conceived without B (Def. 2 of this part); but this is against our hypothesis. Therefore, it is not part of essence B, nor does it constitute the essence of any other particular thing. *Q.E.D.*

PROP. XXXVIII. *That which is common to all things and is equally in a part and in the whole cannot be conceived except adequately.*

Proof. Let A be something that is common to all bodies and which is equally present in the part of any given body and in the whole. I maintain that A cannot be conceived except adequately. For there will necessarily be in God an adequate idea of it (Coroll. Prop. 7 of this part), both in so far as he has the idea of the human body and in so far as he has the ideas of its modifications, which partially involve both the nature of the human body and the nature of external bodies (Prop. 16, 25, and 27); that is, this idea will necessarily be adequate in God in so far as he constitutes the human mind, that is, in so far as he has the ideas that are in the human mind (Prop. 12 and 13). Consequently, the mind necessarily perceives A adequately (Coroll. Prop. 11) and does so both in so far as it perceives itself and in so far as it perceives its own or any external body; nor can A be conceived in any other manner. *Q.E.D.*

Corollary. It follows that there are certain ideas or notions common to everybody. For all bodies agree in certain respects

(Lemma 2), which must be perceived adequately, that is, clearly and distinctly by everyone (previous Prop.).

PROP. XXXIX. *Of anything that is common to and a property of both the human body and some other bodies that are wont to affect it and which is present in the part just as much as in the whole of each, there will be an adequate idea in the mind.*

Proof. Let A be that which is common to and a property of the human body and external bodies and is equally present in the human body and in said external bodies, and finally is equally present in any part of each external body and in the whole. There will be an adequate idea of A in God (Coroll. Prop. 7 of this part) both in so far as he has the idea of the human body and in so far as he has the ideas of the posited external bodies. Let it now be posited that the human body is affected by an external body through what it has in common with it, namely A; the idea of this modification will involve property A (Prop. 16); therefore, the idea of this modification, in so far as it involves property A, will be adequate in God in so far as he is affected by the idea of the human body (same Coroll. Prop. 7), that is, in so far as he constitutes the nature of the human mind (Prop. 13). Consequently, this idea is also adequate in the human mind (Coroll. Prop. 11). *Q.E.D.*

> So Spinoza is only saying here that if the human body is affected by something that can only be conceived adequately (because the idea cannot be fragmented), then the idea of that cause will be adequate. This seems to follow clearly, but the following corollary does not seem to follow.

Corollary. It follows that the more a mind's body has in common with other bodies, the more capable that mind is of perceiving more things adequately.

> The problem with this claim is that the adequacy of the idea of the effect in the above scenario comes not from the similarity of the body with the external body, but from the fact that the effect can only be conceived adequately. This reasoning is extraordinarily abstract and so it is not at all clear how Spinoza derives this Corollary or what additional claims he needs to derive it.

PROP. XL. *Whatever ideas follow in the mind from ideas that are adequate in it are also themselves adequate.*

Proof. This Proposition is self-evident. For when we say that an idea in the human mind follows from ideas that are adequate in it, we are saying nothing other than that in the divine intellect itself there is an idea of which God is the cause, not in so far as he is infinite, nor in so far as he is affected by the ideas of very many particular things, but only in so far as he constitutes the essence of the human mind; <and it must therefore be adequate [*Adaequata*]> (Coroll. Prop. 11 of this part).

Scholium I. I have thus set forth the cause of those notions that are called *common* and form the basis of human reasoning. But there are other causes of certain axioms, or notions, that it would fit the present context to set forth by this method of ours; for it would thus appear which notions are more useful than others and which ones have scarcely any use at all. Further, we would see which ones are commonplace and which ones are only clear and distinct to those who are unshackled by prejudice, and finally which ones are ill-founded. It would also be clear where the notions called *secondary* and, consequently, the axioms that are founded on them have their origin, as well as other points on which I once reflected in connection with those matters. I have decided, however, to pass over the subject here, partly because I have devoted to it another treatise, partly because I am afraid of wearying the reader due to the excessive length of the required disquisitions.

Spinoza's reference here to secondary notions is quite obscure and he seems to be referring to a technical aspect of Scholastic philosophy.

Nevertheless, in order not to omit anything that it is necessary to know among these things, I will briefly deal with the causes in which originate the terms called *transcendental*, such as Being, thing, something. These terms arise from the fact that the human body, being limited, is only capable of distinctly forming a certain number of images (what an image is I explained in the Schol. Prop. 17 of this part) within itself at the same time. If this number is exceeded, the images will start to become confused; and if the number of images that the body is capable of forming distinctly within itself is exceeded by a large margin, they will all become entirely confused with one another. This being so, it is evident from Coroll. Prop. 17 and from Prop. 18 of this part that the human mind can distinctly imagine as many bodies simultaneously as images can be formed simultaneously in its body. Now when the images become fully confused in the body, the mind will also imagine all bodies confusedly without any distinction and will comprehend them, as it were, under one attribute, namely under the attribute of Being, thing, etc. The same conclusion can be drawn from the fact that images are not always equally vivid, and from other analogous causes, which there is no need to explain here, as for our present purpose we need consider only one of them. For all may be reduced to this, that these terms represent ideas that are confused to the highest degree.

> There is a tension in Spinoza's views at this point. He rejects some concepts, such as being, thing, or something, as being "confused to the highest degree," but accepts other equally abstract concepts like substance, attribute, and mode. One may wonder what the difference is between these ideas that are always adequate and these "transcendental" ideas that are always maximally inadequate. The difference appears to be in how the ideas are formed. An adequate idea, like the idea of Extension, is a fragment of an idea of a body. But since the idea of Extension is so simple, it cannot be conceived inadequately. However, the ideas that Spinoza is objecting to here are ideas that are formed when we try to think many particular things at once. So instead of "cutting" the ideas down into smaller parts, these ideas "add" different ideas on top of one another. Whether this approach, or something like it, can fully resolve the tension here is an open question.

From similar causes also arise those notions that we call *general*, such as human being, horse, dog, etc., to wit, from the fact that so many images, for instance, of human beings, are formed simultaneously in the human body that they overwhelm the powers of imagination—not completely, to be sure, but to the point that the mind finds itself unable to imagine the small differences between individual things (for instance, each one's colour, size, etc.) and their definite number, and only distinctly imagines that in which all people agree in so far as the body is affected by them. For this is where each of the aforementioned individual things has chiefly affected the body; this the mind expresses by the name *human being*, and this it predicates of an infinite number of particular individuals, since, as we have said, it is unable to imagine the definite number of individuals. We must note, however, that these notions are not formed by everybody in the same way but vary in each individual depending on which thing has more often affected the body and which one the mind more easily imagines or remembers. For example, those who have most often regarded with admiration the stature of people will by the name *human being* understand an animal of erect stature; those, on the other hand, who have accustomed themselves to contemplating some other attribute will form a different general image of a human being; for instance, that man is a laughing animal, a two-footed animal, without feathers, a rational animal; likewise, everyone will form general images of all other things according to the disposition of their own body. It is no surprise, therefore, that so many controversies have arisen among philosophers, who seek to explain things in nature merely by the images formed of them.

> This passage too would seem to be in tension with the remainder of the *Ethics*. Parts III–V concern human beings as a class or kind. In fact, Spinoza will make many general claims about what human beings are like and how they can be happy. So Spinoza cannot be saying here that all of the different ideas of human beings that we have are inadequate or illusory. Rather Spinoza is only rejecting those ideas that "seek to explain things in nature merely by the images formed of them," not to those ideas that arise from the nature of reason.

Scholium II. From all that has been said above it is clear that we perceive a large number of things and form our general notions (1) from particular things represented to our intellect fragmentarily, confusedly, and without order through our senses (see Coroll. Prop. 29 of this part); I have accustomed myself to calling such perceptions 'knowledge from random experience';[1] (2) from symbols, e.g., from the fact that, having heard or read certain words, we remember things and form certain ideas of them that resemble those through which we imagine things (see Schol. Prop. 18); I will from now on call both of these ways of contemplating things 'knowledge of the first kind', 'opinion', or 'imagination'; (3) lastly, from the fact that we have notions common to everybody and adequate ideas of the properties of things (see Coroll. Prop. 38, Prop. 39 with Coroll. and Prop. 40); this I will call 'reason' and 'knowledge of the second kind'. Besides these two kinds of knowledge, there is, as I will show afterwards, a third kind of knowledge, which we will call 'intuition' (*scientia intuitiva*). This last kind of knowledge proceeds from an adequate idea of the formal essence of certain attributes of God to an adequate knowledge of the essence of things. I will illustrate all of this through a single example. Three numbers are given for

---

1   A Baconian phrase. Nov. Org. Aph. 100. [Pollock, p. 126, n.] (Elwes)

finding a fourth, which shall be to the third as the second is to the first. Tradesmen without hesitation multiply the second by the third and divide the product by the first, either because they have not forgotten the rule they heard from their teacher without any proof, or because they have often made trial of it with very simple numbers, or by virtue of the proof of the nineteenth Proposition of the seventh book of Euclid, namely out of the general property of proportionals. But with very simple numbers there is no need of this: for instance, given the numbers one, two, and three, everyone can see that the fourth proportional is six; and this is much clearer because we infer the fourth number from the ratio that we can see at first glance the first bears to the second.

> This passage is important because the organization of knowledge into three types will be an organizing principle for Spinoza. But his presentation here is unusually confusing. First, to summarize, the three types of knowledge are:
>
> 1. Opinion (of which there are two kinds: perceptions and those that arise from symbols). These ideas are always inadequate and so false.
>
> 2. Reason. These ideas are based on simple properties that are adequately understood. The paradigm case is mathematics. These ideas are always adequate and true.
>
> 3. Intuition. These ideas arise when we suddenly grasp how an attribute of God relates to a particular essence. This kind of knowledge is always adequate and concerns a particular thing.
>
> The third kind of knowledge is the most mysterious and Spinoza will elaborate on it later, especially in Part V of the Ethics. One controversy that has arisen among scholars about these passages is whether the same thing can be understood in three ways (as suggested by Spinoza's example) or whether each kind of knowledge is of a different kind of thing (e.g., that the second kind of knowledge concerns simple kinds and the third only particular individuals).

PROP. XLI. *Knowledge of the first kind is the only source of falsity; knowledge of the second and third kinds is necessarily true.*

Proof. In the foregoing Schol. we said that knowledge of the first kind comprises all those ideas that are inadequate and confused; therefore, this kind of knowledge is the only source of falsity (Prop. 35 of this part). Further, we said that knowledge of the second and third kind comprises those ideas that are adequate; consequently, it is necessarily true (Prop. 34). *Q.E.D.*

PROP. XLII. *Knowledge of the second and third kinds, not knowledge of the first kind, teaches us to distinguish what is true from what is false.*

Proof. This Proposition is self-evident: whoever knows how to distinguish between true and false must have an adequate idea of true and false, that is, know true and false by the second or third kind of knowledge (Schol. 2 Prop. 40 of this part).

PROP. XLIII. *Whoever has a true idea simultaneously knows that they have a true idea and cannot doubt the truth of the thing in question.*

Proof. A true idea in us is an idea that is adequate in God in so far as he is explained through the nature of the human mind (Coroll. Prop. 11 of this part). Let us now suppose that there is in God, in so far as he is explained through the nature of the human mind, an adequate idea A. Of this idea there must also necessarily be an idea in God, and this idea must relate to God in the same way as idea A (Prop. 20 of this part, the proof of which is of universal application <and can be applied to all ideas>). Now idea A is supposed to relate to God in so far as he is explained through the nature of the human mind; therefore, the idea of idea A must relate to God in the same manner; that is, this adequate idea of idea A will be in the very mind that has the adequate idea A (Coroll. Prop. 11). Therefore, whoever has an adequate idea—that is, knows a thing truly (Prop. 34)—must at the same time have an adequate idea—that is, true knowledge—of their knowledge; in other words, they must have certainty (as is self-evident). *Q.E.D.*

Scholium. I explained in Schol. Prop. 21 of this part what the idea of an idea is; however, we need to note that the foregoing Proposition is in itself sufficiently plain to see, since no one who has a true idea is unaware of the fact that a true idea involves the highest certainty. For to have a true idea means nothing other than knowing a thing perfectly, or as well as possible. No one, indeed, can doubt this, unless they think that an idea is something inanimate, like a picture on a panel, and not a mode of thinking, namely the very act of understanding; and who, I ask, can know that they understand anything unless they do first understand it? In other words, who can know that they are sure of a thing unless they are first sure of that thing? Further, what can there be that is clearer and more certain as a standard of truth than a true idea? Just as light manifests both itself and darkness, so truth is a standard both of itself and of falsity.

> It is important to keep in mind that according to Spinoza ideas are not like static pictures, but are instead active affirmations that something exists. So my idea of my cat in my mind is not a mere picture of the cat, but the mental assertion that the cat exists.

And I think I have thus answered the following questions, namely: If a true idea is distinguished from a false one <not in so far as it is a mode of thinking [*Modus cogitandi*], but> only in so far as it is said to agree with its object (*ideatum*)—is it the case, then, that a true idea possesses no more reality or perfection than a false one (since the two are only distinguished through an external mark <and not through an internal mark [*Interna denominatio*]>) and, consequently, neither does a person <— in other words, a human mind—> who has true ideas possesses any more reality or perfection than somebody who has only false ones? Further, why do people have false ideas? Lastly, how can anyone know for sure that they have ideas that agree with their <metaphysical or> epistemic objects?[1] These questions, I repeat, I think I have already answered. For as far as the difference between a true idea and a false one is concerned, from what I said in Prop. 35 of this part it is clear that the former is related to the latter just as being is Prop. 35. From these arguments it also becomes apparent what is the difference between someone who has true ideas and someone who only has false ones. As for the last question (how one can be sure one has an idea that agrees with its <metaphysical or> epistemic object), I have just more than sufficiently demonstrated that this stems from the simple fact that they have an idea that corresponds to its <metaphysical or> epistemic object; in other words, that truth is its own standard. We may add that our mind, in so far as it perceives things truly, is part of God's infinite intellect (Coroll. Prop. 11); therefore, the clear and distinct ideas of the mind are as necessarily true as the ideas of God.

---

1 Here and below, see p. 115, n. 1 (on Prop. 32 of this part). (D.A.)

Spinoza provides a number of different arguments for his conclusion in this passage, but the most important one seems to be that we could not recognize false ideas if we did not already know true ideas. Because we just compare the false ideas to the true ones and see that the false ones are lacking. Consider the following analogous case. Suppose Spinoza were asked how he knows that he is not dreaming. Spinoza could reply that we would not even recognize dreaming if we did not have waking conscious states. So we must be able to recognize waking conscious states as a precondition for recognizing a dream state. So the possibility that "everything is a dream" is incoherent because in that case we wouldn't be able to even think that thought because we wouldn't know anything other than dream states.

Spinoza's arguments here, however, have an interesting consequence. If you can genuinely doubt the truth of a given idea, then you do not know it with certainty. But if you don't know it with certainty, then it's false. So all ideas in Spinoza are either false or known with complete certainty.

PROP. XLIV. *It is not in the nature of reason to regard things as contingent, but as necessary.*

Proof. It is in the nature of reason to perceive things truly (Prop. 41 of this part), that is, as they are in themselves (Ax. 6 Pt. 1)—in other words, not as contingent but as necessary (Prop. 29 Pt. 1). *Q.E.D.*

Corollary I. It follows that it is only through our imagination that we regard things, whether with respect to the future or to the past, as contingent.

Scholium. How this way of looking at things arises, I will briefly explain. We have shown above (Prop. 17 of this part with Coroll.) that the mind always imagines things as present to itself even if they do not actually exist, unless some causes arise which exclude their present existence. Further, we showed (Prop. 18) that, if the human body has once been affected by two external bodies simultaneously, the mind, when it afterwards imagines one of said external bodies, will immediately remember the other, too—that is, it will regard both as present to itself, unless causes arise which exclude their present existence. Further, no one doubts that we imagine time: it is clear from the fact that we imagine some bodies to move more slowly than others, some faster, some at equal speed. So let us suppose that yesterday morning a young boy saw Peter for the first time, at noon Paul, and in the evening

Simon; then, today he again sees Peter in the morning. It is evident from Prop. 18 of this part that, as soon as he sees the morning light, he will imagine the sun traversing the same parts of the sky as it did when he saw it on the preceding day—in other words, he will imagine a complete day—and at the same time as he sees the morning hour he will imagine Peter, at noon Paul, and in the evening Simon; in other words, he will imagine the existence of Paul and Simon in relation to a future time. On the other hand, if he sees Simon in the evening, he will relate Peter and Paul to a past time by imagining them simultaneously with that past time, and he will do so more constantly the more often he has seen them in this order. If it should at any time happen that on some other evening the boy sees James instead of Simon, he will, on the following morning, associate with his imagination of evening sometimes Simon, sometimes James, but not both together; for he is posited to have seen in the evening one or the other of them but not both together. His imagination will therefore vacillate and he will imagine now one, now the other in connection with the coming evening hour; that is, he will think of neither of them as certainly but both as contingently future. And this vacillating of the imagination will be the same if the imagination is concerned with things that we contemplate in the same manner in relation to the past or the present; consequently, we will imagine things as contingent whether they relate to the present, the past, or the future.

> Spinoza seems to argue in this passage both that our uncertainty about the future is due only to ignorance, but also that the experience of the passage of time itself is illusory. We only experience time as "passing" because we have inadequate ideas.

Corollary II. It is in the nature of reason to perceive things under a certain form of eternity (*sub quadam aeternitatis specie*).

Proof. It is in the nature of reason to regard things not as contingent but as necessary (previous Prop.). Reason perceives this necessity of things truly (Prop. 41 of this part), that is, as it is in itself (Ax. 6 pt. 1). Now this necessity of things is the very necessity of God's eternal nature (Prop. 16 Pt. 1); therefore, it is in the nature of reason to regard things under this form of eternity. We may add that the foundations of reason are the notions that explain things common to all (Prop. 38 of this part) and which do not explain the essence of any particular thing (Prop. 37); consequently, these must be conceived without any relation to time, but under a certain form of eternity. *Q.E.D.*

> Notice that in this passage Spinoza says that when we regard things with reason and so see them as they are, they "must be conceived without any relation to time."

PROP. XLV. *Any idea of any body, that is, of any particular thing actually existing, necessarily involves God's eternal and infinite essence.*

Proof. The idea of a particular thing actually existing necessarily involves both the existence and the essence of said thing (Coroll. Prop. 8 of this part). Now particular things cannot be conceived without God (Prop. 15 Pt. 1); on the contrary, since they have God for their cause in so far as he is regarded under the attribute of which the things in question are modes (Prop. 6 of this part), their ideas must necessarily involve the conception of their attribute (Ax. 4 Pt. 1), in other words, God's eternal and infinite essence (Def. 6 Pt. 1). *Q.E.D.*

Scholium. By 'existence' I do not here mean duration, that is, existence in so far as it is conceived abstractedly and as a certain form of quantity. I am speaking of the very nature of existence, which is assigned to particular things because they follow in infinite numbers and in infinite ways from the eternal necessity of God's nature (Prop. 16 Pt. 1). I am speaking, I say, of the very existence of particular things in so far as they are in God. For although each of them is determined by another particular thing to exist in a given way, the force through which each of them perseveres in existing follows from the eternal necessity of God's nature. On this subject see Coroll. Prop. 24 Pt. 1.

PROP. XLVI. *The knowledge of God's eternal and infinite essence that every idea involves is adequate and perfect.*

Proof. The proof of the previous Proposition is universal; and whether a thing is considered as a part or a whole, the idea thereof, whether of the whole or of a part, will involve God's eternal and infinite essence (previous Prop.). Therefore, what gives knowledge of God's eternal and infinite essence is common to all, and is equally in the part and in the whole. Thus, this knowledge will be adequate (Prop. 38 of this part). *Q.E.D.*

PROP. XLVII. *The human mind has an adequate knowledge of God's eternal and infinite essence.*

Proof. The human mind has ideas (Prop. 22 of this part) through which it perceives itself (Prop. 23), its own body (Prop. 19) and external bodies (Coroll. Prop. 16 and Prop. 17) as actually existing; therefore, it has an adequate knowledge of God's eternal and infinite essence (Prop. 45 and 46). *Q.E.D.*

Scholium. Hence we see that God's infinite essence and his eternity are known to all. Now as all things are in God and are conceived through God, it follows that we can infer from this knowledge many things that we may adequately know, so that we can form that third kind of knowledge of which we spoke in Schol. Prop. 40 in this part and of whose excellence and usefulness we will have occasion to speak in Part 5. That people lack as clear a knowledge of God as they have of general notions is due to their inability to imagine God as they do bodies as well as to the fact that they have associated the name *God* with the images of things that they are wont to see, as indeed people can hardly avoid doing since they are continually affected by external bodies. Many errors, in truth, can be traced back to the fact that we do not apply names to things correctly. For instance, if somebody says that the lines drawn from the centre of a circle to its circumference are not of equal length, they certainly mean by 'circle'—at least in that particular instance—something different from what mathematicians do. Likewise, when people make mistakes in calculation, they have one set of figures in their mind and another on the paper. Thus, if one looks at their minds, they are not making a mistake, but they seem to be because we think that they have the same numbers in their mind as on the paper. If this were not so, we would not believe them to be in error, any more than lately I thought someone to be in error, <even though his words were nonsensical,> when I heard him exclaim that his entrance hall had flown into a neighbour's hen, for his meaning seemed sufficiently clear to me. And this is where most controversies arise: from the fact, that is, that people fail to express themselves correctly or misinterpret other people's meaning. For in truth, whenever they most crassly contradict each other, they are having either the same thought or completely unrelated ones, so that the errors or absurdities they think the other is engaging in are not actually there.

PROP. XLVIII. *In the mind there is no absolute, that is, free will, but the mind is determined to want one thing or another by a cause, which has also been determined by another cause, which, in turn, has been determined by another cause, and so on to infinity.*

Proof. The mind is a definite and determined mode of thought (Prop. 11 of this part); thus, it cannot be the free cause of its actions (Coroll. 2 to Prop. 17 Pt. 1); in other words, it cannot have an absolute ability to want or not to want something. Instead, it must be determined to want one thing or another by a cause, which has also been determined by another cause, which, in turn, has been determined by another cause, etc. (Prop. 28 Pt. 1). *Q.E.D.*

Scholium. In the same way it is proved that there is in the mind no absolute ability to understand, desire, love etc. From this it follows that these and similar abilities are either entirely fictitious or nothing but metaphysical, that is, universal entities, which we are accustomed to forming from particular things. Thus, the intellect and the will stand in the same relation to this or that idea or to this or that volition as 'stoniness' to this or that stone or as 'human being' to Peter and Paul. The reason why people consider themselves free, on the other hand, has been put forth in the Appendix to Part 1. Before I proceed further, however, it bears pointing out that by 'the will to affirm or deny' I mean the ability, not the desire: I mean, I say, the ability by which the mind affirms or denies what is true or false, not the desire with which the mind wishes for or turns away from a thing. Now after we have proved that these faculties are general notions that cannot be distinguished from the particular instances out of which we form them, we must inquire whether volitions themselves are anything besides the ideas of things themselves. We must inquire, I say, whether there is in the mind any affirmation or negation beyond the one that the idea, in so far as it is an idea, involves. On this subject see the following Proposition as well as Def. 3 of this part, lest the idea of pictures suggest itself: for by 'ideas' I do not mean images such as are formed at the back of the eye or, if you will, in the midst of the brain, but the conceptions of thought, <in other words, the objective being [*Esse objectivum*] of a thing in so far as it exists in thought alone>.

> The question Spinoza is asking here is a subtle but important one. He is asking whether we have a *capacity* to understand in addition to lots of particular understandings. Should we think of our mind as a thing that affirms certain truths? Or is our mind just the collection or bundle of affirmations of certain truths? Spinoza answers these questions in the next proposition.

PROP. XLIX. *There is in the mind no volition, that is, affirmation and negation, save that which an idea involves in so far as it is an idea.*

Proof. There is in the mind no absolute ability for positive or negative volition, but only particular volitions, namely this or that affirmation and this or that negation (previous Prop.). Now let us conceive some particular volition, to wit, a mode of thinking by which the mind affirms that the three interior angles of a triangle are equal to two right angles. This affirmation involves the conception, that is, the idea of a triangle; in other words, it cannot be conceived without the idea of a triangle: it is the same thing to say that concept A must involve concept B as it is to say that A cannot be conceived without B. Further, this affirmation cannot be made without the idea of a triangle, either (Ax. 3 of this part); consequently, this affirmation can neither exist nor be conceived without the idea of a triangle. Also, this idea of a triangle must involve this same affirmation, namely that its three angles are equal to two right angles. Therefore, and vice versa, this idea of a triangle can neither exist nor be conceived without this affirmation; thus, this affirmation belongs to the essence of the idea of a triangle and is nothing beyond it (Def. 2 of this part). What we have said of this particular volition—as we have picked and chosen it totally at random—must be said of any other, namely that it is nothing but an idea. *Q.E.D.*

Corollary. The will and the intellect are one and the same.

> By 'will' here Spinoza seems to mean the will to affirm something's existence with the mind (say to yourself, "Thing X exists"), not the will to move your body, because the mind does not move the body in Spinoza, but rather the mind's thinking and the body's movements are

one and the same thing considered under two different attributes. What Spinoza is saying here is that to mentally affirm that something exists and to understand something are one and the same mental act.

Proof. The will and the intellect are nothing beyond the individual volitions and ideas (Prop. 48 of this part with Schol.). Now a particular volition and a particular idea are one and the same thing (previous Prop.); therefore, the will and the intellect are one and the same. *Q.E.D.*

Scholium. We have thus removed what is commonly believed to be the cause of error. For above we have shown that falsity consists solely in the privation that fragmentary and confused ideas involve. Therefore, a false idea, to the extent that it is false, does not involve certainty. When we say, then, that someone acquiesces in what is false and has no doubts on the subject, we are not saying that they are certain but only that they do not doubt, or that they acquiesce in what is false because there are no causes that make their imagination vacillate, <that is, which make them doubt it> (on this subject see Schol. Prop. 44 of this part). Thus, although the person in question is assumed to hold on to something false, <so that one in no way can make them doubt it,> we will never say that they are certain. For by 'certainty' we mean something positive (see Prop. 43 with Schol.), not merely the absence of doubt, and by 'absence of certainty' we mean falsity.

> Spinoza is here replying to Descartes's theory of error which is explained in his *Meditations on First Philosophy, Meditation Four.* According to Descartes, we err because we are able to affirm truths that we do not sufficiently understand. Descartes says that we can avoid error by only affirming truths that we clearly and distinctly know to be true. Spinoza disagrees with Descartes here because he thinks that the affirmation is a part of the very idea itself. Therefore, according to Spinoza, it makes no sense to have an idea and not affirm its reality. The only way to not affirm the present existence of something that I am thinking about is if there are other ideas in my mind that exclude its present existence.

However, in order that the foregoing Proposition may be fully explained, there are left a few things to point out; it also remains to answer the objections that may be put forward against our doctrine. Lastly, in order to remove every scruple, I have thought it worthwhile to point out some of the advantages of this doctrine. I say 'some' because they will be better understood from what we shall put forth in the fifth part.

I begin, then, with the first point, and urge my readers to make an accurate distinction between an idea, that is, a conception of the mind, and the images of the things we imagine. It is further necessary to distinguish between the idea and the words through which we signify things. For as many either entirely confuse these three—images, words, and ideas—or fail to distinguish them with sufficient accuracy or, finally, with sufficient care, they have remained utterly ignorant of this doctrine of the will, whose knowledge is absolutely necessary both for philosophical speculation <and science> and for the wise ordering of life. In fact, those who think that ideas consist in images formed in us through contact with external bodies persuade themselves that the ideas of things <that can leave no trace in our brains, that is,> of which we can form no like mental image, are not ideas but only figments that we make up by the free decree of our will; they thus regard ideas as though they were inanimate pictures on a panel and, filled with this prejudice, do not see that an idea, in so far as it is an idea, involves an affirmation or negation. Further, those who confuse words with an idea or with the affirmation itself that an idea involves think that they can wish something contrary to what they feel, while they are, in fact, affirming or denying something contrary to their feelings with words only. One can easily lay aside such misconceptions by reflecting on the nature of knowledge, which does not involve in any way the conception of extension. Thus, one will clearly understand that an idea (being a mode of thinking) does not consist in the image of anything or in words: the essence of words and images is made up solely of bodily motions, which in no way involve the conception of thought. Let it suffice for me to have made these few points; now I will go on to address the objections I mentioned.

The first of these is put forward by those who take it as read that the will has a wider scope than the intellect and is therefore different from it. The reason they hold the belief that the will has a wider scope than the intellect is because they experience—they say—that in order to assent to an infinite number of other things we do not perceive, they do not need an increase in their ability to assent, that is, to affirm or negate, but do need an increase in their ability to understand. The will is thus distinguished from the intellect in that the latter is finite and the former infinite.

Secondly, it may be objected that experience seems to teach us especially clearly that we are able to suspend our judgment so as not to assent to things that we perceive; this is also confirmed by the fact that no one is said to be deceived in so far as they perceive anything, but only in so far as they assent or dissent. For instance, somebody who thinks of a winged horse is not admitting that there is such a thing as a winged horse; that is, they are not in that sense deceived unless they also admit that there is such a thing as a winged horse. Thus, experience seems to teach nothing more clearly than that the will, that is, the ability to assent, is free and different from the ability to understand.

Thirdly, it may be objected that one affirmation does not seem to contain more reality than another; in other words, that we do not seem to need any greater power to affirm that what is true is true than to affirm that what is false is true. However, <with the ideas [*Ideae*] it is another matter, because> we perceive that one idea has more reality or perfection than another, since just as much more excellent some objects are than others, so much more perfect their ideas are than the others' as well. This fact too seems to prove that there is a difference between the will and the intellect.

Fourthly, it may be objected that if man does not act out of free will—what will happen if the incentives to action are equally balanced, as in the case of Buridan's ass? Will he perish of hunger and thirst? If I say that he would, I will seem to be thinking of an ass or the statue of a person rather than of an actual human being; but if I say that he would not, then he will determine his own actions and will consequently possess the ability to go wherever and do whatever he likes. Other objections might also be raised, but, as I am not bound to cram in here everything anyone may dream, I will only care to answer the objections I have mentioned, and that as briefly as possible.

To the first objection I respond that I concede that the will has a wider scope than the intellect, if by 'intellect' they mean only clear and distinct ideas. I dispute, however, that the will has a wider scope than the perceptions, that is, the ability to form conceptions, nor do I see why the ability to form volition should be called infinite any more than the ability to form feelings, since just as we can affirm an infinite number of things (one after the other: we cannot affirm an infinite number of things simultaneously) through the same ability for volition, so also can we feel, or perceive, an infinite number of bodies (one after another <and

not at the same time, which is impossible>) through the same ability for perception. If they should say that there is an infinite number of things we cannot perceive, I retort that we cannot attain such things by any thinking nor, consequently, by any ability for volition. But—they will claim—if God wished to make us perceive them as well, he would have to provide us with a greater ability for perception but not with a greater ability for volition than he has given us. This is the same as saying that, if God wished to cause us to understand an infinite number of other entities, it would be necessary for him to give us a greater intellect but not a more universal idea of entity than he has given us so that we may grasp those same countless entities. For we have shown that will is a universal entity, that is, an idea through which we explain all particular volitions—in other words, that which is common to all such volitions. As, then, our opponents maintain that this common, or universal, idea of all volitions is an ability <of our mind>, it is no wonder that they assert that this ability extends itself into infinity, beyond the limits of the intellect; for what is universal is predicated of one, of many, and of an infinite number of individual things alike.

To the second objection I reply by disputing the claim that we have a free power of suspending our judgment. For when we say that anyone suspends their judgment, we merely mean that they see that they do not adequately perceive the matter in question. Therefore, suspension of judgment is, in truth, a perception, not free will. In order that this point may be clearer, let us suppose a boy imagining a horse and perceiving nothing else. Since this imagination involves the existence of the horse (Coroll. Prop. 17 of this part) and the boy does not perceive anything that would remove the existence of the horse, he will necessarily regard the horse as present and be unable to doubt its existence, although he is not certain of it. We even have daily experience of such a state of affairs in dreams; and I do not suppose that there is anyone who would maintain that while they are dreaming they have the free power to suspend their judgment concerning the things of which they are dreaming and to stop themselves from dreaming the things they see in their dreams; nonetheless, it happens that even in dreams we suspend our judgment, namely when we dream that we are dreaming. I also concede that no one is deceived as far as actual perception is concerned; that is, I concede that the mind's imaginations, regarded in themselves, do not involve error (Schol. Prop. 17 of this part); I dispute, however, that a person does not make any affirmation in so far as they perceive. For what is the perception of a winged horse if not an affirmation that a horse has wings? For if the mind perceived nothing but the winged horse, it would regard it as present to itself and have no reason to doubt its existence or any ability to dissent, unless the imagination of a winged horse were combined with an idea that removed the existence of said horse or unless the mind perceived that the idea it possessed of a winged horse was inadequate; in this case it will necessarily either deny the existence of that horse or be in doubt on the subject.

With this rebuttal I think I have answered the third objection, too: the will is something universal that is predicated of all ideas and signifies only what is common to all ideas, namely an affirmation. Consequently, the will's adequate essence must, in so far as it is thus conceived in the abstract, be in every idea, and only in this respect must it be the same in all of them <like the definition [*Definitio*] of man as a whole and must be equally applied to each particular person. In this way we can conceive that the will [*Voluntas*] is at all times the same in all ideas [*Ideae*],> but not in so far as it is considered as constituting the idea's essence: in this last respect particular affirmations differ from one another just as much as the ideas themselves. For instance, the affirmation involved by the idea of a circle differs from the one involved by the idea of a triangle just as much as the idea of a circle differs from the idea of a triangle. Further, I by no means grant that we need an equal power of thinking both to affirm that what is true is true and to affirm that what is false is true. In truth, these two affirmations, if we regard <only> the mind <and not the becoming>, are in the same relation to one another as being and not-being, since in ideas there is nothing positive that constitutes the form of falsehood (Prop. 35 of this part with Schol. and Schol. Prop. 47 of this part). Thus, at this point it is most necessary to note how easily we are deceived when we confuse universals with singulars and the entities of reason and abstractions with realities.

As far as the fourth objection is concerned, I respond that I fully admit that somebody placed in the balance described (namely as perceiving nothing but hunger and thirst, a certain food and a certain drink, each equally distant from them) will die of hunger and thirst. Should they ask me whether such a person ought not to be regarded as an ass rather than as a human being, I answer that I do not know, just as I do not know how we ought to regard someone who hangs themselves, or how to regard children, fools, lunatics, and so on.

Here Spinoza addresses the classic philosophical question about Buridan's ass. This thought question imagines an ass placed equidistant between two equally nourishing and appealing piles of feed. Given that the ass would have no reason to direct itself towards one side or the other, without any additional (agent causal) power to self-determine, the ass would stand in the middle and starve. This thought question is often posed as a way to motivate the intuition that people must have some additional faculty of choice that distinguishes us from animals. Spinoza affirms without hesitation that people lack any additional faculty for choice. This faculty would conflict with necessitarianism, and would seem to violate the principle of sufficient reason. As such, Spinoza rejects this idea out of hand and seems to take the question as being of little importance for dealing with a study of normal human operations. In reality, according to Spinoza, all that exists occurs by the unfolding of logical necessity. In such a world, there would never be an event, as in such a case whichever outcome occurred would do so without an adequate explanation. Accordingly, the Buridan's ass concern does not concern Spinoza and is dismissed as abstruse metaphysics, whereas Spinoza has a more practical focus.

In the following passage, Spinoza gives a brief summary of some of his most important conclusions from Parts IV–V of the *Ethics*. Spinoza's central focus in this text is not abstruse metaphysics for its own sake, but to find a better way to live and deal with our inevitable human suffering. Spinoza in this book is doing a kind of philosophical therapy.

It remains to point out how much the knowledge of this doctrine helps us in our life, which is easy to gather from the following:

1. This doctrine teaches us that we act solely according to God's decrees and are partakers in the divine nature, the more so the more perfect the actions we perform are and the more we understand God. Therefore, this doctrine not only completely calms our spirit but also teaches us where our highest happiness, or blessedness, is, that is, solely in the knowledge of God, by which we are led to act only as love and piety bid us. We thus clearly understand how far astray from a true estimate of virtue are those who expect to be decorated by God with the highest rewards for their virtue and their best actions, as if for being the most sub-

missive slaves—as though virtue itself and bondage to God were not in itself happiness and the highest freedom.

2. It teaches us how to conduct ourselves with respect to matters of fate, that is, matters that are not under our control—in other words, matters that do not follow from our own nature. This means that we should await and endure fortune's smiles or frowns with an even mind, seeing as everything follows from the eternal decree of God by the same necessity by which it follows from the essence of a triangle that its three angles are equal to two right ones.

3. This doctrine helps improve our social life, as it teaches us not to hate, despise, or deride anybody and not to be angry with anybody or envy anybody. Also, it tells us that everyone should be content with their own lot and helpful to their neighbour, not out of feminine pity, partisanship, or superstition, but solely following the guidance of reason, in the way time and occasion demand, as I will show in Part 4.

4. Lastly, this doctrine benefits to no small extent society at large, in so far as it teaches under which system the citizens should be governed and led—namely not so as to act like slaves but so that they may freely do whatever is best.

I have thus fulfilled what I had undertaken to do in this Scholium, and I thus bring the second part of my treatise to a close. I think that in it I have explained the nature and properties of the human mind at sufficient length and—considering the difficulty of the subject—with sufficient clarity, and that I have expounded such teachings as can form a basis for deducing many things that are excellent, extremely useful and necessary to know, as the following will in part show.

End of Part 2.

PART III
ON THE ORIGIN AND NATURE
OF THE AFFECTS

PREFACE

Most writers on the affects and on how people should live seem to deal with matters outside nature rather than natural phenomena following nature's general laws; they even appear to imagine man to be situated in nature as a kingdom within a kingdom, since they believe that he disturbs rather than follows nature's order, that he has absolute control over his actions, and that he is determined solely by himself. Further, they see the cause of human powerlessness and fickleness not in the power of nature in general but in some mysterious flaw of human nature, and accordingly they bemoan said nature, deride it, despise it, or—most frequently—curse it; and whoever knows how to snipe at the weakness of the human mind particularly eloquently or acutely is looked upon as a seer. Still, there has been no lack of excellent authors (to whose toil and industry I confess myself much indebted) who have written many worthy things concerning the right way of life and have given much wise advice to humankind. However, as far as I know no one has defined the nature and strength of the affects nor, conversely, what the mind is capable of doing to restrain them. I know very well that the illustrious Descartes, although he believed that the mind has absolute power over its actions, strove nevertheless to explain human affects by their primary causes and, at the same time, to point out a way for the mind to attain absolute control over them; however, in my opinion he did nothing but display the acuteness of his own great intellect, as I will show at the proper place. For I want to go back to those who would rather curse or deride human affects and actions than understand them. These people will doubtless think it strange that I should endeavour to deal with human vice and folly geometrically (more Geometrico) and that I should intend on analyzing with precise reasoning what they cry out against as repugnant to reason, frivolous, absurd, and dreadful. But my reasoning is the following: nothing happens in nature that can be blamed on a flaw therein, for nature is always the same, and her efficacy and power of action is one and the same everywhere; that is, nature's laws and rules, in accordance with which all things happen and change from one form to another, are everywhere and always the same, so that the method of understanding the nature of things of any kind must be one and the same too, namely through nature's universal laws and rules. Thus, the passions of hatred, anger, envy, and so on, considered in themselves, follow from the same necessity and efficacy of nature as any other individual thing; they answer to certain definite causes through which they are understood and possess certain properties no less worthy of being known than the properties of any other thing that delights us solely through its contemplation. I will therefore deal with the nature and strength of the affects and the mind's ability to control them following the same method that I have employed thus far in my investigations concerning God and the mind; and I will consider human actions and desires in exactly the same manner as though my inquiry were about lines, planes, and bodies.

Having examined general metaphysical questions in Part I and the nature of the mind in Part II, Spinoza now turns to the nature of emotions (affects) in general. His approach here is quite distinctive insofar as Spinoza does not attempt to moralize about which emotions we *ought* to feel or not feel. Nor does he try to provide moral inspiration towards living more charitable lives. Rather, he simply seeks to understand the nature of emotions as objectively as he can. As he thinks all of reality follows the same necessary causal determination (including human actions, desires, and emotions), the emotions can be handled as dispassionately as any other investigation of reality. Spinoza thus seeks simply to clarify how necessary causal forces direct our emotions.

DEFINITIONS

I. By *adequate cause* I mean a cause whose effect can be clearly and distinctly perceived through that cause itself. By *inadequate* or *partial cause* I mean one whose effect cannot be understood through it alone.

II. I say that we *act* when anything takes place, either within us or externally to us, of which we are the adequate cause, that is, when from our nature something follows within us or externally to us which can be clearly and distinctly understood through our nature alone (previous Def.). On the other hand, I say that we are *acted upon* when something happens within us or follows from our nature of which we are only a partial cause.

III. By *affect* I mean the modifications of the body by which its power of action is increased or diminished, aided or constrained, and also the ideas of such modifications.

N.B.: If we can be the adequate cause of any of these modifications, by 'affect' I mean an action; otherwise I mean by it a passion.[1]

> So an affect is a change in a complex body's health or power (a physical change) and the corresponding experience of that change. When the body's own complex internal activities create an increase in health, then the experience of that increase is an action; when external bodies are partly responsible for the change, then it is a passion. It is interesting to note that Spinoza conceives of emotions as physical as much as psychological.

POSTULATES

> It is interesting to note here that Spinoza terms the following two claims "postulates" rather than "axioms." This may be because he considers them derivable from earlier propositions. But in that case, it is unclear why he did not just make these two claims the first two propositions of Part III.

I. The human body can be affected in many ways (*modi*) by which its power of action is increased or diminished, and also in other ways that neither increase nor diminish its power of action.

N.B.: This postulate, or axiom, rests on Postulate 1 and Lemmas 5 and 7 after Prop. 13 Pt. 2.

II. The human body can undergo many changes and nevertheless retain the impressions, or traces, of objects (see Post. 5 Pt. 2) and, consequently, the same images of things (see their definition in Schol. Prop. 17 Pt. 2).

PROP. I. *Our mind in certain cases acts and in certain cases is acted upon; namely, it necessarily acts in so far as it has adequate ideas and it is necessarily acted upon in so far as it has inadequate ones.*

Proof. In every human mind there are some adequate ideas and some ideas that are fragmentary and confused (Schol. Prop. 40 Pt. 2). Those ideas in someone's mind that are adequate are also adequate in God in so far as he constitutes the essence of that mind (Coroll. Prop. 11 Pt. 2); also, those that are inadequate in the mind are likewise adequate in God (same Coroll.), not in so

---

1 *Passio* refers back to *pati*, here rendered as 'to be acted upon'. Consequently, when we encounter this word we should always bear in mind the connotation, obvious in Latin, of being acted upon rather than being the agent oneself. (D.A.)

far as he contains in himself the essence of the given mind alone, but in so far as he contains at the same time the minds of other things. Further, from any given idea some effect must necessarily follow (Prop. 36 Pt. 1); of this effect God is the adequate cause (Def. 1 of this part), not in so far as he is infinite but in so far as he is regarded as affected by that given idea (Prop. 9 Pt. 2). Now of that effect of which God is the cause in so far as he is affected by an idea that is adequate in somebody's mind—of that effect that same mind is the adequate cause (Coroll. Prop. 11 Pt. 2). Therefore, our mind, in so far as it has adequate ideas, necessarily acts (Def. 2 of this part); this was our first point. Also, anything that necessarily follows from an idea that is adequate in God not in so far as he possesses in himself the mind of one person only, but in so far as he contains, along with the mind of that one person, the minds of other things as well—of such a thing the mind of the given person is not an adequate but only a partial cause (same Coroll. Prop. 11 Pt. 2). Thus, the mind, in so far as it has inadequate ideas, is necessarily acted upon (Def. 2 of this part); this was our second point. Therefore our mind, etc. *Q.E.D.*

To understand Spinoza's proof here we have to keep in mind how different his general picture of reality is from our own. When we consider substance under the attribute of thought we understand it as one infinite mind. Our own mind is just a small bundle of those ideas. The ideas in God's mind are all logically related to one another. God knows his own nature and everything that logically follows from it. But when we zoom down to one individual human mind, we have only a relatively small number of ideas considered in isolation from the rest of the infinite mind of God. Nevertheless, these ideas that exist outside of the individual human mind are still logically related to it, and so are partly related to other ideas outside that mind (making the ideas inadequate insofar as the small human bundle of ideas is just a finite fragment of an infinite whole). This small bundle corresponds to the ideas of themselves conceived under the attribute of extension.

Corollary. It follows that the more inadequate ideas the mind possesses, the more passions it is subject to; conversely, the more adequate ideas it possesses, the more often it acts.

PROP. II. *Neither can the body determine the mind to think, nor can the mind determine the body to move or rest or do anything different from these two (if there is such a thing).*

Proof. All modes of thinking have as their cause God in so far as he is a thinking thing, and not in so far as he is explained under any other attribute (Prop. 6 Pt. 2). Therefore, what determines the mind to think is a mode of thought, not a mode of extension; that is, it is not a body (Def. 1 Pt. 2). This was our first point. Also, the motion and rest of a body must arise from another body, which has also been determined to move or rest by a third body; and in general, everything that arises in a body must arise from God in so far as he is regarded as affected by some mode of extension, and not by some mode of thought (Prop. 6 Pt. 2). That is, it cannot originate from the mind, which is a mode of thought (Prop. 11 Pt. 2). This was our second point. Therefore, the body cannot determine the mind, etc. *Q.E.D.*

Scholium. This is more clearly understood from what I said in Schol. Prop. 7 Pt. 2, namely that mind and body are one and the same thing conceived in one case under the attribute of thought and in the other under the attribute of extension. Hence, the order or concatenation of things is identical whether nature is conceived under the one attribute or the other; consequently, the order of actions and passions in our body is simultaneous in nature with the order of actions and passions in the mind. The same conclusion is evident from the manner in which we proved Prop. 12 Pt. 2. Nevertheless, although things are such in this respect that there can be no further room for doubt, I believe that, unless I prove my point by referring to common experience, people can hardly be induced to consider the question calmly and fairly, so firmly are they convinced that it is merely at the bidding of the mind that the body now moves, now rests, and performs most actions depending solely on the mind's will or ingenuity.

> Here Spinoza presents a number of different arguments against the claim that the mind moves the body, as in the philosophies of Descartes and Aristotle.

However, no one has so far laid down the limits to the powers of the body; that is, no one has as yet been taught by experience what the body can do solely through the laws of nature in so far as she is regarded as extension, and what it cannot do unless it is so determined by the mind. For nobody has so far gained such accurate knowledge of the bodily mechanism as to be able to explain all its functions—not to speak of the fact that in the lower animals we observe many actions that surpass human capabilities by far, and that sleepwalkers do many things in their sleep that they would not venture to do when awake: these instances are enough to show that the body itself, by the sole laws of its nature, is capable of many things that its own mind finds astounding. Also, no one knows in what manner or by what means the mind moves the body, nor how many various degrees of motion it can impart to the body, nor how quickly it can move it. Thus, when people say that this or that physical action has its origin in the mind, which has dominion over the body, they do not know what they are saying and are doing nothing but confessing in specious phraseology that they are ignorant of the true cause of the action at hand without any feeling of wonder. They will say, though, that whether or not they know the means by which the mind moves the body, they at any rate experience that unless the human mind were fit to think, the body would remain inert. Moreover, they experience—they say—that the mind alone can determine whether to speak or to stay silent, as well as many other such cases, where they think, consequently, that the mind's decree is the deciding factor. As to the first point, however, I ask such objectors whether experience also teaches that, if conversely the body is inactive, the mind is at the same time unfit to think? For when the body is at rest in sleep, the mind is at the same time in a state of torpor, too, and has no power of thinking as it does when the body is awake. Moreover, I think everyone has experienced that the mind is not at all times equally fit to reflect on the same object but is more or less so depending on whether the body is more or less fit to have the image of one or another particular object conjured up in itself. They will say, however, that it is impossible that solely from the laws of nature, to the extent that nature is considered as material, we should be able to deduce the causes of buildings, pictures, or any other things that are the product of human ingenuity alone; nor would the human body, unless it were determined and led by the mind, be capable of building a temple. However, I have already pointed out that the objectors do not know what the body can do or what can be concluded merely from a consideration of its nature and that they themselves experience as being accomplished solely by the laws of nature many things they would never have believed possible except under the direction of a mind, such as those that sleep-walkers do while asleep and then themselves wonder at when awake.

> The purpose of Spinoza's reference to sleepwalking here is to try to make less counterintuitive the idea that everything that happens in the physical world must be determined by a mind. Since the mind is not directing the body during sleep (even under the assumption that the mind moves the body), the body must be walking around entirely as a consequence of physical laws only. Spinoza suggests that this occurrence should lessen our doubt that physical causes may be adequate to explain effects that seem as though they should require input from human ingenuity. In both cases, the body succeeds in performing independent actions that would normally be conceived as requiring the intervention of a mind.

I further call attention to the mechanism of the human body itself, which far surpasses in craftsmanship all those created by human ingenuity—not to speak of the fact that, as I have already shown, from nature, under whatever attribute she is considered, infinite results follow. As for the second objection, the world would be much happier if people were as fully able to stay silent as they are to speak; however, experience abundantly shows that they have nothing less under control than their tongues and are capable of controlling nothing less than they are their appetites. This is why most believe that we are only free with respect to things we desire moderately, because our desire for them can easily be controlled by the thought of something else frequently remembered, but that we are by no means free with respect to what we seek with violent affect and where such affect cannot be allayed with the remembrance of anything else. However, if they had not experienced people doing many things that they regret afterwards and often—namely when they are torn between contrary affects—seeing the better but following the worse,[1] there would be nothing to prevent them from believing that we are free in all things. Thus, an infant believes that it desires milk out of its own free will; an angry child, that it freely desires revenge; a coward, that he freely desires to run away. Further, a drunken man believes that he utters by the free decision of his mind words that, when he is sober, he wishes he had not spoken; likewise, a

---

1 An Ovidian phrase: *Video meliora proboque, deteriora sequor* (*Metamorphoses* 7.20–21). (D.A.)

delirious man, a chattering woman, a child, and others of this sort believe that they speak by the free decision of their mind, while in reality they are just unable to restrain their impulse to talk.

It is interesting to note that Spinoza claims here that, as experienced, one would believe that both the desire and the actions that arise from those desires were freely chosen. As such, Spinoza indicates that the actual causes of our own actions may frequently be hidden from our awareness.

Thus, experience teaches us no less clearly than reason that people think themselves free simply because they are conscious of their actions but not of the causes that prompt them, and that the dictates of the mind are nothing but the appetites themselves and, consequently, vary according to the varying state of the body. For everyone moderates everything according to their own affects, and those who are torn between conflicting affects do not know what they wish, whereas those who are not governed by any are readily swayed one way or the other. All these considerations clearly show that a mental decision as well as an appetite and a determined state of the body are by nature simultaneous, or rather are one and the same thing, which we call a decision when it is regarded under and explained through the attribute of thought, and a determination when it is regarded under the attribute of extension and deduced from the laws of motion and rest. This will be seen even more plainly as we continue; for the time being, I wish to call attention to another point, namely that we cannot do anything by the decision of the mind unless we can remember it. For instance, we cannot say a word without remembering it. Further, it is not within the free power of the mind to remember or forget a thing at will; this is why it is believed that the only thing that is within the power of the mind is for us to either say or not say something we remember based solely on the mind's decree.

This is an interesting argument. Its purpose seems to be to try to reduce the strangeness of Spinoza's position that all of our thoughts and decisions are fully causally determined and so not freely chosen. In this case, he is comparing this hidden causality of our thoughts to the causality through which remembering occurs. The mere will to remember something does not guarantee or result in remembering actually occurring. Whether or not one succeeds in remembering is somehow determined by the hidden force of the "mind's decree." Since one cannot will something that is not remembered, all willings are dependent on something being remembered. Accordingly, every will depends on a hidden mental decree. In this way, Spinoza points out that mental acts that we regularly take to be freely chosen are in fact (at least partially) dependent on causal facts that are beyond an agent's control.

But when we dream that we speak, we believe that we are speaking by a free decision of the mind, yet we are not actually speaking or, if we are, it is by a spontaneous motion of the body. As well, we dream that we are hiding something from people and doing so by the same decision of the mind that, when we are awake, makes us stay silent about something we know. Lastly, we dream that through the free decision of our mind we do something that we would not dare to do when awake. Now I would like to know whether there are in the mind two sorts of decisions, one fanciful, the other free. If we do not want to reach that point of craziness, we must admit that this decision of the mind, however much we believe it to be free, is not distinguishable from mere imagination or memory and is nothing more than the affirmation an idea necessarily involves in so far as it is an idea (see Prop. 49 Pt. 2). Consequently, these decisions of the mind arise in the mind by the same necessity as the ideas of things actually existing. Thus, those who believe that they speak or stay silent or act in any way by the free decision of their mind are just dreaming with their eyes open.

PROP. III. *The actions of the mind arise solely from adequate ideas; the passions, on the other hand, depend solely on inadequate ones.*

Proof. The first element that constitutes the essence of the mind is nothing other than the idea of the actually existing body (Prop. 11 and 13 Pt. 2), which is composed of many other ideas (Prop. 15 Pt. 2), some of which are adequate (Coroll. Prop. 38 Pt. 2), some inadequate (Coroll. Prop. 29 Pt. 2). Consequently, whatever follows from the nature of the mind and has the mind as its proximate cause through which it must be understood must necessarily follow either from an adequate or from an inadequate idea. Now in so far as the mind has inadequate ideas, it is necessarily acted upon (Prop. 1 of this part); therefore, the actions of the mind follow solely from adequate ideas, and accordingly the mind is only acted upon in so far as it has inadequate ideas. *Q.E.D.*

Scholium. Thus we see that passions do not relate to the mind except in so far as it contains something involving negation, or in so far as it is regarded as a part of nature that cannot be clearly and distinctly perceived through itself without other parts. In this way I could show that the passions relate to individual things in the same way as to the mind and cannot be perceived otherwise; my object, however, is to deal solely with the human mind.

> The next four propositions are sometimes called the "Conatus (Endeavour or Striving) Argument."

PROP. IV. *Nothing can be destroyed except by a cause external to itself.*

Proof. This Proposition is self-evident, for the definition of anything affirms the essence of that thing but does not negate it; in other words, it posits (*ponit*) the essence of the thing but does not remove (*tollit*) it. Thus, so long as we regard only the thing itself and not the external causes, we will not be able to find in it anything that could destroy it. *Q.E.D.*

> The reader may think that suicide suggests a clear counterexample to this proposition. In the case of a suicide, Spinoza must infer that the person was actually killed by some disease of the body/mind which acted against their own internal striving. The case of a bomb is harder because it not only seems to destroy itself, but seems to be self-destructive essentially. But even here Spinoza could hold that a bomb's essence is to exist in potential explosion, and that it is only when impacted by an external agent that it is destroyed. Its destruction is not the result of its own nature, but of the outside person who triggers it. Of course, as a bomb is an artifact, a tougher case may be the apparently natural occurrence of radioactive decay. Spinoza would need to argue for a similarly external agency in this type of destruction as well.

PROP. V. *Things are naturally contrary, that is, cannot exist in the same object, to the extent that one is capable of destroying the other.*

Proof. If they could agree with each other or co-exist in the same object, there could then be in that object something able to destroy it. This, however, is absurd (previous Prop.). Therefore, things, etc. *Q.E.D.*

> Spinoza claims in this proof that this proposition follows from the previous one. Many scholars have questioned Spinoza's reasoning here. One way to read Spinoza here is as providing us with criteria to distinguish what parts belong to a thing. If a complicated body has two

parts that can destroy each other, then they are not, to that extent, part of the same body, because then we would have a self-destroying object.

PROP. VI. *Everything, in so far as it lies in its power, endeavours to persist in its own being.*

Proof. Individual things are modes by which God's attributes are expressed in a definite and determinate manner (Coroll. Prop. 25 Pt. 1); that is, they are things that express in a definite and determinate manner God's power, through which God is and acts (Prop. 34 Pt. 1). Furthermore, nothing contains in itself anything by which it can be destroyed, in other words, anything that can remove its existence (Prop. 4 of this part); on the contrary, each thing is opposed to anything that can remove its existence (previous Prop.). Therefore, everything, in so far as it can and it lies in its power, endeavours to persist in its own being. *Q.E.D.*

Here Spinoza moves from the claim that no complex thing has internal parts that can destroy it (previous proposition) to the conclusion that each thing strives, endeavors, or struggles to persist in existence. It is clear that Spinoza cannot infer this conclusion from the mere fact that each thing includes no internal self-destroying parts. Instead, Spinoza needs to add another assumption, which he gets from Part I, namely that each finite mode expresses the infinite active power of substance in a finite and particular way. From the joint claims that (i) nothing has self-destructive parts *and* that (ii) each finite thing is active, he infers that each thing strives or endeavors to continue to exist.

PROP. VII. *The endeavour of every single thing to persist in its own being is nothing other than the actual essence of the thing in question.*

Proof. From the given essence of each thing certain consequences necessarily follow (Prop. 36 Pt. 1); also, things cannot do anything but what necessarily follows from their nature as determined (Prop. 29 Pt. 1). Thus, the power of any given thing, that is, the endeavour through which it does something either alone or with other things or tries to do something—in other words, its power, or endeavour, to persist in its own being (Prop. 6 of this part)—is nothing but the given, that is, actual essence of the thing in question. *Q.E.D.*

This claim moves beyond the previous one in that Spinoza is claiming not only that each thing strives to exist, but that this very act of striving is the essence of the thing. The argument seems to be something like this: Each thing is actively striving to continue in existence, and the moment it stops doing so it is destroyed. Thus, this striving must be essential to each thing. Whether this striving activity is the whole essence, or only one part of a more complex essence, may be a meaningless question in this context because every part of the thing is involved in this striving activity. But it is important to note that the essence of each thing in Spinoza is a certain kind of complex activity or movement. A thing continues to exist so long as this complex movement continues to exist. Such a conclusion may be intuitive when it comes to animals, but it might be hard to see how it applies to things like rocks. But note that breaking a rock apart is often hard, and so it strives by resisting the attempts to break it apart.

PROP. VIII. *The endeavour of each thing to persist in its own being involves no finite time but an indefinite one.*

Proof. If it involved a limited time that determined the duration of the thing, it would then follow from the very power by which the thing exists that it could not exist beyond that limited time but would have to be destroyed; this, however, is absurd (Prop. 4 of this part). Therefore, the endeavour of each thing to exist involves no definite time but, on the contrary, an indefinite one, since it will always continue to exist by the same power by which it already exists unless it is destroyed by some external cause (same Prop.).

PROP. IX. *The mind, both in so far as it has clear and distinct ideas and in so far as it has confused ones, endeavours to persist in its being for an indefinite time and is conscious of this endeavour.*

Proof. The essence of the mind is constituted by adequate and inadequate ideas (as is shown in Prop. 3 of this part); therefore, both in so far as it possesses the former and in so far as it possesses the latter, it endeavours to persist in its own being (Prop. 7 of this part), and that for an indefinite time (Prop. 8). Now as the mind is necessarily conscious of itself through the ideas of the modifications of the body (Prop. 23 Pt. 2), the mind is conscious of its own endeavour (Prop. 7 of this part).

When considering the arguments above it is often easier to imagine how they apply to substance considered under the attribute of Extension (i.e., an infinite number of small bodies bouncing around and forming complex patterns). Here however, Spinoza focuses on substance considered under the attribute of Thought (i.e., an infinite number of ideas of physical bodies that stand in complex logical relationships to one another). These ideas group themselves into small bundles just like the bodies do. But whereas the activity of a body is to move, the activity of an idea is to affirm something's existence. Affirming that something exists is what the "will" does. But, of course, there is no will as a capacity to affirm in Spinoza. There are only particular acts of affirming. So the human mind is a complex series of affirmations about what exists. To think about something is to affirm that it exists unless there are other ideas in the mind which invalidate that affirmation.

Scholium. When this endeavour relates solely to the mind, it is called 'will'; when, on the other hand, it relates to the mind and body in conjunction, it is called appetite, which is, consequently, nothing but man's very essence, from whose nature necessarily follows all that helps with his preservation; and man has thus been determined to perform all that. Further, there is no difference between appetite and desire (*cupiditas*), except that the term 'desire' is generally applied to people in so far as they are conscious of their appetite, and may accordingly be defined as follows: *Desire is appetite with consciousness thereof.* It is thus plain from what has been said that in no case do we strive for, wish for, long for, or desire anything because we deem it to be good, but on the contrary we deem a thing to be good because we strive for it, wish for it, long for it, or desire it.

Because a complex body, such as a human body, is a complicated, self-maintaining activity, it will act a certain way in certain contexts. If my hand is cut, then my body naturally bleeds and then heals, restoring the original complex motion. Because this healing is the effect of the body's striving to sustain, and is supportive of this striving, healing is "good." Under the attribute of Thought, the mind will likewise strive to affirm the existence of the body undamaged. These two processes are, of course, the same process considered in two ways. Because the body is a complex self-maintaining motion, certain "appetites" will naturally follow. For example, food is necessary to support the self-maintaining motion of the body. As such, an appetite for food is just a natural consequence of the body's striving.

PROP. X. *An idea that excludes the existence of our body cannot be postulated in our mind, but is contrary to it.*

Proof. Whatever can destroy our body cannot exist in it (Prop. 5 of this part). Therefore, the idea of such a thing cannot exist in God, either, in so far as he has the idea of our body (Coroll. Prop.

9 Pt. 2); that is, the idea of that thing cannot exist in our mind (Prop. 11 and 13 Pt. 2), but on the contrary, since the first element that constitutes the essence of the mind is the idea of the human body as actually existing (same two Prop.), the first and chief endeavour of our mind is to affirm the existence of our body (Prop. 7 of this part). Consequently, an idea that negates the existence of our body is contrary to our mind, etc. *Q.E.D.*

PROP. XI. *Whatever increases or diminishes, helps or hinders our body's power of action, the idea thereof increases or diminishes, helps or hinders our mind's power of thought.*

Proof. This Proposition is evident from Prop. 7 Pt. 2, and also from Prop. 14 Pt. 2.

Scholium. Thus we see that the mind can undergo (*pati*) great changes (*mutationes*) and pass now to a state of greater perfection, now to a state of lesser perfection. These passions explain to us the affects of joy (*laetitia*) and sadness (*tristitia*). In the following, by *joy* I mean a *passion through which the mind passes to a greater perfection*; by *sadness*, on the other hand, I will signify a *passion by which the mind passes to a lesser perfection.*

> So, in other words, joy is just an idea of the body increasing in health (i.e., in its ability to self-sustain), while sadness is just an idea of the body decreasing in health. These two ideas, plus the idea of desire or endeavor, are the three foundational principles from which Spinoza will deduce his entire theory of emotion. All of human psychology, Spinoza argues, can be explained using only sadness, joy, and desire (i.e., pain, pleasure, and striving).

Further, I will call 'stimulation' (titillatio) or 'merriment' (hilaritas) the affect of joy in reference to both the body and the mind together; conversely, I will call the affect of sadness under the same condition 'pain' (dolor) or 'melancholy' (melancholia).

> While it is difficult to understand exactly what Spinoza is saying here, the basic reasoning is clear. A human being is just a complicated collection of millions of little modes that are engaged in a complicated self-maintaining activity. This complicated activity can increase or decrease in its "health" or perfection. When there is an increase or decrease in the health or perfection of this activity, then that change can be understood in one of three ways: in relation to the body only, the mind only, or in relation to both.

However, we must bear in mind that stimulation and pain are referred to man when one part of him is more affected than the rest, merriment and melancholy, on the other hand, when all parts are equally affected. Further, I have explained what 'desire' is in Schol. Prop. 9 of this part. Beyond these three I recognize no other primary affect; I will show in the following that all other affects arise from these three. But before I go any further, I would like here to explain at greater length Prop. 10 of this part, in order that it may be more clearly understood in what way one idea may be contrary to another.

> It is not at all clear why Spinoza added this clarification here. He may be responding to an objection given in an earlier draft and adds this clarification to prepare the reader for the next proposition.

In Schol. Prop. 17 Pt. 2 we showed that the idea that constitutes the essence of the mind involves the existence of the body so long as the body itself exists. Also, from what we pointed out in Coroll. Prop. 8 Pt. 2 with Schol. it follows that the present existence of our mind depends solely on its involving the actual existence of the body. Lastly, we showed that the mind's power to imagine and remember things also depends on its involving the actual existence of the body (Prop. 17 and 18 Pt. 2 with Schol.). It follows that the present existence of the mind and its power of imagining are removed (*tolli*) as soon as it ceases to affirm the present existence of the body. Now the cause of the mind's ceasing to affirm this existence of the body cannot be the mind itself (Prop. 4 of this part), nor can it be the body's ceasing to exist. For the cause of the mind's affirming the existence of the body is not that the body began to exist (Prop. 6 Pt. 2); thus, for the same reason, it does not cease to affirm the existence of the body because the body ceases to exist, but this follows from another idea that excludes the present existence of our body and, consequently, of our mind (Prop. 8 Pt. 2). This last idea is, consequently, contrary to the one that constitutes the essence of our mind.

PROP. XII. *The mind endeavours to imagine, as much as it can, those things that increase or help the body's power of action.*

Proof. So long as the human body is affected in a manner (*modus*) that involves the nature of some external body, the human mind will regard that external body as present (Prop. 17 Pt. 2); consequently, so long as the human mind regards an external body as present (Prop. 7 Pt. 2), that is, imagines it (Schol. same Prop.), the human body is affected in a manner that involves the nature of that same external body. Thus, so long as the mind imagines things that increase or help the power of action in our body, the body is affected in manners that increase or help its power of action (Post. 1 of this part); consequently, the mind's power of thinking is for that period increased or helped (Prop. 11 of this part). Thus, the mind endeavours to imagine such things as much as it can (Prop. 6 or Prop. 9 of this part). *Q.E.D.*

In claiming that "the mind endeavours to imagine such things as much as it can," we see a tension in Spinoza that recurs throughout the book. Spinoza argues in the Appendix to Part I that there is no teleology in nature. Nothing acts for an end. So one way to read Spinoza is as saying that all human actions arise mechanically from the internal self-maintaining motions. This internal striving does not need to be conceived in a teleological way. Instead, one might conceive it as just an instance of "an object in motion tends to stay in motion"; as such, this striving is not based on intent so much as it is analogous to the way a hurricane or tornado maintains and strengthens by its internal nature. However, at times, Spinoza does seem to say that humans can act for an end. For consistency, it would be useful to interpret these claims merely as a useful shorthand. Nonetheless, it is reasonable to wonder whether or not Spinoza is entirely consistent on this issue.

PROP. XIII. *When the mind imagines things that diminish or hinder the body's power of action, it endeavours, as much as it can, to remember things that exclude the existence of those things.*

Proof. As long as the mind imagines anything of that kind, the power of the mind and body is diminished or constrained (previous Prop.); nevertheless, it will continue to imagine said thing until it imagines something else that excludes that thing's present existence (Prop. 17 Pt. 2). That means (as I have just shown) that the power of the mind and of the body is diminished or constrained until the mind imagines something else that excludes the existence of that other thing. Thus, the mind will endeavour, as much as it can, to imagine or remember the latter (Prop. 9 of this part). *Q.E.D.*

Corollary. It follows that the mind shrinks from imagining things that diminish or constrain its power and that of the body.

Scholium. From what has been said we can clearly understand what love and hate are: *Love* is nothing but *joy accompanied by the idea of an external cause*; hate is nothing other than *sadness accompanied by the idea of an external cause*. We also see that whoever loves necessarily endeavours to have in their presence and maintain the object of their love; whoever hates, on the other hand, endeavours to remove and destroy the thing they hate. But I will address these matters at greater length later.

> The derivations of his definitions here seem to go something like this. Joy is the idea of an increase in bodily health. When this change is identified with an external cause, then we experience joy at the thought of that external object. That joy that we experience is love, and there is a similar derivation for hate. So, for Spinoza, when one loves another, it is because the person recognizes that the other is somehow good for them (i.e., makes them healthier).

PROP. XIV. *If the mind has once been affected by two affects at the same time, it will afterwards, whenever it is affected by one of these two, be affected by the other as well.*

Proof. If the human body has once been affected by two bodies at once, whenever afterwards the mind imagines one of them, it will straightway remember the other too (Prop. 18 Pt. 2). Now the mind's imaginations point to the modifications of our body rather than to the nature of external ones (Coroll. 2 Prop. 16 Pt. 2); therefore, if the body and, consequently, the mind has once been affected by two affects at the same time (see Def. 3 of this part), it will, whenever it is afterwards affected by one of the two, also be affected by the other. *Q.E.D.*

PROP. XV. *Anything can accidentally be the cause of joy, sadness, or desire.*

Proof. Let us posit that the mind is simultaneously affected by two affects, one of which neither increases nor diminishes its power of action, the other of which either increases or diminishes it (see Post. 1 of this part). From the foregoing Prop. it is evident that, whenever the mind is afterwards affected by the former under the influence of its true cause, which (according to our hypothesis) in itself neither increases nor diminishes the mind's power of thought, it will be at the same time affected by the latter, which does increase or diminish it; that is, it will be affected with joy or sadness (Schol. Prop. 11 of this part). Thus, the former of the two things will, not in itself but accidentally, be the cause of joy or sadness. One could in the same way easily show that the afore-mentioned thing could accidentally be the cause of desire. *Q.E.D.*

Corollary. Simply from the fact that we have regarded a thing with an affect of joy or sadness of which said thing is not the efficient cause, we can either love or hate it.

> An example may be helpful here. An ex-lover's perfume or cologne is only accidentally connected with the person, but when smelled, even years later, can still remind you of the person.

Proof. For this reason alone the mind afterwards, upon imagining something, can be affected by the affect of joy or sadness (Prop. 14 of this part); that is, the power of the mind and body is increased or diminished, etc. (Schol. Prop. 11). Consequently, the mind desires to imagine it (Prop. 12) or shrinks from imag-ining it (Coroll. Prop. 13); in other words, it loves or hates it (Schol. Prop. 13). *Q.E.D.*

> It is important to remember that by "imagining" here Spinoza means any particular mental content: a visual experience, a smell, a taste, a touch, etc. Each of these would be a way that an external body would modify/affect one's body.

Scholium. From all of this we understand how it is possible that we may love or hate a thing without being aware of any cause for it but merely (as people say) from sympathy or antipathy. We should include in the same category those objects that affect us with joy or sadness simply because they are in some way similar to other objects that affect us in the same way, which I will detail in the next Prop. I am aware that the writers who first introduced the terms 'sympathy' and 'antipathy' did so to signify some occult qualities in things; nonetheless, I think we may be permitted to use the same terms to indicate known or even manifest qualities.

PROP. XVI. *From the mere fact that we imagine a given thing as bearing some resemblance with an object that is wont to affect the mind with joy or sadness, then, even though the point of resemblance may not be the efficient cause of these affects, we will still love or hate the thing in question.*

Proof. We have formerly regarded in the object itself the point of similarity to the object with an affect of joy or sadness (according to our hypothesis). Thus, when the mind is affected by the image of it, it will immediately be affected by one or the other affect (Prop. 14 of this part); consequently, the thing in which we perceive this point of resemblance will accidentally be a cause of joy or sadness (Prop. 15). It follows that, even though the point in which it resembles the object may not be the efficient cause of these affects, we will still love or hate that thing (previous Coroll.). *Q.E.D.*

PROP. XVII. *If we imagine a thing that is wont to affect us with an affect of sadness as having any point of resemblance with another thing which is wont to affect us with an equally strong affect of joy, we will both hate and love it at the same time.*

Proof. The thing at hand is in itself a cause of sadness (according to our hypothesis), and in so far as we imagine it with this affect, we will hate it (Schol. Prop. 13 of this part). Further, in so far as we imagine it as having some point of resemblance with another thing that is wont to affect us with an equally strong affect of joy, we will love it with an equally strong endeavour of joy (previous Prop.). Thus, we will hate and love the same thing at the same time. *Q.E.D.*

Scholium. This *disposition of the mind that arises from two contrary affects* is called *vacillation of mind*; it thus stands to the affects in the same relation as doubt does to the imagination (see Schol. Prop. 44 Pt. 2). Vacillation and doubt do not differ from one another except as greater differs from smaller. Note, however, that in the previous Prop. I deduced such vacillations of mind from causes that give rise to one of the affects in themselves and to the other accidentally. I did so because in this way they are more easily deduced from what precedes, not because I dispute that vacillations of mind mostly arise from an object that is the efficient cause of both affects. For the human body is composed of a variety of individual parts of different nature (Post. 1 Pt. 2), so that it can be affected by one and the same body in very many different ways (Ax. 1 after Lemma 3 after Prop. 13 Pt. 2); conversely, as one and the same thing can be affected in many ways, it can also affect one and the same part of the body in many different ways. From this we can easily conceive that one and the same object can be the cause of manifold and conflicting affects.

Given the great complexity of the human body it is possible for an external cause to increase the overall health (power) of one part of the body while diminishing another. For example, chocolate cake may increase the health of the tongue (which is why it is pleasurable), but decrease the health of the stomach or overall organism (which is why we tend to be ambivalent towards it).

PROP. XVIII. *A person is affected with the same affect of joy or sadness by the image of something past or future as by the image of something present.*

Proof. As long as a someone is affected by the image of anything, they will regard that thing as present, even if it does not exist (Prop. 17 Pt. 2 with Coroll.); they will not imagine it as past or future, except in so far as its image is joined to the image of a past or future time (see Schol. Prop. 44 Pt. 2). Therefore, the image of a thing, regarded in itself alone, is the same whether it relates to the past, the future, or the present; that is, the disposition of the body, or the affect, is the same whether the image is of something past, future, or present (Coroll. Prop. 16 Pt. 2). Consequently, the affect of joy or sadness is the same whether the image is of something past, future, or present. *Q.E.D.*

Scholium I. Here I call a thing 'past' or 'future' to the extent that we either have been or will be affected by it, for instance, if we have seen or will see it, or it has recreated or will recreate us, or it has harmed or will harm us, and so on. For to the extent that we imagine it in this way, we affirm its existence—that is, the body is affected by no affect that excludes the existence of the thing, so that it is affected by the image of that thing in the same way as if it were actually present (Prop. 17 Pt. 2). However, as it very often happens that those who have had more experiences vacillate so long as they regard a thing as future or past and are usually in doubt about its issue (see Schol. Prop. 44 Pt. 2), the affects that arise from similar images of things are not so constant but are generally disturbed by the images of other things until one becomes assured of the issue.

Scholium II. From what has just been said we understand what is meant by the terms 'hope' (*spes*), 'fear' (*metus*), 'confidence' (*secu-*

ritas), 'despair' (*desperatio*), 'delight' (*gaudium*), and 'remorse' (*conscientiae morsus*). *Hope* is nothing but an *inconstant joy arising from the image of something future or past of whose issue we are unsure. Fear,* on the other hand, is an *inconstant sadness also arising from the image of something doubtful.* Further, if the element of doubt is removed from these affects, hope becomes *confidence* and fear becomes *despair*, in other words, *joy* or *sadness arising from the image of something we have hoped for or feared.* Further, *delight is joy arising from the image of something past of whose issue we were unsure.* Finally, *remorse* is the *sadness opposed to delight.*

> It is interesting that Spinoza here defines 'hope' and 'fear' not only in relation to the future but also the past. Perhaps an example might be hoping that, before he died, my rich grandfather left me money in his will.

PROP. XIX. *Those who imagine what they love being destroyed will be saddened; conversely, if they imagine it being preserved will rejoice.*

Proof. The mind endeavours, as far as possible, to imagine those things that increase or help the body's power of action (Prop. 12 of this part); in other words, those things that it loves (Schol. Prop. 13 of this part). Now imagination is helped by those things that cause (*ponunt*) the existence of a thing and, conversely, is hindered by those that exclude the existence of a thing (Prop. 17 Pt. 2); therefore, the images of things that posit the existence of a beloved thing help the mind's endeavour to imagine the beloved thing; in other words, they affect the mind with joy (Schol. Prop. 11 of this part). Conversely, those things that exclude the existence of the thing loved hinder the aforementioned mental endeavour; in other words, they affect the mind with sadness (same Schol.). Thus, those who imagine what they love being destroyed will be saddened, etc. *Q.E.D.*

> In this way, Spinoza rejects the view of the Stoic philosopher Epictetus, who counseled equanimity in the face of the death of a loved one. Not being upset by the loss of something loved is, according to Spinoza, actually impossible. Since a loved-things aids one's self-sustaining motion, the loss of the aid, is a loss to one's own striving. Not to be saddened by the loss of something loved would be like not feeling a loss of breeze after turning off the fan. Likewise, in the next proposition, one cannot help but rejoice at the destruction of a hated thing. One will naturally feel the difference of whether one is rowing with or against a current. Despite the fact, however, that one cannot avoid

feeling an increase or decrease in their striving, Spinoza will later (in Parts IV and V) discuss ways to minimize the problematic effects of these inevitable disruptions.

PROP. XX. *Those who imagine what they hate being destroyed will rejoice.*

Proof. The mind endeavours to imagine what excludes the existence of things by which the body's power of action is diminished or constrained (Prop. 13 of this part); that is, it endeavours to imagine things that exclude the existence of what it hates (Schol. same Prop.). Therefore, the image of a thing that excludes the existence of what the mind hates helps the aforesaid mental effort; in other words, it affects the mind with joy (Schol. Prop. 11). Consequently, those who imagine the object of their hate being destroyed will rejoice. *Q.E.D.*

PROP. XXI. *Those who imagine what they love being affected with joy or sadness will themselves be affected with joy or sadness; and the one or the other affect will be stronger or weaker in the lover depending on whether it is stronger or weaker in the thing loved.*

Proof. The images of things that cause (*ponunt*) the existence of the thing loved help the mind's endeavour to imagine said thing (as we proved in Prop. 19 of this part). Now joy posits the existence of something feeling joy, the more so the greater the affect of joy is; for it is a transition to a greater perfection (Schol. Prop. 11). Therefore, the image of joy in the thing loved helps the mental endeavour of the lover; that is, it affects the lover with joy, the more so the greater this affect has been in the thing loved (same Schol.). This was our first point. Secondly, to the extent that a thing is affected with sadness, it is destroyed, the more so the greater the sadness it is affected with (Schol. Prop. 11 of this part). Consequently, those who imagine what they love being affected with sadness will themselves be so affected (Prop. 19), the more so the greater this affect has been in the thing loved. *Q.E.D.*

Since a joyful person is just the person ably striving, and to love something is to be supported in this striving, the more powerful the aid (the loved thing), the more able (joyful) is the striving of the one who loves. Thus, one's own striving is aided by those things that aid the striving of the external cause that aids you. Or, the more fully the loved things exists (that is, the healthier they are, or the more powerful they are in maintaining themselves), the more you will experience pleasure in them. It is important to remember here that it is unlikely that joy will be the only emotion felt. Spinoza is here attempting to trace the basic emotional facts about humans. Insofar as objects are complex, the interactions between them can be more or less complex. As such, there may be other emotions happening too, because of other causal relations that are occurring simultaneously. In discussing love, he is attempting to isolate particular elements of a complex system.

PROP. XXII. *If we imagine someone affecting something we love with joy, we will be affected with love towards that person. Conversely, if we imagine them affecting something we love with sadness, we will be affected with hatred towards them.*

Proof. Anybody who affects the thing we love with joy or sadness affects us too with joy or sadness, provided that we imagine the thing loved as affected with that same joy or sadness (previous Prop.). Now this joy or sadness is postulated to exist in us accompanied by the idea of an external cause; therefore, if we imagine somebody affecting a thing we love with joy or sadness, we will be affected with love or hatred towards them (Schol. Prop. 13 of this part). *Q.E.D.*

The reader may object that Spinoza has not taken into account jealousy. If my spouse takes a lover who gives her great pleasure, then Spinoza says here that I will feel love towards him, because he gives pleasure to someone I love. Empirically, that seems implausible. Spinoza discusses jealousy in Prop XXXV, but it's worth noting here that given the complexity of the body/mind we rarely if ever experience only one emotion. But Spinoza does seem committed to the claim that I will to some extent love him for giving her pleasure, even if I also hate him for harming me in other ways.

Scholium. Prop. 21 explains to us the nature of *pity* (*commiseratio*), which we may define as *sadness arising from another's ill.* What term we ought to use for joy arising from another's good, I do not know. Further, we will call *love towards someone who has done good to another approval* (*favor*); and *the hatred towards someone who does harm to another* we will call *indignation* (*indignatio*). We must further note that we feel pity not only for a thing we have loved (as shown in Prop. 21) but also for one we have thus far regarded without affect, provided that we deem it to resemble ourselves (as I will show below). Thus, we bestow approval on somebody who has done good to something resembling ourselves and, conversely, are indignant with somebody who has injured it.

PROP. XXIII. *Those who imagine something they hate being affected with sadness will rejoice; conversely, if they imagine it being affected with joy, they will be saddened. Either affect will be stronger or weaker depending on whether its contrary is stronger or weaker in the thing hated.*

Proof. In so far as the thing hated is affected with sadness, it is destroyed, the more so the stronger the sadness it is affected with (Schol. Prop. 11 of this part). Therefore, whoever imagines something they hate being affected with sadness will, conversely, rejoice, the more so the stronger the sadness they imagine the thing hated to be affected with (Prop. 20). This was our first point. Secondly, joy posits (*ponit*) the existence of a thing feeling joy (Schol. Prop. 11), the more so the stronger the joy is conceived to be. If anyone imagines somebody they hate being affected with joy, this imagination will hinder their own endeavour (Prop. 13); in other words, whoever hates will be affected with sadness, etc. (Schol. Prop. 11). *Q.E.D.*

Scholium. This joy can hardly be steadfast and without any mental conflict. For (as I am going to show in Prop. 27) in so far as one imagines something similar to oneself being affected with an affect of sadness, one will be saddened; and one will have the contrary affect if the same thing is imagined to be affected with joy. But here we are dealing with hatred only.

PROP. XXIV. *If we imagine someone affecting with joy something we hate, we will be affected with hatred towards them as well. If, on the other hand, we imagine them affecting that same thing with sadness, we will be affected with love towards them.*

Proof. This Proposition is proved in the same way as Prop. 22 of this part, to which I refer the reader.

Scholium. These and similar affects of hatred relate to *envy* (*invidia*),[1] which, accordingly, is nothing but *hatred* itself *in so far*

---

1 I have translated *invidia* as 'envy' throughout; it is however worth noting that the Latin word connotes having ill-will towards another, and this entails not only sadness at one's enemy's good fortune (which puts it in the vicinity of the English concept of 'envy') but also joy at their misfortune. This connotation is contained in Spinoza's gloss on the word (see below, Def. of the affects, 23). (D.A.)

as it is regarded as disposing a person to delight in another's ill and, conversely, to be saddened by another's good.

Because we are all very similar, emotions are contagious. If I envy my rival's success at getting a certain job, then I hate him because he harms me, and so rejoice in his sadness. Nevertheless, I experience a type of joy at this success because he is similar to me. We are beginning to see how Spinoza's psychology is full of complex emotional reactions and inner conflicts.

PROP. XXV. *We endeavour to affirm about ourselves and what we love everything that we imagine affecting ourselves or the thing loved with joy. Conversely, we endeavour to negate everything that we imagine affecting ourselves or the thing loved with sadness.*

Proof. What we imagine affecting something we love with joy or sadness affects us with joy or sadness as well (Prop. 21 of this part). Now the mind endeavours, as far as it can, to imagine those things that affect us with joy (Prop. 12), in other words, to regard them as present (Prop. 17 Pt. 2 with Coroll.) and, conversely, to exclude the existence of the things that affect us with sadness (Prop. 13 of this part). Therefore, we endeavour to affirm about ourselves and what we love everything we imagine affecting ourselves or what we love with joy, and the opposite. *Q.E.D.*

PROP. XXVI. *We endeavour to affirm about what we hate everything that we imagine affecting it with sadness and, conversely, to negate everything which we imagine affecting it with joy.*

Proof. This Proposition follows from Prop. 23 as the foregoing Prop. followed from Prop. 21 of this part.

Scholium. Thus we see that it can easily happen that somebody thinks too highly of themselves or something they love and, conversely, too meanly of something they hate. This imagining is called 'pride' (*superbia*) when the haughty feeling in question refers to the person themselves, and is a form of madness since therein one dreams with one's eyes open that one can accomplish anything that falls within the scope of one's imagination and which one thereupon deems real, and exults about it as long as one is unable to imagine those things that exclude its existence and limits one's power of action. *Pride* is, therefore, *joy springing from somebody thinking too highly of themselves.* Also, the *joy that arises from someone thinking too highly of another* is called *partiality* (*existimatio*). Finally, *the joy that arises from thinking too little of somebody* is called *scorn* (*despectus*).

It is important to note here that Spinoza is merely describing the unavoidable fantasies that we have about ourselves and others. He is not advising people to not be proud, since pride will happen to everyone in certain situations where it promotes the person's overall striving. There is no moral condemnation or exultation to "do better." Indeed, since pride brings joy, it seems that it is to that extent a good. Pride is only problematic if the power provided by that joy is out of balance with reality, and thus the overall system is made off-balance by that misplaced power.

PROP. XXVII. *By the very fact that we imagine a thing similar to ourselves, which we have not regarded with any affect, to be affected with some affect, we are ourselves affected with a similar affect.*

Proof. The images of things are modifications of the human body whose ideas represent external bodies as present to us (Prop. 17 Pt. 2), in other words, whose ideas involve the nature of our body and, at the same time, the nature of the external body as present. If, therefore, the nature of the external body is similar to that of our body, the idea of the external body we imagine will involve a modification (*affectio*) of our own body similar to the modification of the external body. Consequently, if we imagine anyone similar to ourselves as affected by some affect, this imagination will express a modification of our body similar to that affect. Thus, from the fact that we imagine a thing similar to ourselves to be affected by some affect, we are ourselves affected with an affect just like that of that thing. If, on the other hand, we hate a thing similar to ourselves, we will, to that extent, be affected by an affect contrary, and not similar, to that of that thing (Prop. 23 of this part). *Q.E.D.*

Scholium. This imitation of affects, when it relates to sadness, is called *pity* (*commiseratio*) (on which see Schol. Prop. 22 of this part); when it relates to desire, it is called *emulation* (*aemulatio*), which is nothing other than *the desire of something that arises in us from our imagining others similar to ourselves to have the same desire.*

Corollary I. If we imagine someone whom we have so far regarded with no affect affecting with joy something similar to ourselves, we will be affected with love towards them. If, on the other hand, we imagine them affecting that same thing with sadness, we will be affected with hatred towards them.

Proof. This is proved from the last Proposition in the same manner as Prop. 22 of this part is proved from Prop. 21.

Corollary II. We cannot hate something we pity just because its misery affects us with sadness.

Proof. If we could hate it for this reason, we would rejoice in its sadness (Prop. 23 of this part), which is contrary to the hypothesis.

> This claim is interesting because it rejects a natural inference that one would draw from the preceding principles about emotional complexity. The natural inference would be something like this: I see a person who is suffering and that causes me suffering by imitation of the affects. That suffering harms my health. So—it seems to follow—to that extent I also hate that suffering person for hurting me. But Spinoza denies that next step. We cannot hate the sad person just because their sadness makes us sad too. So what's the problem? To hate someone is to rejoice in their sadness. So if a suffering person's sadness makes me sad and thus I hate him for that reason, then I would both be happy and sad at his suffering. Spinoza takes this as a logical contradiction, but it's not obvious that he should, since we often love and hate the same thing and in different ways, on Spinoza's view.

Corollary III. We seek to free a thing we pity from misery as much as we can.

Proof. That which affects the thing we pity with sadness affects us with similar sadness, too (previous Prop.); therefore, we will endeavour to remember everything that removes (*tollit*) its existence, in other words, that destroys it (Prop. 13 of this part). That is, we will desire to destroy it (Schol. Prop. 9)—in other words, we will be determined to destroy it; thus, we will endeavour to free a thing that we pity from its misery. *Q.E.D.*

Scholium. This will, or appetite, to do good, which arises from our pitying the thing on which we want to bestow a benefit, is called *benevolence* (*benevolentia*). This affect is nothing but *desire arising from pity*. Concerning love or hate towards someone who has done good or harm to something we imagine to be like ourselves, see Schol. Prop. 22 of this part.

When I see someone like me suffering, then I will naturally work to end their suffering. Of course, this desire is not the only desire in my mind and may be overridden by other desires in actual practice. But Spinoza rules out here the possibility of psychopaths who are indifferent to the suffering of others. It may be that the psychopath's pride has caused him to believe that he is fundamentally different from others, and that may interrupt the automatic pity one feels on seeing suffering. But this is just a possible reconstruction of psychopathology in Spinoza's psychology.

PROP. XXVIII. *We endeavour to facilitate anything we imagine to conduce to joy. Conversely, we endeavour to remove or destroy anything we imagine to be at odds with joy, in other words, to conduce to sadness.*

Proof. We endeavour to imagine, as far as possible, what we imagine to conduce to joy (Prop. 12 of this part); in other words, we will endeavour to regard it, as far as possible, as present, that is, actually existing (Prop. 17 Pt. 2). But the endeavour of the mind, that is, the mind's power of thought, is by nature equal to, and simultaneous with, the endeavour of the body, that is, the body's power of action (as clearly follows from Coroll. Prop. 7 Pt. 2 and Coroll. Prop. 11 Pt. 2). Therefore, we make an absolute endeavour for its existence; in other words, we desire and strive for it (which is the same, see Schol. Prop. 9 of this part). This was our first point. Also, if we imagine something we believe to be the cause of sadness—that is, something we hate (Schol. Prop. 13)— being destroyed, we will rejoice (Prop. 20). Consequently, we will endeavour to destroy it (see the first part of this proof) or to remove it from us (Prop. 13), so that we do not have to regard it as present. This was our second point. Thus, anything that conduces to joy, etc. *Q.E.D.*

PROP. XXIX. *We will also endeavour to do anything that we imagine people[1] to regard with joy and, conversely, we shall shrink from doing what we imagine people to shrink from.*

Proof. From the fact that we imagine people loving or hating anything, we will love or hate the same thing (Prop. 27 of this part); that is, from this mere fact we will rejoice in or be saddened by that thing's presence (Schol. Prop. 13). Thus, we will endeavour

---

1 By 'people' in this and the following Propositions, I mean people whom we regard without any particular affect. (Spinoza)

to do whatever we imagine people loving, that is, regarding with joy, etc. (previous Prop.). *Q.E.D.*

Scholium. This endeavour to do and also to avoid doing something solely in order to please people we call 'ambition' (*ambitio*), especially when we so eagerly endeavour to please the majority that we do or omit certain things to our own or another's detriment; in other cases it is generally called 'human kindness' (*humanitas*). Further, I call 'praise' (*laus*) the joy with which we imagine another person's action by which they have endeavoured to please us, and 'blame' (*vituperium*) the sadness with which, conversely, we feel aversion to their action.

> Because emotions are contagious, we love what people like us love and we hate what people like us hate. Accordingly, when someone loves me, I to some extent then love myself too. Similarly, when someone hates me, I to some extent then hate myself. The more people who love or hate me, the more strongly I feel these emotions. As the people who love me will act in support of my striving and those who hate me will act in opposition to my striving, my striving is aided or supported by those who love and/or hate me. Thus, I am caused to feel joy or sadness by how others feel about me. As such, I try to please others so that they will love me and thereby support my striving.

PROP. XXX. *If someone has done something that they imagine affecting others with joy, they will be affected with joy accompanied by the idea of themselves as cause; in other words, they will regard themselves with joy. On the other hand, if someone has done something they imagine affecting others with sadness, they will regard themselves with sadness.*

Proof. Those who imagine themselves affecting others with joy or sadness will, by that very fact, be affected with joy or sadness themselves (Prop. 27 of this part). Now since man is aware of himself through the modifications by which he is determined to act (Prop. 19 and 23 Pt. 2), it follows that those who have done something they imagine to affect others with joy will be affected with joy together with the awareness of themselves as cause; in other words, they will regard themselves with joy. The same with sadness. *Q.E.D.*

Scholium. As love is joy accompanied by the idea of an external cause and hatred is sadness also accompanied by the idea of an external cause (Prop. 13 of this part), the joy and sadness in question will be forms of love and hatred. But as love and hatred relate to external objects, we will employ other names for the affects now under discussion: we will refer to joy accompanied by the idea of an external cause as 'glory' (*gloria*)[1] and to the affect contrary to it as 'shame' (*pudor*). By this I mean cases where joy or sadness arises from a person's belief that they are being praised or blamed; otherwise, I will call the joy accompanied by the idea of an internal cause 'self-contentment' (*acquiescentia in se ipso*) and the sadness contrary to it 'repentance' (*poenitentia*). Further, as the joy with which somebody imagines themselves affecting others may exist solely in their own imagination (Coroll. Prop. 17 Pt. 2) and as everyone endeavours to imagine concerning themselves all that they imagine will affect them with joy, it can easily happen that somebody who glories a great deal (*gloriosus*) is prideful (*superbus*) and imagines themselves as pleasing to all, when in reality they are an annoyance to everyone.

> If you want to love yourself more, then do good to others that are similar to you. This inference is a plausible one. As Spinoza's psychology unfolds, we see the power of self-deception and the staggering complexity of our emotional lives.

PROP. XXXI. *If we imagine someone to love, desire, or hate something we ourselves love, desire, or hate, we will by that very fact love, etc. the thing in question more steadfastly. If, on the other hand, we imagine that person disliking something we love—or the opposite, <that they love what we hate>—we will undergo a vacillation of mind.*

Proof. From the mere fact of imagining someone loving something we will ourselves love that same thing (Prop. 27 of this part). But in our hypothesis we love it even without this influence; consequently, to the love is added a new cause by which it is fostered; hence, we will by this very fact love it more steadfastly. Further, from the mere fact of imagining somebody disliking something we will ourselves dislike that thing (same Prop.). Now if we assume that at the same time we love it, we will then simultaneously love it and dislike it; in other words, we will be subject to vacillation (Schol. Prop. 17 of this part). *Q.E.D.*

---

1 The Latin word *gloria* often refers not only to outward recognition by others but also to an internal feeling of pride (this is obviously what prompted S. to count *gloria* among the affects). For the sake of terminological consistency, I will always translate it as 'glory'. (D.A.)

Corollary. From the foregoing, and also from Prop. 28 of this part, it follows that everyone endeavours, as far as possible, to cause others to love what they themselves love and to hate what they themselves hate. From this come the poet's verses: "As lovers let us share every hope and every fear: iron-hearted is he who loves what the other lets go."[1]

Scholium. This endeavour to bring it about that our own likes and dislikes should meet with universal approval is really ambition (see Schol. Prop. 29 of this part); thus we see that everyone by nature desires for the rest of humankind to live according to their own individual disposition. When such a desire is equally present in all, everyone equally stands in everyone else's way, and when all want to be praised or loved by all, all become mutually hateful.

> Just as there is inevitable inner conflict, so too is external conflict inevitable. Since we all are made healthier when other people agree with us, we strive to obtain agreement. Yet, because we are all very similar, this agreement results in competition, since we will desire the same things. Since the agreed upon goods support each of us (and thus are desired by each of us), to the degree that a good can only support one or the other of us, there will be conflicting interests. Thus, we can sometimes find agreement, but conflict is inevitable.

PROP. XXXII. *If we imagine someone taking delight in something that only one person can possess, we will endeavour to prevent that person from gaining possession of it.*

Proof. From the mere fact that we imagine another person taking delight in a thing, we will love that thing ourselves and desire to take delight in it (Prop. 27 of this part with Coroll. 1). Now we imagine (according to our hypothesis) that the joy in question would be prevented by another's delight in its object; we will, therefore, endeavour to prevent them from possessing it (Prop. 28). *Q.E.D.*

> Here Spinoza focuses on the element of resource scarcity. If there is only one piece of pizza left and I am hungry, then to that extent I will try to prevent others from getting the pizza. The better the thing is for me, the stronger I try to prevent others from getting it. Again, it's important to remember that this is just one of my many desires, and

---

1 From Ovid, *Amores* 2.19.4–5: *ferreus est, siquis, quod sinit alter, amat/speremus pariter, pariter metuamus amantes.* S. inverts the order of the two verses. (D.A.)

since there are many other desires that support my striving, real world desires are not that simple. I might, for example, both want the piece of pizza and want to act in ways that make others love me (i.e., want to share the pizza). Each of these desires would be seeking to gain an aid towards my striving, and would result in inner (and potentially external) conflict.

Scholium. We thus see that human nature is generally so constituted that people pity those who fare ill and envy those who fare well, and this with the more hatred the greater their own love for the thing they imagine the other to possess (previous Prop.). Further, we see that from the same property of human nature from which it follows that people are merciful, it also follows that they are envious and ambitious. Finally, if we consult experience itself we will find that it teaches all that we have said, especially if we turn our attention to the first years of our life: we find that children, as their body is continually in a balance, as it were, laugh or cry simply because they see others laughing or crying and immediately desire to imitate whatever else they see others doing and, in general, wish for themselves anything they imagine others taking delight in. This is because the images of things are, as we have said, simply the modifications of the human body, that is, the modes in which the human body is affected by external causes and disposed to act in this or that manner.

PROP. XXXIII. *When we love something similar to ourselves, we endeavour, as far as we can, to make it love us in return.*

Proof. When we love something, we endeavour, as far as we can, to imagine it above all else (Prop. 12 of this part). So if that thing is similar to ourselves, we will endeavour to affect it with joy more than we do anything else (Prop. 29); in other words, we will endeavour, as far as we can, to make it so that it is affected with joy accompanied by the idea of ourselves, that is, that it loves us in return (Schol. Prop. 13). *Q.E.D.*

This is an elegant argument. If I love someone, then I want them to exist more (be healthier or more powerful and successful in continuing to exist), and so I will try to cause them joy. But since love is joy accompanied by the idea of an external cause, the person will come to love me the more joy I bring them. Thus, if I love someone, I will act to support their striving, and thereby try to make them love me more in return.

PROP. XXXIV. *The greater the affect with which we imagine a thing loved to be affected towards us, the more we will glory in it.*

Proof. We endeavour, as far as we can, to make it so that the thing we love loves us in return (previous Prop.), in other words, that what we love is affected with joy accompanied by the idea of ourselves (Schol. Prop. 13 of this part). Therefore, the greater the joy with which we imagine the thing loved to be affected because of us, the more this endeavour is fostered, that is, the greater will be our joy (Prop. 11 of this part with Schol.). Now when we rejoice in the fact that we have affected with joy something similar to ourselves, we regard ourselves with joy (Prop. 30); consequently, the greater the affect with which we imagine the thing loved to be affected towards us, the greater the joy with which we will regard ourselves—that is, the more we will glory in it (Schol. Prop. 30). *Q.E.D.*

> If I love someone then I seek to cause them joy which causes them to love me. But if I love a person then I love what they love and so I then come to love myself. So loving someone else improves one's self-love.

PROP. XXXV. *If someone imagines something loved joining itself to another with the same or closer bonds of friendship than those with which they themselves alone possessed it, they will be affected with hatred towards the thing loved and will envy their rival.*

Proof. The greater the love with which someone imagines something loved being affected towards them, the more they will glory (previous Prop.), that is, rejoice (Schol. Prop. 30 of this part). Thus, they will endeavour, as far as they can, to imagine the thing loved as most closely bound to them, and this endeavour, or desire, will be increased if they imagine someone else having the same desire (Prop. 31). Now this endeavour, or desire, is assumed to be checked by the image of the thing loved itself in conjunction with the image of the person it joins to itself; therefore, they will through that very fact be affected with sadness accompanied by the idea of the thing loved as a cause as well as the image of their rival (Schol. Prop. 11). That is, they will be affected with hatred towards the thing they love (Schol. Prop. 13) and also towards their rival (Coroll. Prop. 15), whom they will envy for enjoying the beloved thing (Prop. 23). *Q.E.D.*

Scholium. This hatred towards something one loves joined with envy is called 'jealousy' (*zelotypia*), which accordingly is nothing but a vacillation of mind arising from love and hatred combined, accompanied by the idea of another who is envied. Further, this hatred towards the thing loved will be greater in proportion to the joy with which the jealous person used to be affected by the reciprocated love of the thing loved, and also in proportion to the affect with which they used to be affected towards the person to whom they imagine the thing loved joining itself. For if they hated them, they will for this very reason hate the thing loved, because they imagine it as affecting with joy somebody they themselves hate (Prop. 24 of this part), and also because they are compelled to associate the image of the thing loved with the image of the person they hate (Coroll. Prop. 15). This condition generally comes into play in the case of love for a woman: for a man who imagines a woman he loves prostituting herself to another will not only be saddened because his own desire is restrained but will also feel aversion against her because he is compelled to associate the image of the thing loved with the genitals and excretions of the other. Besides, the jealous man is not received by his beloved with the same countenance that she used to offer him, which for a lover is an additional cause of sadness, as I will now show.

> Spinoza's account of romantic jealousy here is curious. Suppose we have a man whose wife has an affair. Why does this cause the man suffering? Intuitively, it would be that the man feels like he is "not good enough" or inadequate, and suffers from this feeling of inferiority. But this pain is not the pain that Spinoza focuses on here. Instead, the man will feel pain because he will combine the idea of his wife with the idea of the other's "genitals and excretions" and so thoughts of the one will automatically include thoughts of the other. As thoughts of one hated cause pain, associating the one loved with the thing hated corrupts the joy from the one. The more joy was previously gained from the loved one, the greater the loss when the source of joy becomes corrupted by a source of hate.

PROP. XXXVI. *Whoever remembers something they have once enjoyed desires to possess it under the same circumstances as when they first enjoyed it.*

Proof. Everything a person has seen in conjunction with the thing they enjoyed will be to them accidentally a cause of joy (Prop. 15

of this part). Therefore, they will desire to possess all of it in conjunction with the thing they have enjoyed; in other words, they will desire to possess the thing in question under the same circumstances as when they first enjoyed it. *Q.E.D.*

Corollary. A lover will, therefore, be saddened if they find out that one of these circumstances is missing.

Proof. In so far as the lover finds some circumstance to be missing, they imagine something that excludes its existence. Now as they desire, because of love, that thing or circumstance (previous Prop.), they will be saddened in so far as they imagine it to be missing (Prop. 19). *Q.E.D.*

Scholium. This sadness, in so far as it relates to the absence of the thing loved, is called 'longing' (*desiderium*).

PROP. XXXVII. *Desire arising through sadness or joy, hatred or love is greater the stronger the affection at hand.*

Proof. Sadness diminishes or constrains a person's power of action (Schol. Prop. 11 of this part); in other words, it diminishes or constrains the effort with which one endeavours to persist in one's own being (Prop. 7). Therefore, it is opposed to said endeavour (Prop. 5), and all that somebody affected by sadness endeavours to do is to remove that sadness. Now the greater the sadness, the bigger the part of a person's power of action to which it must be opposed (by the Def. of 'sadness'); consequently, the greater the sadness, the greater the power of action one will employ to remove it, that is, the greater will be the desire, or appetite, in endeavouring to remove it (Schol. Prop. 9). Also, since joy increases or aids one's power of action (Schol. Prop. 11), it can easily be shown in a similar manner that anybody affected with joy has no desire other than to preserve it, and the greater the joy, the stronger this desire will be. Lastly, since hatred and love are themselves affects of sadness or joy, it similarly follows that the endeavour, appetite, or desire that arises through hatred or love will be greater in proportion to the hatred or love. *Q.E.D.*

PROP. XXXVIII. *If a person has begun to hate something they used to love, so that the love is thoroughly destroyed, they will, the causes being equal, regard it with more hatred than if they had never loved it, and the stronger the former love, the greater the hatred.*

Proof. If someone begins to hate what they used to love, more of their appetites are put under restraint than if they had never loved it. For love is a joy (Schol. Prop. 13 of this part), which man endeavours to conserve as far as he can (Prop. 28); he does so by regarding the thing loved as present (same Schol.) and by affecting it with joy as far as he can (Prop. 21), an endeavour that is the greater the stronger the love is, as is the endeavour to cause the beloved thing to love him in return (see Schol. Prop. 33). Now these endeavours are constrained by the hatred towards the thing loved (Coroll. Prop. 13 and Prop. 23); thus, the lover will be affected with sadness for this cause, too (Schol. Prop. 11), and this the more so the greater the love was; that is, in addition to the sadness that has caused the hatred, there is another caused by the former love. Consequently, the lover will regard the beloved thing with a greater affect of sadness; in other words, they will hate it more than if they had never loved it (Schol. Prop. 13), and the greater the love was, the greater the hatred. *Q.E.D.*

> So, if I come to hate someone that I used to love, then I hate them for whatever reason the hate exists, and I also hate them for depriving me of the prior love. These are two distinct harms. The greater the loss of love, the greater the transition/decrease in power, i.e., the greater the hate.

PROP. XXXIX. *Whoever hates someone will endeavour to do that person an injury, unless they fear that this will cause a greater injury to themselves; conversely, whoever loves someone will, by the same law, seek to benefit them.*

Proof. To hate somebody is to imagine them as a cause of sadness (Schol. Prop. 13 of this part); thus, whoever hates somebody will endeavour to remove (*amovere*) or destroy them (Prop. 28). But if the hater fears that something more painful or (what is the same) a greater evil will accrue to them out of it and thinks that they can avoid such evil by not carrying out the injury they planned against the person hated, they will desire to abstain from inflicting that injury (same Prop.), and this endeavour will be stronger than the former endeavour to do injury (Prop. 37) and will therefore prevail over it, as we asserted. The proof of the second part of this Prop. proceeds in the same manner: thus, whoever hates[1] somebody, etc. *Q.E.D.*

As always, when reading Spinoza, it is important to keep in mind that each of the consequences drawn does not exist in isolation. They interact with lots of other things going on in the mind/body as well.

Scholium. By 'good' I here mean any kind of joy and, further, all that is conducive to it, especially what satisfies our longings, whatever they may be. By 'evil' or 'injury', on the other hand, I mean any kind of sadness, especially one that frustrates our longings. For I have shown above (Schol. Prop. 9 of this part) that we never desire a thing because we judge it to be good but, on the contrary, we deem a thing good because we desire it; consequently, we deem evil what we shrink from. Thus, everyone judges, or estimates, what is good according to their particular affects, likewise what is bad, what is better, what is worse and, lastly, what is best and what is worst. Thus, a greedy person thinks that abundance of money is the best and want of money the worst; an ambitious one desires nothing so much as glory and fears nothing so much as shame. Further, to an envious person nothing is more delightful than another's misfortune and nothing more painful than another's success. So everybody judges something to be good or bad, useful or useless according to their own affects. Apart from that, the affect that causes somebody not to want what they wish or to want what they do not wish is called *timidity* (*timor*), which accordingly is nothing other than *fear in so far as one is disposed by it to avoid an evil they think is going to happen by means of a lesser one* (see Prop. 28 of this part). But if the evil they fear is shame, timidity is called 'modesty' (*verecundia*). Lastly, if the desire to avoid a future evil is checked by the fear of another evil, so that one does not know which to choose, fear is called 'dismay' (*consternatio*), especially if both the evils feared are among the greatest.

It may be a useful reminder at this point that nothing has inherent value in Spinoza's metaphysics. Everything just is. Something becomes good to a thing when it is desired by that thing. So "goodness" and

---

1 So Spinoza's text itself. This must be an oversight, for at this point we expect a demonstration of a lover's propensity to benefit another unless they hope that an even greater joy will accrue to themselves otherwise. (D.A.)

PROP. XL. *Whoever imagines themselves to be hated by another and believes to have given them no cause for hatred will hate that other in return.*

Proof. Whoever imagines another as affected with hatred will through this very fact be affected with hatred themselves (Prop. 27 of this part), that is, with sadness accompanied by the idea of an external cause (Schol. Prop. 13). Now—according to our hypothesis—they imagine no cause for this sadness except the person who hates them; consequently, as a result of imagining themselves hated by someone, they will be affected with sadness accompanied by the idea of the person hating them; in other words, they will hate their hater in return (same Schol.). *Q.E.D.*

Scholium. Someone who thinks that they have given just cause for hatred will be affected with shame (Prop. 30 of this part with Schol.); but this rarely happens (Prop. 25). This reciprocation of hatred may also arise from hatred being followed by an endeavour to injure the person hated (Prop. 39). Thus, someone who imagines themselves being hated by another will imagine that person as the cause of some evil, that is, sadness; consequently, they will be affected with sadness, that is, fear, accompanied by the idea of the hater as cause; in other words, they will be affected with hatred in return, as I said above.

Corollary I. Whoever imagines someone they love being affected with hatred toward them will be torn between hatred and love. For in so far as they imagine being hated by that person, they are determined to hate them in return (previous Prop.). But (according to the hypothesis) they nevertheless love them; therefore, they will be torn between hatred and love.

Corollary II. If one imagines somebody one has thus far regarded without affect to have done one some injury because of hatred, one will immediately seek to repay the injury in kind.

Proof. Whoever imagines another to be affected with hatred against them will hate that person in return (previous Prop.) and will endeavour to come up with anything that can affect that person with sadness (Prop. 26 of this part) and will strive to inflict it upon them (Prop. 39). Now (in our hypothesis) the first thing of this sort that they imagine is the injury done to themselves; they will, therefore, immediately endeavour to inflict the same thing on them. *Q.E.D.*

Scholium. The endeavour to injure someone we hate is called 'anger' (*ira*); the endeavour to repay in kind injury done to ourselves is called 'revenge' (*vindicta*).

> Anger, according to Spinoza, is an active attempt to hurt another person (or thing). This act can consist in any way in which one's actions are set in opposition to the strivings of the other. If one does not actively hurt the other person, then it is only because some internal or external force has prevented it.

PROP. XLI. *If anyone imagines themselves being loved by another and believes that they have given no cause for such love (which can happen: Coroll. Prop. 15 and Prop. 16 of this part), they will love the other person in return.*

Proof. This Proposition is proved in the same way as the preceding one. See also the Schol. appended to that Prop.

Scholium. If someone believes that they have given just cause for the love, they will glory (Prop. 30 of this part with Schol.); this is what most often happens (Prop. 25), and we said that its contrary takes place whenever someone imagines themselves to be hated by another (Schol. previous Prop.). Further, this reciprocal love and, consequently, the endeavour to benefit those who love us (Prop. 39) and who endeavour to benefit us (same Prop.), is called 'thankfulness' or 'gratitude' (*Gratia seu Gratitudo*). It thus appears that people are much more prone to take revenge than to return benefits.

Corollary. Whoever imagines themselves to be loved by one they hate will be torn between hatred and love. This is proved in the same way as the first Coroll. of the preceding Prop.

Scholium. If hatred prevails, one will endeavour to injure the person who loves one. This affect is called 'cruelty' (*crudelitas*), especially if the lover is believed to have given no ordinary cause for hatred.

PROP. XLII. *Whoever has conferred a benefit on someone out of love or hope for glory will be saddened if they see that the benefit is received without gratitude.*

Proof. Whoever loves something similar to themselves endeavours, as far as they can, to cause it to love them in return (Prop. 33 of this part). Therefore, somebody who confers a benefit on another out of love does so because of the desire they feel to be loved in return, that is, from the hope of glory (Prop. 34), that is, joy (Schol. Prop. 30). Hence, they will endeavour, as far as they can, to imagine this cause of glory, that is, to regard it as actually existing (Prop. 12). Now (in our hypothesis) they imagine something else that excludes the existence of said cause of glory; therefore, they will be saddened for this very reason (Prop. 19). *Q.E.D.*

> Here Spinoza seems to identify gratitude with the same thing as loving the person who benefited you.

PROP. XLIII. *Hatred is increased by reciprocal hatred; on the other hand, it can be destroyed by love.*

Proof. Whoever imagines someone they hate to be affected with hatred against them in return will for this very reason feel a new hatred (Prop. 40 of this part), while the former hatred still remains (according to our hypothesis). But if, on the other hand, they imagine that person to be affected with love toward them, they will, to the extent that they do so, regard themselves with joy (Prop. 30) and will to this extent endeavour to please the other person (Prop. 29)—in other words, they will to that extent endeavour not to hate them and not to affect them with sadness (Prop. 41); this endeavour will be stronger or weaker in proportion to the affect from which it arises (Prop. 37). Therefore, if it is stronger than that which arises from hatred and with which they endeavour to affect with sadness the thing they hate (Prop. 26), it will get the better of it and banish the hatred from the mind. *Q.E.D.*

> So if I hate someone and they respond by loving me, then when I think about them loving me, then I feel joy, because love is but joy accompanied by the idea of an external cause. Insofar as I feel that joy, I will love you in return, and insofar as I love you, I will try to bring you joy. This reaction will be greater or lesser depending upon how intense the hate and love are (that is, how much they harm or help me).

PROP. XLIV. *Hatred that is completely vanquished by love turns into love; and the love is for this reason greater than if hatred had not preceded it.*

Proof. The proof proceeds in the same way as that of Prop. 38 of this part. For anyone who begins to love a thing they used to hate, that is, regard with sadness, rejoices because of the very fact of loving, and to this joy involved by love (see its Def. in Schol. Prop. 13 of this part) is added the one arising from the fact that the endeavour to remove the sadness involved by hatred (as we showed in Prop. 37) is decisively fostered and this process is accompanied by the idea of the person previously hated as cause.

Scholium. Though this is so, no one will endeavour to hate anything, that is, to be affected with sadness, for the sake of enjoying this greater joy; that is, no one will desire to suffer a damage in the hope of recouping the damage or long to be ill in the hope of getting well. For everyone will always endeavour to conserve their being and to remove (*amovere*) sadness as far as they can. Indeed, if the contrary were conceivable, namely that one could desire to hate someone in order to be able to love them all the more thereafter, they will always desire to hate that person. For the stronger the hatred has been, the greater will be the love, so that one will always wish for the hatred to grow stronger and stronger; and for a similar reason, one would endeavour to become more and more ill in order to take a greater joy later in being restored to health; and one would always endeavour to be ill, which is absurd (Prop. 6 of this part).

Here Spinoza argues that we never engage in self-harm for the anticipated joy of its removal. The reasoning here is that as we always strive for greater health, self-harm is impossible. Even if I hate myself to some degree, that hate must have been caused by something external. To support this claim, Spinoza imagines the opposite. Imagine if it were possible to hate oneself as a step towards the anticipated joy of removing the hate/harm. If this were possible, then there would be no rational stopping point because greater harm would always mean greater joy at its removal.

PROP. XLV. *If one imagines someone similar to oneself to be affected with hatred against something also similar to oneself which one loves, one will hate that person.*

Proof. The thing loved hates in turn anybody who hates it (Prop. 40 of this part); therefore, the lover who imagines someone hating the beloved thing imagines, for this very reason, the beloved thing as affected with hatred, in other words, with sadness (Schol. Prop. 13). Thus, they are saddened themselves (Prop. 21), a sadness accompanied by the idea of the hater of the beloved thing as cause; that is, they will hate that person (Schol. Prop. 13). *Q.E.D.*

PROP. XLVI. *If one has been affected with joy or sadness by somebody of a class or nation different from one's own and if this has been accompanied by the idea of that person, under the general category of the class or nation, as cause, then one will love or hate not only the individual at hand but also everyone who belongs to that class or nation.*

Proof. This is evident from Prop. 16 of this part.

> It is interesting that Spinoza adds here that the idea of the person must be "under the general category of the class or nation" because it means that our response will depend in part on how the other person is conceived. If I have the idea of being harmed by Fred, then I will hate Fred, but if I have the idea of being harmed by a physics major, then to that extent I will hate all physics majors.

PROP. XLVII. *Joy arising from the fact that we imagine something we hate being destroyed or affected with some other ill is always accompanied by a certain sadness in our mind.*

Proof. This is evident from Prop. 27 of this part. For in so far as we imagine a thing similar to ourselves to be affected with sadness, we are saddened ourselves.

Scholium. This Prop. can also be proved from Coroll. Prop. 17 Pt. 2. For whenever we remember something, even if it does not actually exist, we still regard it as present and our body is affected in the same manner. Consequently, in so far as the remembrance of the thing is strong, one is determined to regard it with sadness, a determination that, while the image of the thing in question lasts, is indeed checked by the remembrance of other things that exclude the existence of the aforesaid thing, but is not removed (*tollitur*). Hence, one only rejoices in so far as said determination is checked, which is why the joy that arises from the ill befalling what we hate is repeated every time we remember that thing.

For—as we have said—since the image of the thing in question involves its existence, when it is aroused it determines one to regard that thing with the same sadness as one was wont to do when it actually did exist; however, since one has joined to the image of the thing other images that exclude its existence, this determination to be saddened is immediately checked and one rejoices afresh, and this as often as the repetition takes place. This is also the cause why people rejoice every time they recall some evil now past and delight in recounting dangers from which they have been freed. For when they imagine a danger, they imagine it as still upcoming and are determined to fear it; but this determination is checked afresh by the idea of liberation that they associated with the idea of the danger when they were freed from it. This renders them safe again, and therefore they rejoice again.

> Here Spinoza offers a subtle and intricate understanding of the psychology of hate. Even when rejoicing in its destruction, I feel sad at the destruction of something similar to myself.

PROP. XLVIII. *Love or hatred towards, for instance, Peter is destroyed if the joy involved by the former or the sadness involved by the latter is associated with the idea of another cause; and both are diminished to the extent that we imagine Peter not to have been the sole cause of either.*

Proof. This Prop. is evident from the mere definition of love and hatred (see Schol. Prop. 13 of this part). For joy is called 'love towards Peter' and sadness 'hatred towards Peter' solely because Peter is regarded as the cause of one affect or the other. Thus, when this condition of causality is either wholly or partly removed, the affect towards Peter wholly or in part vanishes, too. Q.E.D.

PROP. XLIX. *Love or hatred towards a thing that we imagine to be free must, the cause being equal, be greater than if it were felt towards a thing that is necessary.*

Proof. A thing that we imagine to be free must be perceived through itself without any other (Def. 7 Pt. 1). If, therefore, we imagine it as the cause of joy or sadness, we will for this very reason love or hate it (Schol. Prop. 13 of this part), and we will do so with the utmost love or hatred that can arise from the given affect (previous Prop.). But if we imagine the thing that causes the affect to be a necessary one, we will then imagine it not as the sole cause, but as one of the causes of the affect (Def. 7 Pt. 1); therefore, our love or hatred towards it will be less (previous Prop.). *Q.E.D.*

Scholium. It follows that as people think themselves to be free, they feel more love or hatred towards one another than towards anything else. To this consideration we must add the imitation of affects, on which see Prop. 27, 34, 40, and 43 of this part.

> This claim is an important one for Spinoza's general philosophical psychotherapy. When I am injured by someone, and I believe that that person is the only and sole cause of the injury, then all of the pain is attributed to him. But if the person was understood as having no free will, then many causes contributed to my injury, and so my hate is spread out among them. To see this more clearly consider the different types of anger at finding out that someone has smashed the windshield on your car with a bat because they were mad at you, vs. finding out that the person was in the midst of a psychological delusion and a long-time victim of abuse. I may hate the vandal in each case, but the anger is weaker in the latter case. In the latter case, I may think the person had no choice, or my anger may be spread across the act, the illness, and/or an abusive system, for example.

PROP. L. *Anything without exception can be, accidentally, a cause of hope or fear.*

Proof. This Proposition is proved in the same way as Prop. 15 of this part, which see together with Schol. 2 Prop. 18 of this part.

Scholium. Things that are accidentally causes of hope or fear are called good or evil omens. Further, in so far as these very omens are causes of hope or fear, they are also causes of joy and sadness (see the Def. of hope and fear in Schol. 2 Prop. 18 of this part); consequently, to this extent we love or hate them (Coroll. Prop. 15) and endeavour either to use them as means towards what we hope for or to remove (*amovere*) them as obstacles or causes of fear (Prop. 28). It follows, further, from Prop. 25 that we are naturally so constituted as to believe readily in what we hope for and with difficulty in what we fear, as well as to estimate such things above or below their true value. From this fact have arisen superstitions that assail people everywhere. However, I do not think it worthwhile to describe here the vacillations of mind that spring from hope and fear, as it follows from the definition of these affects alone that there can be no hope without fear nor fear without hope (as I will explain at greater length in the proper place), and also because in so far as we hope for or fear anything, we love or hate it, so that anyone can apply by themselves to hope and fear what we have said concerning love and hatred.

> A concrete example may help. Suppose that I get bad news while wearing my new Christmas Moose tie for the first time. After that I may avoid the tie as bringing "bad luck"—simply because I now associate it with bad news. Given the number of such coincidences that occur in life there is no possible limit to the number of good and bad "signs" that we can find in the world.

PROP. LI. *Different people can be differently affected by one and the same object, and one and the same person can at different times be differently affected by one and the same object.*

Proof. The human body is affected by external bodies in very many ways (Post. 3 Pt. 2). Two people can therefore be differently affected at the same time and, therefore, can be differently affected by one and the same object (see Ax. 1 after Lemma 3 after Prop. 13 Pt. 2). Furthermore, the human body can be affected sometimes in one way, sometimes in another (same Post.); consequently, it can be differently affected at different times by one and the same object (same Ax.). *Q.E.D.*

Scholium. We thus see that it can happen that someone loves what another hates or fears what another does not; likewise, one and the same person may love what they once hated, or may be bold where they once were timid, and so on. Also, as everyone judges according to their affects what is good, what bad, what better, and what worse (Schol. Prop. 39 of this part), it follows that people can vary in their judgments no less than their affects.[1] Hence, when we compare some with others, we distinguish them solely by the diversity of their affects and call some 'brave', others 'fearful', and others some other thing. For instance, I will call someone 'brave' if they look down on an evil that I am wont to fear; if I further take into consideration that their desire to injure those they hate and to benefit those they love is not restrained by

---

1 This is possible even though the human mind is part of the divine intellect, as I have shown in Schol. Prop. 13 Pt. 2. (Spinoza)

the fear of an evil that is sufficient to restrain me, I will call him 'daring'. Further, I will deem 'fearful' anybody who fears an evil that I am wont to look down on; and if I further take into consideration that their desire is restrained by the fear of an evil that is unable to restrain me, I will say that he is 'cowardly'; and everyone else will pass judgment in the same way. Lastly, due to this human nature and fickleness of the judgment, shown for instance in the fact that people often judge things solely through their affects or in the fact that the things they believe to cause joy or sadness, which therefore they endeavour to promote or prevent (Prop. 28 of this part), are often purely imaginary—not to speak of what I expounded in Pt. 2 regarding the uncertainty of things—we may readily imagine how a person may often have a cause either to be saddened or to rejoice, in other words, to be affected either with sadness or with joy, with this state being accompanied by the idea of himself as cause. Hence we can easily understand what is 'repentance' (*poenitentia*) and what 'self-contentment' (*acquiescentia in se ipso*): *repentance* is *sadness accompanied by the idea of oneself as cause*; *self-contentment* is *joy accompanied by the idea of oneself as cause*; and these affects are most intense because people believe themselves to be free (see Prop. 49 of this part).

> If I believe that I have harmed someone, then I will feel sadness accompanied by myself as the cause (which is repentance or hatred). If I believe myself to be free, and so the sole cause of the harm, then I will hate myself intensely. If, however, I believe that my actions are fully determined, then I will hate myself much less. It is important not to apply the usual moral connotations to the terms Spinoza is using.

PROP. LII. *An object that we have formerly seen in conjunction with others or which we imagine not to have any property that is not common to many will not be regarded by us for as long as one that we imagine to have some property peculiar to itself.*

Proof. As soon as we imagine an object that we have seen in conjunction with others, we at once remember those others, too (Prop. 18 Pt. 2 with Schol.); thus, we immediately pass from the contemplation of one object to the contemplation of another. And this is equally the case with an object that we imagine to have no property that is not common to many, since we assume, for this very reason, that in it we are contemplating nothing that we have not already seen in conjunction with other objects. However, when we suppose that we imagine something special about an object, something we have never seen before, we are saying nothing other than that the mind, while contemplating that object, has in itself nothing else into whose contemplation it can fall from the contemplation of the former; therefore, the mind is determined to contemplate that object only. Therefore an object, etc. *Q.E.D.*

> This argument is interesting because we contemplate strange or unique things longer than common things only because the strange thing has no associations yet, and so the train of thoughts stops for a time. The mind is determined to contemplate that object until associations are attached to it in such a way that the thing becomes common.

Scholium. This mental modification, or imagination of a particular thing, in so far as it is alone in the mind, is called 'wonder'; but if it is aroused by an object we fear, it is called 'dismay', because wonder at an evil keeps one so engrossed in the simple contemplation of it that one has no power to think of anything else by which he might avoid the evil. If, however, what we wonder at is somebody's prudence, diligence, or anything of that sort, since we regard that person as far surpassing ourselves thereby, wonder is called 'veneration' (*veneratio*); otherwise, if someone's anger, envy, etc. is what we wonder at, this affect is called 'horror' (*horror*). Also, if what we wonder at is the prudence, diligence, etc. of someone we love, our love will on this account be the greater (Prop. 12 of this part); and when this love is joined to wonder or veneration it is called 'devotion' (*devotio*). We may also imagine hatred, hope, confidence, and the other affects as connected with wonder in the same way, and we should thus be able to deduce more affects than those that are usually signified by established names. Hence it is evident that the names of the affects have been created in accordance with their everyday occurrences rather than with an accurate knowledge of them.

> When there is someone with a rare characteristic benefiting us, then the idea of that person will hold our attention longer because of the lack of associations (that is, wonder). We can then experience wonder in connection with all of the other emotions as well. It is worth noting here, however, that Spinoza has provided us no theory of attention or general phenomenology of perception or emotion.

The affect opposed to wonder is 'contempt' (*contemptus*), which generally arises from the fact that, because we see someone wondering at, loving, or fearing something and the like, or because something appears at first sight to be like things that we wonder at, love, fear, etc., we are determined to wonder at, love, or fear that thing (Prop. 15 with Coroll. and Prop. 27 of this part). But if from the presence or more accurate contemplation of the thing in question we are compelled to deny everything about it that can be the cause of wonder, love, fear, etc., the mind then remains determined by the very presence of it to think of what is not in the object rather than what is (although normally, when the object is present, the mind thinks for the most part of what actually is in it). Further, as devotion (*devotio*) springs from wonder at something we love, so derision (*irrisio*) springs from contempt toward a thing we hate or fear, and disrespect (*dedignatio*) from contempt of folly, just as veneration arises from wonder at prudence. Lastly, we can imagine love, hope, glory, and the other affects as connected with contempt and thus deduce yet other affects that we are not used to distinguishing from the others through any specific words, either.

> We hold something in contempt when we first think it is something wonderful, only to find it common; or something lovable, only to find it neutral, etc. It is interesting to note in this argument that Spinoza says that we contemplate the lack or absence of something. Spinoza himself notes the tension in an aside. The contempt then comes from comparing two existing things and noting that what exists in one does not exist in the contemptible thing.

PROP. LIII. *When the mind contemplates itself and its power of action, it rejoices, the more so the more distinctly it imagines itself and its power of action.*

Proof. One does not know oneself except through the modifications of one's body and the ideas of them (Prop. 19 and 23 Pt. 2). When, therefore, the mind is able to contemplate itself, it is thereby assumed to pass to a greater perfection, in other words, to be affected with joy (Schol. Prop. 11 of this part); and the joy will be the greater the more distinctly it is able to imagine itself and its power of action. *Q.E.D.*

> This is a difficult argument. We only know ourselves through the modifications of our bodies. So when the mind contemplates itself, it is

assumed to pass to a greater perfection (health, power) and so feel joy. The reference helps us reconstruct this reasoning, because the scholia tells us that to imagine something is to affirm its existence, and the better we imagine it the more completely we affirm its existence. This idea, coupled with Spinoza's claim that the more adequately one understands something the more active the mind is, and the more active it is the healthier it is, gets us the conclusion. The better we understand ourselves, the more active the mind. The more active the mind, the healthier it is. The experience of passing to that higher degree of health/activity/power/perfection is joy.

Corollary. This joy is all the more fostered the more one imagines oneself to be praised by others. For the more one imagines oneself as praised by others, the more joy one will imagine them being affected with by oneself, joy accompanied by the idea of oneself (Schol. Prop. 29 of this part); thus, one is oneself affected with greater joy accompanied by the idea of oneself (Prop. 27). *Q.E.D.*

PROP. LIV. *The mind endeavours to imagine only things that assert* (ponunt) *its power of action.*

Proof. The mind's endeavour, or power, is the actual essence of the mind (Prop. 7 of this part); but the essence of the mind only affirms what the mind is and can do, not what it neither is nor can do (as is self-evident). Thus, the mind endeavours to imagine only that which affirms, or asserts *(ponit)*, its power of action. *Q.E.D.*

The essence of a complex body is its self-sustaining activity. When we think about things under the attribute of thought, that self-sustaining activity is understood as an affirmation that that activity exists. So the motions of the body correspond to the affirmations in the mind that those motions exist. Thus, just as the body strives to continue to exist, so too the mind strives to affirm that the body continues to exist.

PROP. LV. *When the mind imagines its own weakness, it is saddened because of this very fact.*

Proof. The essence of the mind only affirms that which the mind is or can do; in other words, it is the mind's nature to imagine only things that assert its power of action (previous Prop.). Thus, when we say that the mind in reflecting on itself imagines its own weakness, we are merely saying that, while the mind is endeavouring to imagine something that asserts its power of action, this endeavour of its is checked; in other words, it is saddened (Schol. Prop. 11 of this part). *Q.E.D.*

> These arguments are hard to reconstruct. But one possibility is something like the following: In addition to affirming the existence of the body, the ideas in the mind also affirm the existence of themselves. When the body is damaged, it strives less well. When this same circumstance is considered under the attribute of thought, the mind would include more ideas which depend on ideas external to the mind, i.e., more inadequate ideas. Accordingly, the mind is less able to affirm the existence of the body clearly and distinctly. As such, the mind is less able to employ its power of action. As sadness is merely the transition from greater to lesser affirmation (power), a weakened mind is a saddened mind.

Corollary I. This sadness is fostered more and more if one imagines being blamed by others. This is proved in the same way as Coroll. Prop. 53 of this part.

Scholium. This sadness, accompanied by the idea of our own weakness, is called 'humility' (*humilitas*); the joy that springs from the contemplation of ourselves is called 'self-love' (*philautia*) or 'self-contentment' (*acquiescentia in se ipso*). And since this affect is renewed as often as one contemplates one's own virtues—that is, one's own power of action—it follows that everyone is fond of narrating their exploits and showing off the force both of their body and of their mind, and also that people, for this reason, are annoying to one another. From this, in turn, it follows that people are naturally envious (see Schol. Prop. 24 and Schol. Prop. 32 of this part), that is, rejoice in the weakness of their equals and are saddened because of their virtues. For whenever each person imagines their own actions, they are affected with joy (Prop. 53 of this part), which is the greater the more perfection they imagine their actions to display and the more distinctly they imagine them—in other words, the more they can distinguish them from others and regard them as something special (see what was said in Schol. 1 Prop. 40 Pt. 2). Therefore, one will take the most delight in contemplating oneself when contemplating in oneself some quality that one denies about others. But if what someone affirms of themselves refers to the universal idea of man or of a living being, they will not be equally pleased; and they will, conversely, be saddened if they imagine their own actions as falling short when compared with those of others. And naturally they will endeavour to remove this sadness (Prop. 28 of this part) by misinterpreting the actions of their peers or by embellishing their own as much as they can. It is thus apparent that human beings are naturally prone to hatred and envy, which latter is additionally fostered by their education, for parents are wont to incite their children to virtue solely by the spur of honour and envy. But perhaps there remains some doubt because we very often wonder at people's virtues and venerate their possessors. In order to remove it, I will add the following corollary.

> Contemplating our own power and activity causes joy. Contemplating our own weakness causes sadness. So there is a strong tendency in our mind's activity (affirmations) to think about our strengths and ignore our weaknesses. At this level of generality, the reasoning seems clear and intuitive. But working out this reasoning in more detail within Spinoza's metaphysics of emotions is not quite so straightforward. To name just one of the questions warranting further exploration: What is the physical correspondent to the contemplation of the mind? Here is one of the places where we can note that Spinoza's conclusions may feel plausible and compelling, but it is less obvious how these conclusions follow from the complex metaphysical arguments that are meant to ground them.

Corollary II. No one envies the virtue of anyone who is not their equal.

Proof. Envy is hatred itself (see Schol. Prop. 24 of this part), that is, sadness (Schol. Prop. 13), that is, a modification by which somebody's power of action, or endeavour to act, is checked (Schol. Prop. 11). But man does not endeavour or desire to do anything that cannot follow from his given nature (Schol. Prop. 9); therefore, a person will not desire any power of action, or virtue (which is the same thing), to be attributed to them which is appropriate to another's nature but foreign to their own. Thus, their desire cannot be checked—that is, they cannot be saddened (Schol. Prop. 11 of this part)—by the contemplation of some virtue in someone unlike themselves; consequently, they cannot envy that person. They can, however, envy their equals, who are assumed to have the same nature as themselves. *Q.E.D.*

> In this way I do not envy the cat's ability to purr, because purring is something that is alien to my nature. I may, however, envy her ability to run fast.

Scholium. Thus, when we said above (Schol. Prop. 52 of this part) that we venerate somebody because we wonder at their prudence, fortitude and so on, this happens because we imagine those qualities as peculiar to them and not as common to our nature (as is apparent from Prop. 52 itself). Therefore, we will no more envy their possessor for them than we do trees for their height, lions for their strength and the like.

PROP. LVI. *There are as many kinds of joy, sadness, and desire and, consequently, of each affect compounded of these, such as vacillation of mind, or derived from these, such as love, hatred, hope, fear etc., as there are kinds of objects by which we are affected.*

Proof. Joy and sadness, and consequently the affects compounded of or derived from them, are passions (Schol. Prop. 11 of this part); now we are necessarily acted upon to the extent that we have inadequate ideas (Prop. 1). And we are acted upon only in so far as we have such ideas (Prop. 3); that is, we are necessarily acted upon only in so far as we imagine (Schol. Prop. 40 Pt. 2), that is, in so far as we are affected by an affect that involves the nature of our own body and the nature of an external one (see Prop. 17 Pt. 2 with Schol.). Therefore, the nature of each passion must perforce be so explained as to express the nature of the object by which we are affected. This means that the joy that arises from, say, object A involves the nature of that same object A, and the joy that arises from object B involves the nature of object B, which is why these two affects of joy are by nature different, since they arise from causes of a different nature. Likewise, the affect of sadness that arises from one object is by nature different from the sadness arising from another cause; the same applies to love, hatred, hope, fear, vacillation of mind etc. Thus, there are necessarily as many forms of joy, sadness, love, hatred etc. as there are forms of objects by which we are affected. Now desire is simply everybody's essence, or nature, in so far as it is conceived as determined to do something according to whatever constitution they may have (see Schol. Prop. 9 of this part); therefore, depending on whether one is affected through external causes with this or that form of joy, sadness, love, hatred, etc.— in other words, depending on whether one's nature is constituted in this or that manner, one's desire will necessarily be of one kind or another, and the nature of one desire must differ from the nature of another just as widely as the affects differ from which each desire arose. Thus, there are as many forms of desire as there are of joy, sadness, love, etc. and, consequently—as follows from what has been shown—as there are kinds of objects by which we are affected. *Q.E.D.*

> The claim here is fascinating because it means that each emotion includes within it the particular cause, and so the joy of ice cream is different in kind from the joy of pizza or a good movie or a hot shower. Joy is, therefore, not a single thing but an unclear abstraction. There are actually an unlimited number of different kinds of joy, which all differ from each other not only in degree but in kind. This claim is in keeping with Spinoza's general tendency towards nominalism.

Scholium. Noteworthy among the forms of affects, which must be very numerous (previous Prop.), are luxury (*luxuria*), drunkenness (*ebrietas*), lust (*libido*), greed (*avaritia*), and ambition (*ambitio*), which are but names for love or desire, explaining the nature of each of these two affects through the object to which they relate. For by luxury, drunkenness, lust, greed, and ambition we mean nothing other than the immoderate love or desire of feasting, drinking, intercourse, riches, and glory. Furthermore, these affects, in so far as we distinguish them from others merely by the object to which they relate, have no contraries: temperance, sobriety, and chastity, which we are wont to oppose to luxury, drunkenness, and lust respectively, are not affects, that is, passions, but signify a power of the mind that moderates those affects. However, I cannot here explain the remaining kinds of affects (seeing as they are as numerous as the kinds of objects), nor, if I could, would it be necessary. For it is sufficient for our purpose, namely to determine the strength of the affects and the mind's power over them, to have a general definition of each affect. It is sufficient, I say, to understand the common properties of the affects and the mind, so as to be able to determine the quality and extent of the mind's power in moderating and checking them. Thus, although there is a great difference between one affect of love, hatred, or desire and another—for instance, between love for one's children and love for one's wife—there is no need for us to know these differences and further inquire into the nature and origin of the affects.

PROP. LVII. *Any affect of any individual differs as much from the affect of another individual as the essence of the one differs from the essence of the other.*

Proof. This Proposition is evident from Ax. 1 after Lemma 3 Schol. Prop. 13 Pt. 2. Nevertheless, we will demonstrate it from the nature of the three primary affects. All affects relate to desire, joy, or sadness, as is shown by their definitions given above. Now desire is each person's very nature, or essence (see its definition in Schol. Prop. 9 of this part); therefore, desire in one individual differs as much from desire in another individual as the nature, or essence, of the one differs from the essence of the other. Also, joy and sadness are passions by which each person's power—that is, endeavour to persist in their being—is increased or diminished, helped or hindered (Prop. 11 of this part with Schol.). Now by 'the endeavour to persist in one's being', in so far as it relates to mind and body at the same time, we mean appetite and desire (Schol. Prop. 9); thus, joy and sadness are just desire or appetite itself in so far as it is increased or diminished, helped or hindered by external causes; in other words, it is each person's nature (same Schol.). It follows that the joy and sadness of one person differ from the joy and sadness of another as much as the nature, or essence, of the one differs from the essence of the other; consequently, any affect of one individual differs as much from the affect of another individual, etc. *Q.E.D.*

There is a difficulty in these passages in that desire seems to be described as both the essence of everything (not just humans, but animals, rocks, trees, and cups too) and an affect of them. If desire were an affect, then it would be a property had by an essence rather than the essence itself. Spinoza addresses this point at the beginning of the Definition of the Affects at the end of Part III.

Scholium. From this it follows that the affects of the animals that are called irrational (for after learning the origin of the mind we can by no means doubt that brutes feel) differ from man's affects as much as their nature differs from human nature. The lust of procreating moves horse and man alike; but the lust of the former is equine, that of the latter is human; likewise, the lusts and appetites of insects, fishes, and birds must be different from each other. Thus, although each individual being lives content with whatever nature happens to be its own and takes delight in it, that life with which each is content and that delight is nothing other than the idea, or soul (*anima*), of that individual; hence the delight of one differs in nature from that of another to the extent that the essence of one differs from the essence of the other. Lastly, it follows from the foregoing Proposition that there is no small difference between the delight by which, say, a drunkard is led and the one possessed by a philosopher, as I just wanted to point out here in passing. This much about the affects that relate to one in so far as one is acted upon. It remains to add a few words about those that relate to one in so far as one acts.

> In this way, my dog feels sadness. But his sadness differs in kind from my own sadness, because it is a decrease in a different kind of activity. We call them both sadness not because they are phenomenologically similar (Spinoza never talks about this) but because they have similar effects on the two complex bodies. At this point, one sees Spinoza shifting from a focus on how things are passively affected to the ways that one actively affects the world around them.

PROP. LVIII. *Besides joy and desire, which are passions, there are other affects derived from joy and desire, which relate to us in so far as we act.*

Proof. When the mind imagines itself and its power of action, it rejoices (Prop. 53 of this part); and the mind necessarily contemplates itself when it conceives a true, or adequate, idea (Prop. 43 Pt. 2). Now the mind does conceive certain adequate ideas (Schol. 2 Prop. 40 Pt. 2); therefore, it rejoices in so far as it conceives adequate ideas, in other words, in so far as it acts (Prop. 1). Further, the mind, both in so far as it has clear and distinct ideas and in so far as it has confused ones, endeavours to persist in its own being (Prop. 9). Now by 'endeavour' we mean desire (Schol. same Prop.); therefore, desire relates to us in so far as we understand, that is, in so far as we act (Prop. 1). *Q.E.D.*

> The argument here is hard to follow (how can a desire "relate" to us more or less when it is our essence?), but the conclusion is important, namely, that there is joy in understanding something better. When thinking about an adequate idea, the mind (or part of the mind) is not dependent upon anything external and so is maximally active. This is healthy and so joyful. But many questions need to be explored: for example, what are the physical correlates of these adequate ideas?

PROP. LIX. *Among all the affects that relate to the mind in so far as it acts, there are none that do not relate to joy or desire.*

Proof. All affects relate to desire, joy, or sadness, as is shown by the definitions we have given of them. Now by 'sadness' we mean what diminishes or checks the mind's power of thinking (Prop. 11 of this part with Schol.); therefore, in so far as the mind is saddened, its power of understanding—that is, of action (Prop. 1)—is diminished or checked. Thus, no affects of sadness can relate to the mind to the extent that it acts, but only affects of joy and desire, which relate to the mind to that extent also (previous Prop.). *Q.E.D.*

> So greater understanding always brings greater joy. If counterexamples seem to readily present themselves, just remember that for Spinoza joy is an increase in power, and not a certain phenomenological experience.

Scholium. All actions that follow from affects relating to the mind in so far as it understands, I set down to strength of character (*fortitudo*), which I divide into courage (*animositas*) and generosity (*generositas*). By *courage* I mean *the desire by which everyone endeavours to preserve their own being in accordance with the dictates of reason alone.* By *generosity* I mean *the desire by which everyone endeavours, solely under the dictates of reason, to help all others and to unite them to themselves in friendship.* Those actions, therefore, that strive solely toward the good of the agent I set down to courage, and those that aim at the good of others I set down to generosity. Thus, temperance, sobriety, presence of mind in danger and the like are forms of courage; humility, mercy, etc. are forms of generosity.

> Courage and generosity both arise out of adequate ideas of something. When one acts in a seemingly courageous way due to external causes (and so inadequate ideas), however, then one is not courageous or generous. In this reasoning, Spinoza has put many different ideas together here and it is hard to keep them all clear. Spinoza has argued that mental *actions* are always adequate, joyful, and healthy. A mental action is power, virtue, perfection, reason, an affirmation of the existence of the body and of the idea itself. On the contrary, mental *passions*, insofar as they relate to external objects, are always inadequate, painful, and unhealthy (i.e., all of the corresponding opposites) (Prop III). Accordingly, a general overall picture emerges. Rational people are healthier, more joyful, and more active, while irrational people are the opposite. The same would also seem to apply to everything else

that exists as well—although many things may be too simple to have any complex adequate ideas.

I think I have thus explained and shown through their primary causes the main affects and vacillations of mind that arise from the combination of the three primary affects, to wit, desire, joy, and sadness. It is evident from what I have said that we are in many ways driven about by external causes and that, like waves of the sea driven by contrary winds, we toss to and fro without knowledge of the outcome for us and of our fate. I have said, however, that I have only described the main <affects>, not all conflicts of the mind that may exist.[1] For by proceeding in the same way as above, we can easily show that love is united to repentance, disrespect (*dedignatio*), shame, etc. Indeed, I think that from what has been said everyone will agree that the affects could be compounded with one another in so many ways and so many variations could arise in this way as to exceed all possibility of computation. For my purpose, however, it is enough to have enumerated only the most important ones; for all those others that I have omitted would have been more for the sake of curiosity than of profit. Nonetheless, it remains to remark about love that it very often happens that while we are enjoying a thing we longed for, the body acquires from the act of enjoyment a new constitution by which it is determined in another way, other images of things are aroused in it, and the mind begins at the same time to imagine new things and desire new things. For example, when we imagine something that generally delights us with its flavour, we desire to enjoy it, that is, to eat it. But whilst we are thus enjoying it, the stomach is filled and the body is constituted otherwise. If, therefore, when the body is thus otherwise disposed, the image of the food is stimulated through the presence of the food itself, and consequently the endeavour, or desire, to eat it is stimulated as well, the new disposition of the body will be repugnant to this desire or endeavour, so that the presence of the food that we formerly longed for becomes odious. This is what is called 'nausea' (*fastidium*) or 'weariness' (*taedium*). For the rest, I have neglected the outward modifications of the body observable in affects, such as trembling, pallor,

---

1   In the original Latin edition, *precipuos* goes with *conflictûs*, and the sentence consequently translates as "I have described only the main conflicts of the mind that may exist, not all of them." (D.A.)

sobbing, laughter, etc., for these relate only to the body without any reference to the mind.

> Spinoza's example here is instructive. When thinking about the mental world as Spinoza is here doing, it is important to keep in mind how dynamic and active it is. Our minds are bundles of millions of ideas all making affirmations to various degrees and new ideas are entering and leaving the internal system all the time. Just as Spinoza's physical world is buzzing with activity, so too is Spinoza's mental world. Our minds are a buzz of millions of affirmations and alterations in emotion/affect up or down in various complex ways. There are two interesting things to note about the sheer volume of activity that Spinoza deduces. First, he deduces all of this activity on the basis of a very small number of explicit assumptions (although there are lots of auxiliary ones). Second, the world that Spinoza describes stands in sharp contrast to his geometrical method. Spinoza's geometrical method would seem to describe elegant, unchanging truths, seemingly like those offered by Euclid. However, the world Spinoza describes is far more complex and dynamic.

Lastly, it is necessary to make a few points about the definitions of the affects. I will therefore repeat them in order here and add to them whatever observations need to be made about each of them.

DEFINITIONS OF THE AFFECTS

> This section is the clearest and most succinct discussion of Spinoza's general overall theory. If one wanted to get Spinoza's general theory of emotions in just a few pages, then this is the clearest statement in his collected works. Spinoza will give a similar summary of his conclusions at the end of Part IV. We get the impression that Spinoza's early readers may have had some difficulty with these texts and asked for a summary, which, thankfully, Spinoza provided.

I. Desire (*cupiditas*) is the very essence of man in so far as it is conceived as determined to do something by some given modification of itself.

Explanation. We have said above (Schol. Prop. 9 of this part) that desire is appetite one is aware of and that appetite is the essence of man itself in so far as it is determined to do things that help maintain his existence. In the same Schol., however, I also remarked that, in fact, I recognize no distinction between human appetite and desire. For whether one is aware of one's appetite or not, the appetite remains one and the same; thus, in order to avoid the appearance of tautology, I have refrained from explaining desire through appetite but have taken care to define it in such a manner as to comprehend, under one head, all those endeavours of human nature that we refer to as 'appetite', 'will', 'desire', or 'impulse'. For I might have said that desire is man's essence itself in so far as it is imagined as determined to do something; but from such a definition it would not follow that the mind can be conscious of its desire or appetite (Prop. 23 Pt. 2). Therefore, in order to involve the cause of such awareness, it was necessary to add: *in so far as it is determined by some given modification thereof, etc.* (same Prop.). For by 'modification of man's essence' we understand any disposition of that essence, whether it is innate <or coming from outside>, whether it is conceived solely under the attribute of thought or solely under the attribute of extension or, lastly, whether it relates to both these attributes at the same time. By 'desire', then, I mean in this context all of man's endeavours, impulses, appetites, and volitions, which vary according to each person's constitution and are therefore not seldom opposed to one another, so that people are drawn in different directions and do not know where to turn.

> This passage is valuable for a number of reasons. First, it helps (somewhat) clarify the various distinctions that Spinoza is making in different ways to think about one thing. For example, here is where it is most clear that "desires" for Spinoza do not include any intentional awareness. I can "desire" something (i.e., be determined to strive towards it) without having any conscious realization that I am so striving. As such, as many scholars have pointed out, this shows how Spinoza seems committed to the idea of a vast and important unconscious mind, which would seemingly be constantly interacting with the conscious desires and ideas. While Spinoza does not develop this idea, many later authors, including Freud, will cite Spinoza as one of the thinkers who believed in a "dynamic unconscious."

II. Joy (*laetitia*) is someone's transition from a lesser to a greater perfection.

III. Sadness (*tristitia*) is someone's transition from a greater to a lesser perfection.

Explanation. I say 'transition' because joy is not perfection itself. For if human beings were born with the perfection to which they pass, they would possess it without the affect of joy. This appears more clearly from the consideration of the contrary affect, sadness. No one can deny that sadness consists in the transition to a lesser perfection and not in the lesser perfection itself: for one cannot be saddened in so far as one partakes of any perfection. Neither can we say that sadness consists in the absence of a greater perfection, for absence is nothing, whereas the affect of sadness is an action. Thus, this action can be none other than the action of transition to a lesser perfection; in other words, it is an action by which one's power of action is lessened or constrained (see Schol. Prop. 11 of this part). On the other hand, I will omit the definitions of 'merriment' (*hilaritas*), 'stimulation' (*titillatio*), 'melancholy' (*melancholia*), and 'pain' (*dolor*), because these terms are generally used in reference to the body and are merely forms of joy or sadness.

> It is worth noting that sadness is not a state of being, on Spinoza's view, but a decreasing of power or health (conceived in all the different ways). This means that one cannot be sad (or happy) at a moment of time, but only over time. It also means that prolonged sadness without interruption would inevitably lead to death. Or, to say it differently, that slowing dying is sadness. Under this meaning, one cannot die happy. (See related ideas in Part V.)

IV. Wonder (*admiratio*) is the imagining of anything in which the mind comes to a stand because the particular imagination in question has no connection with other concepts (see Prop. 52 with Schol.).

Explanation. In Schol. Prop. 18 Pt. 2 we showed the reason why the mind falls immediately from the contemplation of one thing into the contemplation of another: namely because the images of those things are interconnected and arranged in such a way that one follows the other. This state of interconnection cannot be conceived when the image of the thing is new, but the mind will then be stuck in the contemplation of the same thing until it is determined by other causes to think of something else. Thus, the imagination of a new object, considered in itself, is of the same nature as others; hence, I do not include wonder among the affects, nor do I see why I should do so since this distraction of the mind arises from no positive cause distracting the mind away from other objects, but merely from the absence of a cause determining the mind to pass from the contemplation of one object to the contemplation of another.

I therefore recognize only three primitive, or primary, affects (as I pointed out in Schol. Prop. 11 of this part), namely joy, sadness, and desire. I have spoken of wonder only because it has become customary to refer to certain affects that spring from the three primitive ones by different names whenever they relate to objects one wonders at. This same reasoning now compels me to add here a definition of 'contempt', too.

V. Contempt (*contemptus*) is the imagining of anything that touches the mind so little that the mind itself is prompted by its presence to imagine those qualities that are not in it rather than those that are (see Schol. Prop. 52 of this part).

> Spinoza's language here is interesting because he rephrases his earlier discussion in entirely positive terms. Instead of contemplating a lack (which is problematic given Spinoza's other commitments), the mind is touched "so little" by the thing that its lack in comparison to something else becomes prominent.

I here omit the definitions of 'veneration' and 'disrespect', because no affects I am aware of are named after them.

VI. Love (*amor*) is joy accompanied by the idea of an external cause.

Explanation. This definition explains with sufficient clarity the essence of love; the one given by those authors who say that *love is the lover's wish to unite themselves to the thing loved* expresses not the essence of love but a property; also, as those authors have not sufficiently discerned love's essence, they have been unable to acquire a clear concept of this property, either; accordingly, their definition is judged by all to be very obscure. It must however be noted that when I say that it is a property in the lover to unite themselves in their volition to the thing loved, by 'volition' I do not mean consent or a deliberation of the mind, that is, a free decision (for I have shown in Prop. 48 Pt. 2 that this is fictitious); nor do I mean a desire of being united to the thing loved when it is absent, or of continuing in its presence when it is at hand; for love can be imagined without either of these desires. Instead, by 'volition' I mean the contentment that is in the lover on account of the presence of the thing loved, by which the lover's joy is strengthened, or at least fostered.

This note is interesting because Spinoza argues that the essence of love is the increase in health or perfection. The motivation to then unite with the lover is an accidental fact, and not part of the essence of love itself. In terms of contemporary theories of emotion, Spinoza is claiming that the motivation that emotions provide is not essential, and so motivational theories of emotions are wrong. He also uses 'volition' in this passage to indicate not the affirmation of the existence of something, but the contentment that the lover feels. If he is referring here to the phenomenological character of being in love, then such a reference is exceedingly rare in Spinoza. It is also hard to square this claim with his other uses of the term, and so perhaps it is best just to think of these uses of this word as totally unrelated.

VII. Hatred (*odium*) is sadness accompanied by the idea of an external cause.

Explanation. What needs pointing out in this context is easily grasped after what has been said in the Explanation of the preceding Def. (See also Schol. Prop. 13 of this part).

VIII. Inclination (*propensio*) is joy accompanied by the idea of something that is accidentally a cause of joy.

The accidental nature is, of course, epistemological and not metaphysical.

IX. Aversion (*aversio*) is sadness accompanied by the idea of something that is accidentally the cause of sadness. (On these two see Schol. Prop. 15 of this part).

X. Devotion (*devotio*) is love towards someone we wonder at.

Explanation. We have shown in Prop. 52 of this part that wonder springs from the novelty of a thing. If, therefore, we happen to imagine what we admire quite often, we will cease to wonder at it; thus we see that the affect of devotion readily degenerates into simple love.

XI. Derision (*irrisio*) is joy arising from our imagining the presence of a quality we despise in something that we hate.

Explanation. In so far as we despise a thing we hate, we deny existence to it (Schol. Prop. 52 of this part), and we rejoice to that extent (Prop. 20). But since we have posited that the person who derides something nonetheless hates it, it follows that the joy in question is not substantial (see Schol. Prop. 47 of this part).

XII. Hope (*spes*) is an inconstant joy arising from the idea of something future or past about whose result we are somewhat in doubt.

XIII. Fear (*metus*) is an inconstant sadness arising from the idea of something future or past about whose result we are somewhat in doubt. (On these see Schol. 2 Prop. 18 of this part.)

Explanation. From these definitions it follows that there is no hope without fear and no fear without hope. For those who depend on hope and doubt the result of something are posited to imagine something that excludes the existence of that thing in the future; therefore, to this extent they are saddened (Prop. 19 of this part). Consequently, while dependent on hope, they fear that the thing in question may not happen. On the other hand, whoever is in fear—in other words, has doubts about the future existence of something they hate—imagines something that excludes the existence of the thing in question, too; to this extent they feel joy and, consequently, to this extent hope that that thing will not happen (Prop. 20).

XIV. Confidence (*securitas*) is joy arising from the idea of something future or past from which all cause of doubt has been removed (*tollere*).

XV. Despair (*desperatio*) is sadness arising from the idea of something future or past from which all cause of doubt has been removed.

Explanation. Thus, confidence springs from hope and despair from fear when all cause for doubt as to the issue of a thing has been removed. This happens because one imagines something past or future to be present and regards it as such, or else because one imagines other things that exclude the existence of the causes of one's doubt. For although we can never be certain of the issue of any particular thing (Coroll. Prop. 31 Pt. 2), it can nevertheless happen that we feel no doubt concerning it. Indeed, we have shown that to feel no doubt concerning a thing is not the same as to possess certainty of it (see Schol. Prop. 49 Pt. 2); thus, it can happen that we are affected with the same affect of joy or sadness from imagining something past or future as from imagining something present, as I have already shown in Prop. 18 of this part, which the reader is invited to read along with its Scholia.

XVI. Delight (*gaudium*) is joy accompanied by the idea of something past that has happened beyond our hope.

XVII. Remorse (*conscientiae morsus*) is sadness accompanied by the idea of something past that has happened beyond our fear.

XVIII. Pity (*commiseratio*) is sadness accompanied by the idea of an evil that has befallen someone else whom we imagine to be like ourselves (see Schol. Prop. 22 and Schol. Prop. 27 of this part).

Explanation. Between pity and mercifulness (*misericordia*) there seems to be no difference, except perhaps that 'pity' refers to a specific action whereas 'mercifulness' refers to the habit thereof.

XIX. Approval (*favor*) is love towards someone who has done good to another.

XX. Indignation (*indignatio*) is hatred towards someone who has done evil to another.

Explanation. I am aware that these terms commonly bear meanings different from these. My object, however, is to explain, not the meanings of words, but the nature of things, and to designate them with terms whose usual meaning does not differ too much from that in which I want to use them. May it suffice to have stated this once. As for the cause of the above-named affects, see Coroll. 1 Prop. 27 and Schol. Prop. 22 of this part.

XXI. Partiality (*existimatio*) is thinking too highly of someone out of love.

XXII. Scorn (*despectus*) is thinking too little of someone out of hatred.

Explanation. Thus, partiality is an effect, or property, of love and scorn an effect, or property, of hatred; therefore, *partiality* can also be defined as *love in so far as it affects someone in such a way that they think too highly of the beloved thing*. Conversely, *scorn* can be defined as *hatred in so far as it affects someone in such a way that they think too little of the person they hate* (see Schol. Prop. 26 of this part).

XXIII. Envy (*invidia*) is hatred in so far as it affects one in such a way that one is saddened by another's good fortune and, conversely, rejoices in another's ill.

Explanation. Envy is generally regarded as opposed to mercifulness, which, by stretching the meaning of the word somewhat, may therefore be defined as follows:

XXIV. Mercifulness (*misericordia*) is love in so far as it affects somebody in such a way that they delight in another's good and are saddened by another's ill.

Explanation. Concerning envy see Schol. Prop. 24 and Schol. 32 of this part. And these are affects of joy or sadness accompanied by the idea of something external as cause either in itself or accidentally. I now pass on to other affects, which are accompanied by the idea of something internal as cause.

XXV. Self-contentment (*acquiescentia in se ipso*) is joy that arises from contemplating oneself and one's power of action.

XXVI. Humility (*humilitas*) is sadness that arises from contemplating one's powerlessness, or weakness.

Explanation. Self-contentment is opposed to humility in so far as we thereby mean joy arising from a contemplation of our own power of action; but in so far as by this word we also mean joy accompanied by the idea of any action that we believe we have performed by the free decision of our mind, it is opposed to repentance, which I define as follows:

XXVII. Repentance (*poenitentia*) is sadness accompanied by the idea of some action that we believe we have performed by the free decision of our mind.

Explanation. I have described the causes of these affects in Schol. Prop. 51 of this part and in Prop. 53, 54, and 55 with Schol. Concerning the free decision of the mind see Schol. Prop. 35 Pt. 2. But this is also the place to call attention to the fact that it is no surprise that all those actions which are commonly called *evil* (*pravi*) are followed by sadness and all those which are called *right* (*recti*) are followed by joy. For we can easily gather from what has been said that this depends in great measure on education: parents, by reprobating the former class of actions and frequently chiding their children because of them and, conversely, by recommending and praising the latter, have made it so that the former are associated with the physical motions of sadness and the latter with those of joy. This is confirmed by experience itself: custom and religion are not the same among all people, but what some consider sacred others consider profane, and what some consider honourable others consider disgraceful. Thus, each person will regret or glory in one and the same action depending on how they have been educated.

> Spinoza's claims here of cultural relativity fit well with his general theory of value, whereby something is good because it is desired. This is evident insofar as what is desired is dependent on certain historical facts, such as education, cultural influences, etc. As what is good depends on what is desired, and what is desired depends on these relative influences, the good is culturally relative.

XXVIII. Pride (*superbia*) is thinking too highly of oneself out of love.

Explanation. Thus pride is different from partiality, for the latter term refers to an external object whereas pride refers to somebody thinking too highly of themselves. However, as partiality is an effect or property of love, so *pride* is an effect or property of self-love, which may therefore be defined as *love of self or self-contentment in so far as it affects one in such a way that one thinks too highly of oneself* (see Schol. Prop. 26 of this part). To this affect there is no contrary. For no one thinks too little of themselves because of self-hatred; I shall even say that no one thinks too little of themselves in so far as they imagine themselves as being unable to do this or that. For whatever people imagine themselves as incapable of doing, they necessarily imagine it and are disposed by this imagining in such a way that they really cannot do what they imagine they cannot do. For as long as they imagine themselves as being unable to do this or that, they are not determined to do it and, consequently, it is so long impossible for them to do it. However, if we consider only such matters as depend merely on opinion, we shall find it conceivable that someone may think too little of themselves; for it can happen that somebody, while sorrowfully regarding their own weakness, imagines themselves as despised by everyone, while the rest of the world are thinking of nothing less than of despising them. People may also think too little of themselves if they deny in the present something about themselves that relates to a future time of which they are uncertain, as, for instance, if they should say that they are unable to form any clear conceptions, or that they can desire or do nothing except evil or disgraceful things, and so on. We may also say that somebody thinks too little of themselves when we see them, out of excessive fear of shame, not dare to do things that others, who are their equals, dare. Thus, we can oppose this affect to pride, an affect that I will call 'self-abasement' (*abjectio*), for as from self-contentment springs pride, so from humility springs self-abasement, which I will accordingly define as follows:

> Spinoza's implied argument against self-hatred is interesting. I cannot hate myself because I cannot seek my own destruction: that would be against my essence. I am always destroyed by other things. But I can feel pain by imagining that others hate me and I can misjudge my own abilities. Often, it seems, when people talk about self-hatred what they mean is that they imagine that they are hated *by* or hateful *to* others.

XXIX. Self-abasement (*abjectio*) is thinking too little of oneself out of sadness.

Explanation. We are nevertheless generally accustomed to oppose pride to humility, but in so doing we are paying more attention to the effect of either affect than to its nature. We are wont to call 'prideful' anyone who glories too much (see Schol. Prop. 30 of this part), who talks of nothing but their own virtues and other people's faults, who wants to be preferred to everybody and, lastly, who walks with such gravitas and pomp as those are wont to do who are of much higher rank than them. On the other hand, we call 'humble' somebody who blushes particularly often, who confesses their faults and recounts other people's virtues, who gives in to everybody and who, lastly, walks with bent head and neglects to adorn themselves. However, these affects, humility and self-abasement, are extremely rare, for human nature, considered in itself, strives against them as much as it can (see Prop. 13 and Prop. 54 of this part); hence, those who are believed to be most self-abased and humble are in reality for the most part the most ambitious and envious.

Since humility is so socially useful, and so contrary to human nature, Spinoza infers that most humble people are just pretending to be humble in order to advance themselves in some way. More than just making a claim that seems to capture empirical experience, Spinoza is drawing a conclusion that is entailed by his general theory of emotion. If humility was intentionally weakening one's own power, then this would contradict striving to endure and succeed.

XXX. Glory (*gloria*) is joy accompanied by the idea of some action of our own which we imagine to be praised by others.

XXXI. Shame (*pudor*) is sadness accompanied by the idea of some action we imagine to be blamed by others.

Explanation. On this subject see Schol. Prop. 30 of this part. But we should here notice the difference which exists between shame and modesty (*verecundia*). Shame is the sadness following the deed of which we are ashamed; modesty is the fear or dread of shame which restrains one from doing something disgraceful. Modesty is usually opposed to shamelessness (*impudentia*), but the latter is not an affect, as I will show at the proper place; however, the names of the affects (as I have already demonstrated) have regard more to common usage than to nature. I have now fulfilled the task of explaining the affects of joy and sadness. I therefore proceed to deal with those that I refer to as desire.

XXXII. Longing (*desiderium*) is the desire, or appetite, to possess something fostered by the remembrance of that thing and at the same time constrained by the remembrance of other things that exclude the existence of the one desired.

Explanation. When we remember a thing, we are by that very fact, as I have already said more than once, disposed to regard it with the same affect as if it were present; but while we are awake, this disposition, or endeavour, is generally checked by the images of things that exclude the existence of the thing we remember. Thus, when we remember something that has affected us with a certain kind of joy, we endeavour, because of this very fact, to regard it as present with the same affect of joy; but this endeavour is at once checked by the remembrance of things that exclude the existence of the thing remembered. Therefore, longing is, strictly speaking, a sadness opposed to the joy that arises from the absence of something we hate (on which see Schol. Prop. 47 of this part). But, as the name *longing* seems to refer to desire, I classify this affect among the affects springing from desire.

> Longing is an affect of desire because it is a person's desire (essence) modified by the circumstances, so that it cannot be satisfied. The circumstances result in that part of the person's striving to be frustrated.

XXXIII. Emulation (*aemulatio*) is the desire of something, engendered in us by our imagining that others have the same desire.

Explanation. Whenever somebody runs away because they see others running away, or fears because they see others in fear, or even when someone, on seeing that another has burnt their hand, draws their own hand toward themselves and moves their body as though their own hand were being burnt, we will say that that person is imitating another's affect, but not that they are emulating it. This is not because we know the cause of emulation and that of imitation to be different, but because it has become customary to speak of emulation only with respect to someone who imitates what we deem to be honourable, useful, or pleasant. As for the cause of emulation, see Prop. 27 of this part with Schol. And as for the reason why this affect is generally coupled with envy, I refer to Prop. 32 of this part with Schol.

XXXIV. Thankfulness or gratitude (*gratia seu gratitudo*) is the desire or zeal springing from love by which we endeavour to benefit someone who, with a similar affect of love, has conferred a benefit on us (see Prop. 39 with Schol. Prop. 41 of this part).

XXXV. Benevolence (*benevolentia*) is the desire of benefitting someone we pity (see Schol. Prop. 27 of this part).

XXXVI. Anger (*ira*) is the desire by which we are induced out of hatred to injure someone we hate (see Prop. 39 of this part).

XXXVII. Revenge (*vindicta*) is the desire by which we are induced, through mutual hatred, to injure somebody who, with a similar affect, has injured us (see Coroll. 2 Prop. 40 of this part with Schol.).

XXXVIII. Cruelty or savageness (*crudelitas seu saevitia*) is the desire by which one is impelled to injure somebody whom we love or pity.

Explanation. To cruelty is opposed clemency (*clementia*), which is not a passion but a power of the mind by which one moderates one's anger and revenge.

XXXIX. Timidity (*timor*) is the desire to avoid a greater evil which we dread by undergoing a lesser one (see Schol. Prop. 39 of this part).

XL. Daring (*audacia*) is the desire by which one is impelled to do something with a danger that one's equals fear to undergo.

XLI. Cowardice (*pusillanimitas*) is said of somebody whose desire is checked by the fear of some danger that their equals dare to undergo.

Explanation. Cowardice is, therefore, nothing but the fear of some evil which most people are wont not to fear; hence I do not reckon it among the affects springing from desire. Nevertheless, I have chosen to explain it here because, in so far as we look to desire, it is truly opposed to the affect of daring.

XLII. Dismay (*consternatio*) is said of somebody whose desire of avoiding evil is checked by wonder at the evil they fear.

Explanation. Dismay is, therefore, a form of cowardice. But since it arises from a double fear, it can be more conveniently defined as a *fear that keeps one so bewildered or vacillating that one is not able to remove the evil*. I say *bewildered* in so far as we understand this person's desire of removing the evil to be constrained by their wonder. I say *vacillating* in so far as we understand that desire to be constrained by the fear of another evil that equally torments them, so that they are in doubt as to which of the two to avert (on this subject see Schol. Prop. 39 and Schol. Prop. 52 of this part. As for cowardice and daring, see Schol. Prop. 51 of this part).

XLIII. Human kindness or moderation (*humanitas seu modestia*) is the desire to do things people like and to refrain from doing things they dislike.

XLIV. Ambition (*ambitio*) is the immoderate desire of glory.

Explanation. Ambition is the desire by which all the affects are fostered and strengthened (Prop. 27 and 31 of this part); therefore, this affect is almost impossible to overcome. For as long as one is bound by any desire, one is at the same time necessarily bound by this one, too. "The best men," says Cicero,[1] "are driven mainly by the desire of glory. Even when philosophers write books about spurning glory, they sign their name to them ..."

XLV. Luxury (*luxuria*) is excessive desire, or even love, of feasting.

XLVI. Drunkenness (*ebrietas*) is the excessive desire and love of drinking.

XLVII. Greed (*avaritia*) is the excessive desire and love of riches.

XLVIII. Lust (*libido*) is desire and love in matters of sexual intercourse.

Explanation. Whether this desire is moderate or not, it is still called 'lust'. Besides, these last five affects have no contraries (as I have pointed out in Schol. Prop. 56 of this part). For humility (*modestia*) is a form of ambition, on which I refer to Schol. Prop. 29; and I have already pointed out that temperance, sobriety, and chastity indicate a power of the mind, not a passion. It can nevertheless happen that a greedy, an ambitious, or a timid person abstains from too much food, drink, or sexual intercourse; yet greed, ambition, and timidity are not contraries to luxury, drunkenness, or lust. For someone greedy is often glad to gorge themselves on someone else's food and drink; an ambitious person will restrain themselves in nothing so long as they think their indulgences are secret, and if they live among drunkards and debauchees, they will, from the mere fact of being ambitious, be more prone to those vices. Lastly, a timid person does things they

---

1 *Pro Archia poeta*, ch. 11. (D.A.)

would rather not do. For although a greedy person may throw their wealth into the sea to avoid death, they will nonetheless remain greedy; and if a lustful person is saddened because they are unable to indulge themselves, they do not therefore cease to be lustful. And in general these affects are concerned not so much with the actual feasting, drinking, etc. as with the appetite and love thereof itself. Nothing, therefore, can be opposed to these affects except for generosity and courage, of which I will speak in the following.

The definitions of 'jealousy' and other vacillations of the mind I pass over in silence, both because they arise from the compounding of the affects already described and because many of them lack their own names, which shows that it is sufficient for practical purposes to have merely a general knowledge of them. However, it is established from the definitions of the affects we have dealt with that they all spring from desire, joy, or sadness; or, rather, that there is nothing besides these three and each of them is wont to be called by a variety of names due to its various relations and external denominations. If we now direct our attention to these primitive affects and to what we said above concerning the nature of the mind, we shall be able to define the affects, in so far as they relate to the mind only, as follows.

GENERAL DEFINITION OF THE AFFECTS

An affect, which is called a passion (*pathema*) of the mind, is a confused idea by which the mind affirms a force of existence (*existendi vis*) of its body—or any of its parts—greater or smaller than before, and by the presence of which the mind is determined to think of one thing rather than another.

Explanation. I say, first, that an affect, or passion of the mind, is a confused idea. For we have shown that the mind is only acted upon in so far as it has inadequate, that is, confused ideas (Prop. 3 of this part). I say, further, *by which the mind affirms a force of existence of its body—or any of its parts—greater or smaller than before.* For all the ideas of bodies that we possess indicate the actual constitution of our own body rather than the nature of an external body (Coroll. 2 Prop. 16 Pt. 2). Now the idea that constitutes the form of an affect must indicate or express the constitution of the body itself or some part of it, a constitution the body itself—or one of its parts—possesses because its power of action, or force of existence, is increased or diminished, helped or hindered. But it must be noted that, when I say *a greater or smaller force of existence than before*, I do not mean that the mind compares the present constitution of the body with a past one, but that the idea that constitutes the form of an affect affirms something of the body that, in fact, involves more or less reality than before.

> This claim is an interesting one because Spinoza has previously defined an affect as a transition from one state of perfection/power to another. Here he makes the different claim that it is an affirmation of a lower state of perfection/power, not the transition from one state to the other. Perhaps to deal with this discrepancy, he then adds the following:

And since the essence of the mind consists in the fact that it affirms the actual existence of its own body (Prop. 11 and 13 Pt. 2) and by 'perfection' we understand the very essence of a thing, it follows that the mind passes to greater or smaller perfection when it happens to affirm concerning its own body, or any part thereof, something involving more or less reality than before. Thus, when I said above that the power of the mind is increased or diminished, I merely meant that the mind had formed of its own body, or of some part thereof, an idea involving more or less reality than it had already affirmed concerning its body. For the excellence of ideas and the actual power of thinking are measured by the excellence of the object. Lastly, I have added *by the presence of which the mind is determined to think of one thing rather than another* in order that, besides the nature of joy and sadness, which is explained by the first part of the definition, I might also express the nature of desire.

End of Part 3.

PART IV
OF HUMAN BONDAGE, OR
THE STRENGTH OF THE AFFECTS

PREFACE

Human powerlessness in moderating and checking the affects I name 'bondage'. For when a person is a prey to their affects, they are not their own master but are at the mercy of fortune, which has such power over them that they are often compelled, while seeing what is better for them, to follow what is worse. [1] *Why this is so, and what is good or evil about the affects, I intend to show in this part of my treatise. Before I begin, however, it would be well to preface a few observations on perfection and imperfection, good and evil.*

> In Part III Spinoza gave a descriptive account of human emotions, and now he turns in Part IV to an evaluation of human emotions. How do emotions fit into the good human life? But before Spinoza can engage in this project, he reminds us of his theory of value, whereby nothing is good or bad in itself, but only insofar as it relates to someone's striving.

*When somebody has decided to make a given thing and has completed it, not just they themselves, but anyone who accurately knows the mind of the author of that work (or thinks they do) will call it 'completed' (*perfectam*). For instance, suppose that someone sees a work (which I assume to have not been finished yet) and knows that the aim of the author of that work is to build a house; they will call the house 'incomplete' (*imperfectam*); they will, on the other hand, call it 'completed' (*perfectam*) as soon as they see that it is carried through to the end that its author had established for it. But if someone sees a work the like of which they have never seen before and if they do not know the intention of its author, they plainly cannot know whether that work is completed or not. Such seems to have been the original meaning of the terms 'perfect' and 'imperfect'. However, after people began to form general ideas, think out types of houses, buildings, towers, etc., and to prefer certain types to others, they began each to call 'perfect' what appeared to them to match the universal idea they had formed of the thing in question, and to call 'imperfect' what appeared to agree less with their own pre-imagined type, even when according to its maker it*

---

1 The same Ovidian phrase we have encountered above, cf. Schol. Prop. 2 Pt. 3 with p. 145, n. 1. (D.A.)

had been completed flawlessly. *This seems to be the only reason people call natural things, which, indeed, are not made by human hands, 'perfect' or 'imperfect': people are wont to form universal ideas of things natural as well artificial and hold such ideas as types, believing that nature (which they think does everything for a purpose) has them in view and has set them as types before itself. Therefore, when they see something happen in nature which does not wholly conform to the pre-imagined type they have of the thing in question, they think that nature herself has fallen short or has blundered and has left that thing incomplete (*imperfectam*). Thus we see that people are wont to refer to natural phenomena as 'perfect' or 'imperfect' because of their own prejudices rather than from true knowledge of such things. Now we showed in the Appendix to Part 1 that nature does not work with an end in view; for the eternal and infinite Being, which we call 'God' or 'nature', acts by the same necessity by which it exists. We have shown, in fact, that it acts by the same necessity of its nature by which it exists (Prop. 16 Pt. 1). The reason or cause why God—or nature—acts and the reason why he exists are one and the same. Consequently, as he does not exist for a purpose, so neither does he act for one; on the contrary, of his existence and of his action there is neither origin nor end. Thus, that cause which is called 'final' is nothing but human appetite itself in so far as it is considered as the origin or primary cause of something. For example, when we say that to be inhabited is the final cause of this or that house, we mean nothing more than that somebody, imagining the conveniences of household life, had a desire to build a house. Therefore, the inhabiting, in so far as it is regarded as a final cause, is nothing but this particular appetite, which is really the efficient cause; it is regarded as the primary cause because people are generally ignorant of the causes of their appetites. They are, as I have often said already, conscious of their actions and appetites but ignorant of the causes by which they are determined to desire any particular thing. The fact that they even commonly say that nature sometimes falls short or blunders and produces things that are imperfect I count among the comments I dealt with in the Appendix to Part 1. Perfection and imperfection, then, are in reality merely modes of thinking, namely notions that we are wont to form by comparing individual things of the same species or kind to each other; hence I said above (Def. 6 Pt. 2) that by 'reality' and 'perfection' I mean the same thing. For we are wont to refer all the individual things in nature to a single kind, which is called the most general, namely the category of Being (*ens*), which pertains to absolutely all individual things in nature. Thus, in so far as we refer the* individual things in nature to this category, compare them to one another, and find that some possess more of being, that is, reality than others, we say that some are more perfect than others; and in so far as we attribute to them anything implying negation, such as term, end, inability, and so on, we call them 'imperfect', since they do not affect our mind as much as the things we call 'perfect', and not because they have any intrinsic deficiency or because nature has blundered. For nothing lies within the scope of the nature of anything except for what follows from the necessity of the nature of its efficient cause, and anything that follows from the necessity of the nature of its efficient cause necessarily happens.

As for the terms 'good' and 'bad', they point to no positive quality in things—if regarded in themselves—but are merely modes of thinking, in other words, notions that we form by comparing things to one another. Indeed, one and the same thing can be at the same time good, bad, and indifferent. For instance, music is good for a melancholic person, but bad for one who mourns; for the deaf, on the other hand, it is neither good nor bad. Nevertheless, though this is so, we must hold on to these terms; for seeing as we desire to form an idea of man as a type of human nature which we may hold in view, it will be useful for us to retain the terms in question in the sense I have indicated. In what follows, then, I mean by 'good' what we know with certainty to be a means of getting closer and closer to the type of human nature that we have set before ourselves; by 'bad', on the other hand, that which we know with certainty to prevent us from mirroring that same type. Also, we will refer to people as being more perfect or more imperfect to the extent that they come more or less close to said type. For it must be specially remarked that, when I say that someone passes from a lesser to a greater perfection or vice versa, I do not mean that they are changed from one essence, or form, to another: for instance, a horse would be as completely destroyed by being changed into a human being as by being changed into an insect; but what I mean is that we conceive their power of action, in so far as it is understood based on their own nature, to be increased or diminished. Lastly, by 'perfection in general' I mean, as I have said, reality—in other words, each thing's essence in so far as it exists and acts in a particular manner, without paying any regard to its duration. For no particular thing can be said to be more perfect just because it has persisted in existing for a longer time.

This last claim is at first puzzling because the perfection of a body is the body's ability to maintain itself in existence. As such, the more perfect a thing is, the better able it is to continue to survive. Despite this, Spinoza denies that the mere fact that one thing endures longer than another is not grounds for claiming that the first is more perfect than the second. To see that there is no contradiction in this, consider the following example. Suppose there are two similar people. One is healthy and goes to the gym often, whereas the other is lazy, never works out, and eats nothing but junk food. Now suppose that the healthy man is killed in a tragic bus accident. It would be strange to say that the lazy man was actually the healthier one in the end, just because he happened to live longer.

For the duration of things cannot be determined by their essence, since the essence of things involves no definite and determined period of existence; but anything, whether it be more perfect or less, will always be able to persist in existence through the same power through which it began to exist; thus, in this respect, all things are equal.

DEFINITIONS

I. By 'good' I mean that which we know for sure to be useful to us.

> It is interesting that Spinoza does not say what is actually useful, but what we know to be useful. As such, this is an epistemic claim rather than a metaphysical one. It is a claim about what can be understood. Of course, for Spinoza, anything adequately understood is correct, so this definition carries metaphysical import.

II. By 'evil' I mean that which we know for sure to prevent us from possessing some good.

(Concerning these terms, see the foregoing Preface towards the end.)

III. I call particular things 'contingent' in so far as, while regarding their essence only, we find nothing that necessarily asserts (*ponit*) their existence or necessarily excludes it.

> It is "contingent" whether or not the airplane I will ride on tomorrow will crash. This means not that it could go either way given the past and laws of nature, but only that given my state of knowing both outcomes are consistent. This epistemic contingency exists because my nature, considered in isolation of external causes, does not prove my necessary existence (i.e., substance itself) or my necessary non-existence (i.e., a square circle).

IV. I likewise call particular things 'possible' in so far as, while regarding the causes by which they must be produced, we do not know whether such causes are determined to produce them.

> When asked if I will ever finish writing a book that I have been working on for years, one may respond that it is "possible." But that does not mean that it really could go either way, but only that we don't know if I'm up to the job or not. You see Spinoza again emphasizing that these claims are epistemological and not metaphysical.

(In Schol. 1 Prop. 33 Pt. 1 I drew no distinction between possible and contingent because there was no need to distinguish them precisely at that point.)

V. By 'conflicting affects' I mean those that draw one in different directions although they are of the same kind, such as luxury and greed, which are both forms of love and are opposites not by nature but by accident.

VI. What I mean by 'affect felt towards a thing future, present, and past' I explained in Schol. 1 and 2 Prop. 18 Pt. 3, to which I refer the reader.

(At this point, however, I should also remark that we can distinctly imagine distance of both space and time only up to a certain definite limit; that is, we are wont to imagine all objects that are more than two hundred feet away from us, or whose distance from the place where we are exceeds that which we can distinctly imagine, to be equally distant from us and, therefore, as if they were on the same surface. Likewise, we imagine objects whose time of existing we imagine as removed from the present by a larger gap than we are wont to distinctly imagine to be all equally distant from the present, and we refer them all, as it were, to the same moment of time.)

> Spinoza's willingness to treat space and time as strictly analogous is interesting. These claims are not as implausible as they first seem. Consider two dinosaurs that lived 65 million years apart. Despite how far these dinosaurs are temporally divided, it is hard to really feel the difference in time between them. Instead of really conceiving this difference, we often imagine (wrongly) that all dinosaurs more or less existed together. We link both of those far separated dates into one "prehistoric time," which is singularly conceived.

VII. By an 'end for the sake of which we do something' I mean a desire.

> A goal or end is a desire, in the sense that if my goal or end is to build a house, that is the same thing as saying that I desire a house.

VIII. By 'virtue' (*virtus*) and 'power' (*potentia*) I mean the same thing; this means that virtue, in so far as it relates to man, is man's very essence, or nature (Prop. 7 Pt. 3), in so far as it has the power to bring about what can only be understood through the laws of his nature.

> Here we get another one of Spinoza's identity claims. So our essence is to strive to exist, that is the same thing as our power in general, our health, our perfection, our degree of knowledge, and now our virtue. So to be healthier is to be more active and less passive. When healthier/more active, one is also more knowledgeable and more virtuous. Accordingly, there is an identity between essence, power, virtue, health, perfection, and knowledge. It is often difficult to keep all of these identities in mind and, of course, they raise a lot of difficult questions.

AXIOM

There is no individual thing in nature than which there is not another more powerful and stronger. On the contrary, for any given thing there is a more powerful one by which it can be destroyed.

> Given that substance expresses itself in an infinite number of finite modes we can keep finding larger and larger complex finite objects (or minds) indefinitely. Spinoza makes the same point in Part II in the "Short Treatise on Bodies."

PROPOSITIONS

PROP. I. *No positive quality possessed by a false idea is removed* (tollitur) *by the presence of what is true in so far as it is true.*

Proof. Falsity consists solely in the privation of knowledge that inadequate ideas involve (Prop. 35 Pt. 2); there is no positive quality to them on account of which they are called false (Prop. 33 Pt. 2). Conversely, in so far as they relate to God, they are true (Prop. 32 Pt. 2). Consequently, if the positive quality possessed by a false idea were removed by the presence of what is true in so far as it is true, a true idea would then be removed by itself, which is absurd (Prop. 4 Pt. 3). Therefore, no positive quality possessed by a false idea, etc. *Q.E.D.*

So an idea is false only insofar as it is a fragment of the truth. (Think of one stone in a mosaic.) Everything is true in God's mind, because nothing is fragmented and everything is considered in its full context. So there is nothing "positive" in a false idea that is wrong. It's only wrong because it is removed from its context, which changes or obscures its meaning.

Scholium. This Proposition is more clearly understood from Coroll. 2 Prop. 16 Pt. 2. For imagination is an idea that indicates the present constitution of the human body rather than the nature of an external body—not distinctly, however, but confusedly; on account of this fact the mind is said to err. For instance, when we look at the sun, we imagine that it is about two hundred feet from us, about which we are fooled as long as we are ignorant of its true distance; but once its true distance is known, the error is removed, but not the imagination, that is, that idea of the sun which only explains its nature in so far as our body is affected by it, so that, although we know its real distance, we will nonetheless imagine it to be near us. For as we said in Schol. 35 Pt. 2, we imagine the sun to be so near us not because we are ignorant of its true distance, but because the mind conceives the size of the sun to the extent that the body is affected by it. In the same way, when the sun's rays, falling on the surface of water, are reflected into our eyes, we imagine the sun as if it were in the water, though we are aware of its real position; and similarly, all the other imaginations that deceive the mind—whether they refer to the natural constitution of the body or to its power of action being increased or diminished—are not contrary to the truth and do not vanish in its presence.

These are cases where a false idea when put into a better context is understood more clearly, and so becomes truer (more adequate). It may be difficult to conceptualize all falsity as being merely a lack of truth.

It happens indeed that, when we mistakenly fear an evil, the fear vanishes when we hear the true news; but the contrary also happens, namely that, when we fear an evil that is sure to come, our fear vanishes when we hear false news. Thus, imaginations do not vanish through the mere presence of the truth in so far as it is the truth, but because there come along other imaginations, stronger than the first, which exclude the present existence of the things we imagine, as I have shown in Prop. 17 Pt. 2.

PROP. II. *We are acted upon in so far as we are a part of nature that cannot be conceived by itself without other parts.*

Proof. We are said to be acted upon when something arises in us of which we are only a partial cause (Def. 2 Pt. 3), that is, something that cannot be deduced solely from the laws of our nature (Def. 1 Pt. 3). Consequently, we are acted upon in so far as we are a part of nature that cannot be conceived by itself without other parts. *Q.E.D.*

PROP. III. *The force by which one persists in existing is limited and is infinitely surpassed by the power of external causes.*

Proof. This is evident from the Axiom of this part, since for a given human being there is something else—say A—more powerful, and when A is given, there is something else—say B—more powerful than A, and so on to infinity; thus, the power of a human being is limited by the power of some other thing and is infinitely surpassed by the power of external causes. *Q.E.D.*

> Now at first it might seem that Spinoza is conflating two different claims. First, that there is some one thing that is more powerful. Second, that for everything there will always be a collection of other things that are more powerful. This follows Spinoza's views on part-whole relations. Insofar as things work together to cause a single outcome, they are to that extent one thing. Whereas the second claim seems far less controversial than the first, it is not clear whether he intends to make the more controversial former claim. If so, it would seem to require more defense than is here provided.

PROP. IV. *It is impossible for man not to be a part of nature, nor can he be exempt from undergoing changes beyond those that can be understood through his nature and of which he is an adequate cause.*

Proof. The power by which each particular thing, and consequently man, preserves its being is the power of God or of nature itself (Coroll. Prop. 24 Pt. 1), not in so far as it is infinite, but in so far as it can be explained by the actual essence of man (Prop. 7 Pt. 3). Thus, man's power, in so far as it is explained through his own actual essence, is a part of the infinite power of God or nature, in other words, of the essence thereof (Prop. 34 Pt. 1). This was our first point. Further, if it were possible for man to undergo no changes beyond those that can be understood solely through his nature, it would follow that he would not be able to die, but would always necessarily exist (Prop. 4 and 6 Pt. 3). This situation would have to follow from a cause whose power was either finite or infinite, namely either of man's power alone, who would be capable of removing from himself all those changes that could spring from external causes, or of nature's infinite power, which would order all individual things in such a way that man could not undergo any changes but those that worked towards his preservation. Now the first alternative is absurd (previous Prop., the proof of which is universal and can be applied to all individual things). Therefore, if it were possible for man to be unable to undergo any changes except for those that can be explained solely through his own nature—so that, as we have already shown, he would always necessarily exist—this would have to follow from God's infinite power; consequently, the whole order of nature, in so far as it is imagined under the attributes of extension and thought, would have to be deduced from the necessity of God's nature in so far as he is regarded as affected by the idea of some given human being (Prop. 16 Pt. 1). From this it would follow that man is infinite (Prop. 21 Pt. 1), which is absurd (first part of this Proof). Therefore, it is impossible for man to undergo no changes beyond those of which he is an adequate cause. *Q.E.D.*

Corollary. It follows that man must always be subject to passions, follow and obey the general order of nature, and accommodate himself to it as much as the nature of things demands.

> The reasoning here is not new, and Spinoza is largely repeating arguments that he has made a few times already. What is new here is that he concludes that we cannot avoid negative emotions. The Stoic or Buddhist ideal of emotional detachment is, for Spinoza, in principle impossible. Humans cannot avoid feeling sadness, anger, hate, etc.

PROP. V. *The power and increase of every passion and its persistence in existing are not defined by the power by which we ourselves endeavour to persist in existing, but by the power of an external cause compared to our own.*

Proof. The essence of a passion cannot be explained through our essence alone (Def. 1 and 2 Pt. 3); that is, the power of a passion cannot be defined by the power by which we ourselves endeavour to persist in existing (Prop. 7 Pt. 3), but must necessarily be defined by the power of an external cause compared with our own (as is shown in Prop. 16 Pt. 2). *Q.E.D.*

PROP. VI. *The force of any passion, or affect, can overcome the rest of a person's activities, or power, so that the affect becomes obstinately fixed to them.*

Proof. The force and increase of any passion and its persistence in existing are defined by the power of an external cause compared with our own (previous Prop.); therefore, it can overcome someone's power (Prop. 3 of this part), etc. *Q.E.D.*

Our emotions are more powerful than our reasoning because their strength depends upon the external world, which has far more power than we do. Thus, it seems, the ability to live a rational life, not dominated by emotions, is often impossible and likely only occurs for limited periods of time in very particular circumstances. So when asked whether reason is more powerful than emotion, Spinoza's answer is clearly no. Reason is my own power of acting, which is infinitely surpassed by the power of the rest of nature.

PROP. VII. *An affect cannot be constrained or removed except by another affect contrary to and more powerful than the affect to be constrained.*

Proof. An affect, in so far as it relates to the mind, is an idea through which the mind affirms a greater or smaller force of existence of its body than before (see the general Definition of the affects at the end of Part 3). When, therefore, the mind is assailed by any affect, the body is at the same time affected with a modification by which its power of action is increased or diminished. Further, this modification of the body receives from its cause the force to persist in its being (Prop. 5 of this part); thus, it can only be checked or removed by a bodily cause (Prop. 6 Pt. 2) affecting the body with a modification contrary to it (Prop. 5 Pt. 3) as well as stronger than it (Ax. of this part). Consequently, the mind is affected by the idea of a modification stronger than and contrary to the previous one (Prop. 12 Pt. 2); in other words, the mind will be affected by an affect stronger than and contrary to the former affect (see the general Definition of the affects), which will exclude or remove (*tollere*) the existence of the former one.

Thus, an affect cannot be removed or constrained except by a contrary and stronger affect. *Q.E.D.*

> This conclusion is interesting because it tells us that we cannot reason away an emotion. It will normally be no help to give yourself arguments about why you ought not to feel a certain way, or why some emotion is bad for you. The only thing that is powerful enough to change a powerful emotion is another more powerful emotion that contradicts it. You can't talk yourself out of hate by a dispassionate study. The only way to change hate is through feeling love or kindness.

Corollary. An affect, in so far as it relates to the mind, cannot be constrained or removed except through the idea of a modification of the body contrary to and stronger than that which is acting upon us. For the affect that acts upon us cannot be constrained or removed except by an affect stronger than and contrary to it (previous Prop.)—in other words, by the idea of a modification of the body stronger than and contrary to the modification by which we are being acted upon (general Definition of the affects).

PROP. VIII. *The knowledge of good and evil is nothing but the affect of joy or sadness in so far as we are conscious of it.*

Proof. We call a thing 'good' or 'evil' when it serves or hampers the preservation of our being (Def. 1 and 2 of this part), that is, when it increases or diminishes, helps or hinders our power of action (Prop. 7 Pt. 3). Thus, in so far as we perceive a thing affecting us with joy or sadness, we call it 'good' or 'evil' (see the Def. of 'joy' and 'sadness' in Schol. Prop. 11 Pt. 3); therefore, the knowledge of good and evil is nothing but the idea of joy or sadness that necessarily follows from the affects of joy and sadness themselves (Prop. 22 Pt. 2). Now this idea is united to the affect in the same way as the mind is united to the body (Prop. 21 Pt. 2); that is, there is in truth no distinction between this idea and the affect itself—in other words, the idea of the modification of the body (general Def. of the affects)—except in conception only (as I showed in Schol. Prop. 21 Pt. 2). Therefore, the knowledge of good and evil is nothing but the affect in so far as we are conscious of it. *Q.E.D.*

> A few interesting things to note in this passage. First, Spinoza seems again to imply the existence of non-conscious emotions and partly-conscious emotions. Second, Spinoza claims that the idea and the affect are one and the same thing conceived in two ways. It is hard to

flesh this idea out further, but perhaps an example may help. When I am angry at someone, I have an idea of them "shaped" in an angry way: it's an angry idea of them. When I love someone, I have an idea of them that is "shaped" in a loving way. These two ideas are just two different ways of thinking about the person. But my idea of them and my emotion towards them are ultimately aspects of the same thing. In this way, it is important to note that in Spinoza, affects seem to have representational content. They are about something (namely, the cause).

PROP. IX. *An affect whose cause we imagine to be with us in the present is stronger than if we did not imagine it to be present.*

Proof. Imagination is the idea through which the mind regards a thing as present (see its Def. in Schol. Prop. 17 Pt. 2). However, it indicates the constitution of the human body rather than the nature of an external thing (Coroll. 2 Prop. 16 Pt. 2). An affect is therefore imagination in so far as it indicates the constitution of the body (general Def. of the affects). Now imagination is stronger so long as we imagine nothing that excludes the present existence of the external thing (Prop. 17 Pt. 2); thus, an affect is likewise stronger, or more intense, when we imagine its cause to be with us at the present time than if we did not do so. *Q.E.D.*

Scholium. When I said above (Prop. 18 Pt. 3) that we are affected by the image of something future or past with the same affect as if the thing imagined were present, I expressly cautioned that this is only true in so far as we look solely to the image of the thing in question itself, for the image's nature remains the same whether we imagine things as present or not. I did not deny, however, that the image becomes weaker when we contemplate other things present to us which exclude the present existence of the future thing; I did not expressly call attention to this fact because I planned on dealing with the strength of the affects in this part of my work.

Here we see one of Spinoza's core "psychotherapy" ideas, which will become more important later in the work. Emotions are strongest when they are related to something that is considered in isolation. When it is considered in its context, then the greater the context, the more reduced the emotion. He makes this point by describing the affect of imagining a thing's cause to be present with us. In making the cause present, one imagines the thing apart from the infinite series that gives rise to it. This is clearly a fragmented/inadequate idea.

Corollary. The image of something future or past, that is, of a thing that we contemplate in relation to time future or time past to the exclusion of the present, is, all else being equal, weaker than the image of something present; consequently, an affect felt towards a thing future or past is less intense, all else being equal, than an affect felt towards something present.

PROP. X. *Towards something future that we imagine to be just about to occur we are affected more intensely than if we imagine the time of its existence to be farther away from the present; similarly, we are affected by the memory of something we imagine to have not long passed away more intensely than if we imagined it to have long passed away.*

Proof. In so far as we imagine something to be just about to occur or to have not long passed away, by this very fact we imagine something that excludes the presence of that thing less than if we imagined the time of its future existence to be more distant from the present or if it had long passed away (as is self-evident). Therefore, we will, to that extent, be more intensely affected towards it (previous Prop.). *Q.E.D.*

> It is important to note that "excluding the existence" of something is a matter of degree. If I know that my brother will arrive at 2:00 pm, then at noon my thought of him includes something that excludes his present existence (I know he is somewhere else). But, Spinoza says this exclusion is less than the exclusion that we get if I knew that he would not be arriving until Christmas, in six months. That knowledge excludes his existence more and so, to that extent, any related affects are diminished.

Scholium. From the remarks made in Def. 6 of this part it follows that, if objects are separated from the present by a longer period than we can define by way of imagining, they all affect us equally faintly, even if we are aware that their dates of occurrence are widely separated from one another.

PROP. XI. *An affect towards something we imagine as necessary is, all else being equal, more intense than an affect towards something possible or contingent, that is, not necessary.*

Proof. To the extent that we imagine a thing to be necessary, we affirm its existence; conversely, we deny a thing's existence to the extent that we imagine it not to be necessary (Schol. 1 Prop. 33 Pt. 1). Therefore, an affect towards something necessary is, all else being equal, more intense than an affect toward something not necessary (Prop. 9 of this part). *Q.E.D.*

> This conclusion follows from the same principle mentioned above; namely, that affects are stronger when the cause is imagined in isolation. This follows insofar as imagining something as contingent requires imagining more things than just the essence of the thing itself. Contingency can only be conceived in this way, since a thing's essence will only establish its existence. To thereby imagine a thing's possible non-existence (i.e., to imagine contingency), is to think of other causes that may interact with and thereby exclude the thing's existence.

PROP. XII. *An affect towards a thing that we know not to exist at the present time and which we imagine as possible is more intense, all else being equal, than an affect towards a contingent one.*

Proof. In so far as we imagine a thing to be contingent, we are not affected by the image of any other thing that would assert (*ponit*) the existence of the former (Def. 3 of this part), but, on the contrary, we imagine—in our hypothesis—certain things that exclude its present existence. Now in so far as we imagine a thing to be possible in the future, we imagine things that assert (*ponunt*) its existence (Def. 4 of this part), that is, things that promote hope or fear (Prop. 18 Pt. 3). Consequently, an affect towards something possible is more vehement. *Q.E.D.*

> The distinction Spinoza draws here between the contingent and the possible is interesting. Something is contingent when we can imagine causes that would block it, but don't know if those causes will come about. Something is possible when we imagine causes that would bring it into existence, but don't know if those causes will in fact bring it about. Affects towards possible things are stronger, since to imagine causes consistent with its existence (i.e., possibility) is to imagine the thing's actually existing. On the contrary, to imagine causes inconsistent with the thing's existence (i.e., contingency) is to imagine the non-existence of the thing.

Corollary. An affect towards a thing we know not to exist in the present and which we imagine as contingent is much fainter than if we imagined the thing in question to be with us in the present.

Proof. An affect towards a thing that we imagine to exist in the present is more intense than it would be if we imagined it as future (Coroll. Prop. 9 of this part), and is much more vehement than if we imagined the future time as far distant from the present (Prop. 10 of this part). Therefore, an affect towards a thing whose period of existence we imagine to be far away from the present is much fainter than if we imagined the thing as present; nevertheless, it is more intense than if we imagined the same thing as contingent (previous Prop.). Thus, an affect towards a contingent thing will be much fainter than if we imagined the thing to be with us in the present. *Q.E.D.*

PROP. XIII. *An affect towards something contingent that we know not to exist in the present is, all else being equal, fainter than an affect towards something past.*

Proof. In so far as we imagine a thing as contingent, we are not affected by the image of any other thing that asserts (*ponit*) the existence of that thing (Def. 3 of this part) but, on the contrary, we imagine (in our hypothesis) certain things that exclude its present existence. However, to the extent that we imagine it in relation to the past, we are posited to imagine something that recalls it to memory, that is, excites the image thereof (see Prop. 18 Pt. 2 with Schol.), thereby causing us, to that extent, to regard that thing as if it were present (Coroll. Prop. 17 Pt. 2). Consequently, an affect towards something contingent that we know does not exist in the present is fainter, all else being equal, than an affect towards a thing past (Prop. 9 of this part). *Q.E.D.*

PROP. XIV. *True knowledge of good and evil cannot constrain any affect in so far as it is true, but only in so far as it is regarded as an affect.*

Proof. An affect is an idea through which the mind affirms a greater or smaller force for existing of its body than before (general Def. of the affects); therefore, it has no positive quality that could be removed (*tolli*) by the presence of what is true (Prop. 1 of this part). Consequently, true knowledge of good and evil cannot, by virtue of being true, restrain any affect. But in so far as it is an affect (see Prop. 8 of this part), if it has more strength than the affect to be restrained, it will be able to restrain it, and to that extent only (Prop. 7 of this part). *Q.E.D.*

Here we see one of Spinoza's core therapeutic insights, which is that an emotion can only be changed by another emotion. Say one is feeling sadness: that sad feeling just is the idea of the body becoming less healthy. The only thing that could constrain such an idea is an idea that contradicts it: thus, an idea of the body becoming healthier. The mere knowledge that pain is the body decreasing in health does nothing by itself to cure one's sadness, because affects relate to powers in bodies, and ideas relate to affirmations in minds. Since ideas do not move bodies (Spinoza's interaction doctrine), a clear understanding, as such, does not change the body. However, given parallelism, there are ideas that correlate with the power in the body. Ideas about bodily health correlate with the affect of joy. Thus, ideas of bodily health, which carry the affect of joy, counteract the affect of sadness.

PROP. XV. *Desire arising from true knowledge of good and evil can be extinguished or constrained by many other desires that arise from the affects that assail us.*

Proof. From the true knowledge of good and evil, in so far as it is an affect (Prop. 8 of this part), necessarily arises desire (Def. of the affects, 1), which is the stronger the greater the strength of the affect from which it arises (Prop. 37 Pt. 3). However, as this desire arises (in our hypothesis) from the fact that we truly understand something, it follows in us all by itself in so far as we act (Prop. 3 Pt. 3), and must therefore be understood through our essence only (Def. 2 Pt. 3); consequently, its force and increase must be defined solely by human power (Prop. 7 Pt. 3). Further, the desires arising from the affects that assail us are also stronger the more vehement said affects are; therefore, their force and increase must be defined solely by the power of external causes (Prop. 5 of this part), a power that, when compared to our own, indefinitely surpasses it (Prop. 3). Hence, the desires arising from affects like these can be more vehement than that arising from true knowledge of good and evil, and can, consequently, constrain or extinguish it (Prop. 7). *Q.E.D.*

To know something means to understand it, which is an active process arising out of the mode's own internal motions (or affirmations). But these will always, in principle, be weaker than the external forces which can increase or decrease the body's health.

PROP. XVI. *Desire arising from the knowledge of good and evil, in so far as such knowledge refers to the future, can be more easily constrained or extinguished than desire for what is agreeable in the present.*[1]

Proof. An affect towards a thing that we imagine as future is fainter than one towards a thing that is present (Coroll. Prop. 9 of this part). Now desire that arises from true knowledge of good and evil, even when such knowledge is concerned with things that are good in the present, can be extinguished or constrained by some headstrong desire (previous Prop., whose proof is of universal application). Thus, desire arising from the same knowledge when it refers to the future can be more easily extinguished or constrained, etc. *Q.E.D.*

> This proposition also follows from the previous one. Since the external world has so much more power than we do, it can increase the health of parts of the body, to a much greater extent than we can through our own internal motions. So we are only able to overcome weaker temptations. Another way to think of this is, knowledge about future events is always less clear than knowledge of present things. As such, an affirmation (even if true) about the future will always have the sort of weakness that could be overcome by the affects of a desire now felt. The affect related to a weaker understanding is simply weaker than the affect of a current desire. An example to illustrate: I may currently have a true idea that eating a chocolate cake will cause me not to fit into my skinny jeans in three months. But, even if that understanding is correct, it is not affirmed powerfully. It is only weakly affirmed because it is about the future, and I can imagine that I might suffer an illness, for example, between now and then which could result in the cake not harming my ability to fit those skinny jeans. As such, my desire for the cake today will be more powerful than my affirmation that cake now results in poor fitting pants later.

PROP. XVII. *Desire arising from true knowledge of good and evil, in so far as such knowledge is concerned with contingent things, can be restrained far more easily still than desire for things that are present.*

Proof. This Prop. is proved in the same way as the previous Prop. from Coroll. Prop. 12 of this part.

Scholium. I think I have thus shown the reason why people are more readily moved by opinion than by true reason and why

---

1   Another possible interpretation of this sentence is: "... can be quite easily constrained or extinguished *by* a desire...." The same ambiguity is found in the following Prop. (D.A.)

true knowledge of good and evil stirs up conflicts in the mind and often yields to every kind of passion. Hence the exclamation of the poet:[1] "The better path I see and approve, the worse I follow." The Ecclesiastes[2] seems to have had the same thing in mind when he wrote: "He who increaseth knowledge increaseth sorrow." I am not saying this in order to draw the conclusion that ignorance is preferable to knowledge or that a wise person is on a par with a fool in controlling their affects, but because it is necessary to know both the power and the powerlessness of our nature, so that we can determine what reason can do in restraining the affects and what it cannot do; and I have said that in the present part I shall merely deal with human powerlessness, since I have decided to discuss the power of reason over the affects separately.

PROP. XVIII. *Desire arising from joy is, all else being equal, stronger than desire arising from sadness.*

Proof. Desire is man's very essence (Def. of the affects, 1)—that is, the endeavour through which a human being endeavours to persist in their own being (Prop. 7 Pt. 3). Therefore, desire arising from joy is helped or increased by the very affect of joy (see the Def. of 'joy' in Schol. Prop. 11 Pt. 3), whereas that arising from sadness is diminished or constrained by the very affect of sadness (same Schol.). Hence, the force of the desire that arises from joy must be defined by human power together with the power of an external cause, whereas desire arising from sadness must be defined by human power only; thus, the former is the stronger of the two. *Q.E.D.*

> So, according to Spinoza, we want pleasurable things more than we want to get out of suffering. When we desire something pleasurable then we have the power from our own internal motions (essence) and the power of the external cause that is the source of the joy. But when the external world is causing us pain, the desire to leave that pain comes only from the body's own powers, and is not aided by external forces.

Scholium. In these few remarks I have explained the causes of human powerlessness and inconstancy and shown why people do

---

1 Ovid. See above, p. 145, n. 1 and p. 212, n. 1. (D.A.)
2 1. 18. (D.A.)

not abide by the precepts of reason. It is left for me to show what it is that reason commands us to do and which of the affects are in harmony with the rules of human reason and which ones are at odds with them. Before I begin to demonstrate these things in our detailed geometrical fashion (*ordine Geometrico*), however, I would like to outline reason's precepts themselves, so that everyone may more readily grasp my meaning.

> These kinds of summaries are rare in this work and it is interesting that Spinoza seems to concede here that the geometrical method can make his point harder to grasp. But the core of Spinoza's ethics (the name of the book, after all) is as follows:

As reason makes no demands contrary to nature, it demands that everybody love themselves, seek their advantage—I mean, what is really useful to them—desire everything that really brings a person to greater perfection; in short, that everybody endeavour to preserve their own being as much as they can. This is as necessarily true as that the whole is greater than the part (see Prop. 4 Pt. 3).

> Having defined what reason demands of us (that is, what is in our best interest), Spinoza can then explain his definition of "virtue":

Further, as virtue is nothing other than acting in accordance with the laws of one's specific nature (Def. 8 of this part) and as no one endeavours to preserve their own being if not because of the laws of their own specific nature (Prop. 7 Pt. 3), it follows, *first*, that the foundation of virtue is the endeavour to preserve one's own being and that happiness consists in man's ability to preserve his own being; *secondly*, that virtue is to be desired for its own sake and that there is nothing more excellent or more useful to us for the sake of which we should strive for virtue; *thirdly* and lastly, that those who commit suicide are powerless in their mind and are completely overcome by external causes repugnant to their nature. Further, it follows from Postulate 4 Pt. 2 that we can never make it so that we no longer need anything external to us for the preservation of our being and can live in such a way as to have no relations with things that are outside ourselves. Also, if we consider our mind, we see that our intellect would be more imperfect if the mind were alone and could understand nothing besides itself. There are, then, many things outside ourselves that are useful to us and are therefore to be desired. Among these things we can discern none more excellent than those that are in entire agreement with our nature. For if, for example, two individual things of entirely the same nature are united, they form a single individual thing twice as powerful as either of them singly.

This claim is not immediately obvious. Spinoza argues that two things exactly alike in nature will naturally work together, and so, to that extent, become one thing. It is relatively easy to come up with counter-examples here, but Spinoza would argue that it is only to the extent that things are different that they can come into conflict. Two beings of exactly the same nature would always agree with each other's desires, since the same external causes would aid the striving of both. As such, both would act towards the desired object in the same way. If both are causally working towards the same thing in the same way, then they become a larger, singular object.

Consequently, there is nothing more useful to man than man; nothing, I say, can be wished for by people which is more excellent for preserving their being than that all should agree in all points to such an extent that the minds and bodies of all should form, as it were, one single mind and one single body and that all people together should endeavour to preserve their being as much as they can, and all together should seek their common advantage. It follows that people who are governed by reason— that is, who seek their own advantage under the dictates of reason—desire for themselves nothing that they do not also desire for the rest of humankind and, consequently, are just, faithful, and honourable in their conduct.

Since all people share the same fundamental nature as I do, and since reason directs us towards whatever will best support my striving (as the kind of thing that I am), whatever is good for me is also good for them. If rational, and thereby concerned with improving the power of my striving, then whatever I desire for myself, I should also desire for those around me. This is because, if we are alike and rational, then we will all desire the same empowering things, and thus would all form a larger, more powerful whole that seeks those things. In virtue of our accord, we become something more. The accord increases our power to strive.

Such are the dictates of reason that I undertook to outline at this point, before beginning to prove them in greater detail. I have taken this course in order, if possible, to gain the attention of those who believe that this principle, that everybody is bound to seek what is useful for themselves, is the foundation of impiety rather than of piety and virtue. Therefore, after briefly showing that the contrary is the case, I go on to prove it by the same method by which I have proceeded so far.

PROP. XIX. *Everybody, by the laws of their nature, necessarily desires or shrinks from what they deem to be good or bad.*

Proof. The knowledge of good and evil is the very affect of joy or sadness in so far as we are conscious thereof (Prop. 8 of this part); consequently, everybody necessarily desires what they deem good and shrinks from what they deem bad (Prop. 28 Pt. 3). But this appetite is nothing other than man's very essence, or nature (see the Def. of 'appetite' in Schol. Prop. 9 Pt. 3 and Def. of the affects, 1). Therefore, everybody, solely by the laws of their own nature, desires or shrinks, etc. *Q.E.D.*

> When we feel sad, we have a confused idea of the body in a lesser state of health. The knowledge of this sadness is just this same idea considered in a different way. That is, it is an idea of an idea which is identical to the original idea—just considered in a different way. Likewise, the idea of goodness is the affect of joy considered in a different way. As what brings joy is what improves our power of action, our idea of good is identical with our essence, since our essence is to strive.

PROP. XX. *The more everyone endeavours and is able to seek what is useful to them—in other words, to preserve their own being—the more they are endowed with virtue; conversely, to the extent that one neglects to preserve what is useful to them, that is, their own being, they are powerless.*

Proof. Virtue is human power itself, which is defined solely by man's essence (Def. 8 of this part), that is, solely by a person's endeavour to persist in their own being (Prop. 7 Pt. 3). Therefore, the more one endeavours and is able to preserve their own being, the more they are endowed with virtue; consequently, to the extent that somebody neglects to preserve their own being, they are powerless (Prop. 4 and 6 Pt. 3). *Q.E.D.*

Scholium. No one, therefore, neglects to seek their own good, or preserve their own being, unless they are overcome by causes external and foreign to their nature. No one, I say, is driven by the necessity of their own nature, but only by compelling external causes, to shrink from food or kill themselves; which latter may be done in a variety of ways. For instance, someone may kill themselves under the compulsion of another who twists around their right hand, with which they happened to have taken up a sword, and forces them to turn the blade against their own heart; or they may be compelled to slit open their own veins by a tyrant's command, like Seneca—that is, they wish to escape a greater evil by incurring a lesser one; or, lastly, latent external causes may so dispose one's imagination and so affect one's body that it assumes a nature contrary to its former one, a nature the idea of which cannot exist in the mind (Prop. 10 Pt. 3). But that a person should from the necessity of their own nature endeavour to become non-existent or to change into another form is as impossible as that something should be made out of nothing, as everyone will see for themselves after a little reflection.

PROP. XXI. *No one can desire to be blessed, to act rightly, and to live rightly without at the same time wishing to be, to act, and to live—in other words, to actually exist.*

Proof. The proof of this Proposition, or rather its content itself, is self-evident, and is also plain from the definition of desire. For the desire to live, act, etc. blessedly, that is, rightly, is the very essence of man (Def. of the affects, 1), in other words, the endeavour made by everyone to preserve their own being (Prop. 7 Pt. 3). Therefore, no one can desire, etc. *Q.E.D.*

> In order to desire to be a good person, I first have to desire to be a person at all. Indeed, both desires are the same. A good person is one who is living a human life well. To thrive as a person is to exist.

PROP. XXII. *No virtue can be imagined as prior to this one, namely the endeavour to preserve one's own being.*

Proof. The endeavour for self-preservation is the essence of a thing (Prop. 7 Pt. 3). Therefore, if any virtue could be conceived as prior to this one (that is, this endeavour), the very essence of a thing would have to be conceived as prior to itself (Def. 8 of this part), which is absurd (as is self-evident). Therefore no virtue, etc. *Q.E.D.*

Corollary. The endeavour for self-preservation is the first and only foundation of virtue. For prior to this principle none other can be conceived (previous Prop.), nor can virtue be conceived without it (Prop. 21 of this part).

PROP. XXIII. *Man cannot be absolutely said to act in obedience to virtue in so far as he is determined to do something because he has inadequate ideas, but only in so far as he is so determined because he understands.*

Proof. In so far as someone is determined to do something through having inadequate ideas, they are acted upon (Prop. 1 Pt. 3), that is, they do something that cannot be perceived solely through their essence (Def. 1 and 2 Pt. 3), that is, does not follow from their virtue (Def. 8 of this part). Now in so far as they are determined to do something because they understand, they act (same Prop. 1 Pt. 3); that is, they do something that is perceived through their essence alone, in other words, something that adequately follows from their virtue (Def. 8 of this part). *Q.E.D.*

PROP. XXIV. *To act absolutely in obedience to virtue is in us the same thing as to act, to live, or to preserve one's being (these three terms are identical in meaning) in accordance with the dictates of reason on the basis of seeking what is useful to oneself.*

Proof. To act absolutely in obedience to virtue is nothing but to act according to the laws of one's own nature (Def. 8 of this part). Now we only act in so far as we understand (Prop. 3 Pt. 3); therefore, to act in obedience to virtue is in us nothing but to act, to live, or to preserve our being in obedience to reason, and that on the basis of seeking what is useful for us (Coroll. Prop. 22 of this part). *Q.E.D.*

PROP. XXV. *No one wishes to preserve their being for the sake of anything else.*

Proof. The endeavour with which each thing endeavours to persist in its being is defined solely by the essence of the thing itself (Prop. 7 Pt. 3); from this given essence alone, and not from the essence of anything else, it necessarily follows that everyone endeavours to preserve their being (Prop. 6 Pt. 3). Moreover, this Proposition is evident from Coroll. Prop. 22 of this part; for if one endeavoured to preserve one's being for the sake of anything else, the last-named thing would be the basis of virtue (as is self-evident), which is absurd (previous Coroll.). Therefore, no one, etc. *Q.E.D.*

Take the example of a mother who lives only for her child. She may take care of herself only so that she is able to take care of the child she loves. Isn't this person living for the sake of someone else? Spinoza answers, no. The reason is that the desire to exist comes entirely from the nature of the mother, and so includes no reference to anything external. If the mother were in pain, and staying alive only for the child, then this person is overcome by external forces. But the goal of existing is just to go on existing, and one must desire this in order to desire anything else.

PROP. XXVI. *Whatever we endeavour to do in obedience to reason is nothing other than to understand; and the mind, in so far as it makes use of reason, does not judge anything to be useful to it except for what is conducive to understanding.*

Proof. The endeavour for self-preservation is nothing but the essence of the thing itself (Prop. 7 Pt. 3), which, in so far as it exists such as it is, is conceived to have the strength to persist in existence (Prop. 6 Pt. 3) and to do those things that necessarily follow from its given nature (see the Def. of 'appetite' in Schol. Prop. 9 Pt. 3). Now the essence of reason is nothing other than our mind in so far as it clearly and distinctly understands (see its Def. in Schol. 2 Prop. 40 Pt. 2); therefore, whatever we endeavour to do in obedience to reason is nothing other than to understand (Prop. 40 Pt. 2). Further, since this endeavour of the mind with which it endeavours, in so far as it reasons, to preserve its own being is nothing but understanding (first part of this Proof), this endeavour to understand is the first and single basis of virtue (Coroll. Prop. 22 of this part), and we will not endeavour to understand things for the sake of any particular goal (Prop. 25 of this part). On the contrary, the mind, in so far as it reasons, will not be able to conceive any good for itself except for what is conducive to understanding (Def. 1 of this part). *Q.E.D.*

The mind and body are the same thing. The essence of the body is a complex self-maintaining motion; the essence of the mind is the complex affirmation of the existence of that body. Health in the body comes about when the motion is preserved, and when the motion comes from itself. Understanding in the mind comes about when ideas follow adequately in the mind from ideas we already have. These two processes are, according to Spinoza, the same thing conceived in two ways.

PROP. XXVII. *We know nothing to be good or evil with certainty except for what is really conducive to understanding or what can hinder us from doing so.*

Proof. The mind, in so far as it reasons, desires nothing other than to understand and judges nothing to be useful to itself except for what is conducive to understanding (previous Prop.). Now the mind cannot possess certainty concerning anything except in so far as it has adequate ideas (Prop. 41 and 43 Pt. 2 with Schol.), or (what is the same thing, see Schol. Prop. 40 Pt. 2) in so far as it reasons. Therefore, we know nothing to be good or evil with certainty except for what is really conducive to understanding and, conversely, we know to be bad what can hinder us from understanding. *Q.E.D.*

> Once we know that increased health to the body is just the same thing as increased knowledge in the mind, then we can infer that the only thing we seek (when considered as a mind) is to understand. Joy is to the body as clear and distinct understanding is to the mind. Both are one and the same thing considered under different attributes. As both are also the striving actions of substance (considered under each attribute), what one understands is what brings joy and is what is good for humankind.

PROP. XXVIII. *The mind's highest good is the knowledge of God, and the mind's highest virtue is to know God.*

Proof. The highest thing the mind can understand is God, that is, a being absolutely infinite (Def. 6 Pt. 1), without which nothing can either exist or be conceived (Prop. 15 Pt. 1); therefore, the mind's highest utility—that is, good (Def. 1 of this part)—is the knowledge of God (Prop. 26 and 27 of this part). Also, the mind acts only in so far as it understands (Prop. 1 and 3 Pt. 3), and only to the same extent can it absolutely be said to act virtuously (Prop. 23 of this part). The mind's absolute virtue, therefore, is to understand. Now the highest that the mind can understand is God (as we have already shown); therefore, the highest virtue of the mind is to understand—that is, to know—God. *Q.E.D.*

PROP. XXIX. *No individual thing whose nature is entirely different from ours can help or restrain our power of action, and absolutely nothing can do us good or harm unless it has something in common with us.*

Proof. The power of every individual thing—and, consequently, of man (Coroll. Prop. 10 Pt. 2)—through which it exists and operates, can only be determined by another individual thing (Prop. 28 Pt. 1), whose nature must be understood through the same attribute through which human nature is conceived (Prop. 6 Pt. 2). Therefore, our power of action, however it is conceived, can be determined and, consequently, helped or hindered by the power of another individual thing that has something in common with us, but not by the power of a thing whose nature is entirely different from our own. And since we call 'good' or 'evil' what is the cause of joy or sadness (Prop. 8 of this part), that is, what increases or diminishes, helps or hinders our power of action (Schol. Prop. 11 Pt. 3), something whose nature is entirely different from ours can be neither good nor bad for us. *Q.E.D.*

PROP. XXX. *Nothing can be bad for us through what it has in common with our nature, but to the extent that it is bad for us, it is opposed to us.*

Proof. We call a thing 'bad' when it is the cause of sadness (Prop. 8 of this part), that is, when it diminishes or restrains our power of action (see Def. of 'sadness' in Schol. Prop. 11 Pt. 3). Therefore, if anything were bad for us through what it has in common with us, it would be able to diminish or restrain that very thing which it has in common with us, which is absurd (Prop. 4 Pt. 3). Thus, nothing can be bad for us through that which it has in common with us; on the contrary, in so far as it is bad for us—that is, in so far as it can diminish or restrain our power of action (as we have just shown)—it is opposed to us (Prop. 5 Pt. 3). *Q.E.D.*

> Spinoza infers here, again, that since I cannot destroy myself, I also cannot destroy anything exactly like myself. Which means that I can destroy something only insofar as it is different from me. The more similar it is to me, the less I am able to destroy it. Many counterexamples no doubt come to the reader's mind. But consider whether someone's ability to destroy another is because of what they share, or what they do not.

PROP. XXXI. *To the extent that a thing agrees with our nature, it is necessarily good.*

Proof. In so far as a thing agrees with our nature, it cannot be bad (previous Prop.). Thus, it will necessarily be either good or indifferent. If it is posited to be neither good nor bad, nothing will follow from its nature that fosters the preservation of our nature (Ax. 3 of this part), that is, that fosters the preservation of the thing itself (according to the hypothesis). This, however, is absurd (Prop. 6 Pt. 3); therefore, in so far as a thing agrees with our nature, it will necessarily be good. *Q.E.D.*

Corollary. It follows that, the more something agrees with our nature, the more useful, that is, to a greater extent good, it is to us; conversely, the more useful something is to us, the more it agrees, to that extent, with our nature. For in so far as it does not agree with our nature, it will necessarily be different from it or opposed to it. If different, it can be neither good nor bad (Prop. 29 of this part); if opposed, it will also be opposed to that which agrees with our nature, that is, contrary to what is good (previous Prop.)—in other words, bad. Nothing, therefore, can be good except in so far as it agrees with our nature; hence, the more something agrees with our nature, the more useful it is and vice versa. *Q.E.D.*

PROP. XXXII. *To the extent that people are subject to passions, they cannot be said to agree naturally.*

Proof. Things that are said to agree naturally are understood to agree in power (Prop. 7 Pt. 3), but not in powerlessness—that is, negation—thus not in passion either (Schol. Prop. 3 Pt. 3). Consequently, people, in so far as they are subject to passions, cannot be said to agree naturally. *Q.E.D.*

Scholium. This is self-evident, too; for if someone were to say that white and black only agree in the fact that neither is red, this would amount to absolutely stating that white and black do not agree in anything. Likewise, if one were to say that a stone and a person agree only in the fact that both are finite, powerless, or not existing by the necessity of their own nature or, lastly, indefinitely surpassed by the power of external causes, one would be straightout stating that a stone and a person are not alike in anything; for things that agree only in negation, that is, in what neither possesses, in truth do not agree in anything.

Spinoza's point here may be a bit obscured by his example. But his claim is simply that if the only thing that A and B have in common is that neither is a C, D, or E, and nothing else can be said about what they have in common, then they have nothing in common. Of course, a stone and a person are both modes, have weight, have shape, etc. Thus, stones can, in fact, hurt and help us.

PROP. XXXIII. *People can differ in nature in so far as they are assailed by affects that are passions;*[1] *and to this extent one and the same person is variable and inconstant as well.*

Proof. The nature, or essence, of the affects cannot be explained solely through our essence, or nature (Def. 1 and 2 Pt. 3), but it must be defined by the power—that is, the nature (Prop. 7 Pt. 3)—of external causes in comparison with our own. Consequently, there are as many forms of each affect as there are forms of external objects by which we are affected (see Prop. 56 Pt. 3) and people can be affected differently by one and the same object (see Prop. 51 Pt. 3), and to this extent differ in nature; lastly, one and the same person can be differently affected towards the same object (same Prop.) and can therefore be variable, etc. *Q.E.D.*

PROP. XXXIV. *In so far as people are assailed by affects that are passions, they can be opposed to one another.*

Proof. A man, for instance Peter, can be the cause of Paul's being saddened by virtue of possessing something similar to a thing Paul hates (Prop. 16 Pt. 3) or of having sole possession of a thing Paul too loves (Prop. 32 Pt. 3 with Schol.) or for other causes (the most important of which are enumerated in Schol. Prop. 55 Pt. 3). It can therefore happen that Paul hates Peter (Def. of affects, 7); consequently, it can also easily happen that Peter hates Paul in return (Prop. 40 Pt. 3 with Schol.) and that, therefore, they endeavour to harm one another (Prop. 39 Pt. 3), that is, that they are opposed to each other (Prop. 30 of this part). Now an affect of sadness is always a passion[2] (Prop. 59 Pt. 3); hence, people, in so far as they are assailed by affects that are passions, can be opposed to one another. *Q.E.D.*

Since human nature is the same for everyone—or very similar, if you think Spinoza is committed to nominalism about universals—then the

---

1 See how S. defines 'passion' at the beginning of part 3, with p. 141, n. 1. (D.A.)
2 See note above.

only way that people can really differ from one another is in their passions, not in their reason.

Scholium. I said that Paul may hate Peter because he imagines him to possess something that Paul himself also loves; from this it seems, at first sight, to follow that these two people damage each other because they both love the same thing and, consequently, because they agree with each other in nature. If this were so, Prop. 30 and 31 of this part would be untrue. But if we give the matter our unbiased attention, we shall see that the discrepancy vanishes. For the two men are not disagreeable to each other in so far as they agree in nature, that is, in so far as both love the same thing, but in so far as they differ from one another: in so far as each loves the same thing, the love of each is thereby fostered (Prop. 31 Pt. 3), that is, the joy of each is thereby fostered (Def. of the affects, 6). Therefore, it is far from being the case that they are mutually disagreeable in so far as both love the same thing and through the agreement in their natures; the cause for their opposition lies, as I have said, solely in the fact that they are posited to differ in nature. For we posit that Peter has the idea of the thing loved as in his possession, while Paul has the idea of the loved object as lost. Hence, the one man will be affected with joy, the other with sadness, and thus they will be opposed to each other. We can easily show in a similar manner that all other causes of hatred are due solely to the fact that people are different in nature, not to the points where they agree.

PROP. XXXV. *Only in so far as people live in obedience to reason do they always necessarily agree in nature.*

Proof. In so far as people are assailed by affects that are passions, they can be different in nature (Prop. 33 of this part) and opposed to one another (previous Prop.). But people are only said to act in so far as they live in obedience to reason (Prop 3 Pt. 3); therefore, whatever follows from human nature in so far as it is defined by reason must be understood solely through human nature as its proximate cause (Def. 2 Pt. 3). However, since everybody, by the very laws of their nature, desires what they deem good and endeavours to remove what they deem bad (Prop. 19 of this part), and since, furthermore, what we deem good or bad in accordance with reason necessarily is good or bad (Prop 41 Pt. 2), it follows that it is only in so far as people live in obedience to reason that they necessarily do things that are necessarily good for human nature and, consequently, for each individual human being, in other words, things that agree with each person's nature (Coroll. Prop. 31 of this part). Therefore, in so far as people live in obedience to reason, they necessarily always agree with one another. *Q.E.D.*

Corollary I. There is no individual thing in nature more useful to man than man living in obedience to reason. For the thing most useful to man is that which agrees the most with his nature (Coroll. Prop. 31 of this part), that is, man (as is self-evident). Now man acts absolutely according to the laws of his nature when he lives in obedience to reason (Def. 2 Pt. 3), and only to this extent is he always necessarily in agreement with the nature of another (previous Prop.). Thus, among individual things nothing is more useful to man than man, etc. *Q.E.D.*

Corollary II. People are most useful to each other when each of them seeks particularly what is useful to themselves. For the more each seeks what is useful to themselves and endeavours to preserve themselves, the more they are endowed with virtue (Prop. 20 of this part) or—what is the same thing (Def. 8 of this part)— the more they are endowed with the power to act according to the laws of their own nature, that is, to live in obedience to reason (Prop. 3 Pt. 3). Now people agree the most in nature when they live in obedience to reason (previous Prop.); therefore, they will be most useful to one another when each of them seeks particularly what is useful to themselves (previous Coroll.). *Q.E.D.*

Scholium. What we have just shown is attested by experience itself through so many and so shiny examples that nearly everyone repeats the saying: "Man is a God to man." And yet rarely do people live in obedience to reason, but things are so ordered among them that they are generally envious and troublesome to one another. Nevertheless, they are scarcely able to lead a solitary life, so that the definition of man as a social animal has met with general assent; and as a matter of fact, people do derive from social life much more convenience than injury. Let satirists then laugh their fill at human affairs, let theologians rail against them, and let misanthropes praise to their utmost the life of untutored rusticity and heap contempt on humans and praises on beasts; they will nonetheless find that people can have their needs met much more easily through mutual help and that only by uniting their forces can they escape from the dangers that beset them on every side, not to say how much more excellent and worthy of our knowledge it is to study the actions of humans than those of beasts. But I will treat of this at greater length elsewhere.

PROP. XXXVI. *The highest good of those who follow virtue is common to all and all can equally delight therein.*

Proof. To act virtuously is to act in obedience to reason (Prop. 24 of this part), and whatever we endeavour to do in obedience to reason is to understand (Prop. 26). Therefore, the highest good for those who follow after virtue is to know God (Prop. 28 of this part), that is, a good that is common to all people and can be possessed by all equally in so far as they are of the same nature (Prop. 47 Pt. 2 with Schol.). *Q.E.D.*

Scholium. Someone may ask how it would be if the highest good of those who follow virtue were not common to all? Would it not follow, then, as it did above (see Prop. 34 of this part), that people who live in obedience to reason—that is, people in so far as they agree in nature (Prop. 35)—would be opposed to each other? To this person let it be answered that it follows not accidentally but from the very nature of reason that man's highest good is common to all, namely because it is deduced from man's very essence in so far as it is defined by reason, and because a human being could neither exist nor be conceived without the power to delight in this highest good. For it belongs to the essence of the human mind to have adequate knowledge of God's eternal and infinite essence (Prop. 47 Pt. 2).

> Spinoza responds to this natural objection in a characteristic way. Namely, he argues that what is actual is necessary. There is no other way things could be. So the highest good of humanity is necessarily something that can be shared. To imagine something else is to imagine a logical impossibility.

PROP. XXXVII. *The good that all who follow virtue desire for themselves they will also desire for all other people, the more so the greater their knowledge of God.*

Proof. People are most useful to their fellow humans in so far as they live in obedience to reason (Coroll. 1 Prop. 35 of this part);

therefore, in obedience to reason we will necessarily endeavour to make it so that people live in obedience to reason (Prop. 19). Now the good that everyone, in so far as they are guided by reason—in other words, follow virtue (Prop. 24 of this part)—desires for themselves is to understand (Prop. 24); therefore, the good that each follower of virtue seeks for themselves they will desire for others too. Further, desire, in so far as it relates to the mind, is the very essence of the mind (Def. of the affects, 1); now the essence of the mind consists in knowledge (Prop. 11 Pt. 2), which involves the knowledge of God (Prop. 47 Pt. 2) and can neither exist nor be conceived without it (Prop. 15 Pt. 1). Consequently, the greater the knowledge of God that the mind's essence involves, the greater will be the desire with which the follower of virtue will wish another to possess that which they seek as good for themselves. *Q.E.D.*

Another Proof. The good that someone desires for themselves and loves they will love more constantly if they see that others love it also (Prop. 31 Pt. 3); they will therefore endeavour to make others love it too (Coroll. same Prop.). Also, as the good in question is common to all and all can delight in it (previous Prop.), one will endeavour to make it so that everybody delights in it (by the same reasoning), the more so the greater their own enjoyment of the good (Prop. 37 Pt. 3).

Spinoza now outlines his political views, which are more fully developed in the *Theological-Political Treatise* and the *Political Treatise*.

Scholium I. Anyone who merely out of affect endeavours to cause everyone else to love what they themselves love and to make the rest of the world live according to their own preference acts solely on impulse and is, therefore, loathsome, especially to those who like something different and, accordingly, strive and endeavour, by a similar impulse, to make everybody else live in accordance with their preferences instead. Further, as the highest good sought by people under the guidance of affect is often such that it can only be possessed by a single individual, those who love it are not consistent in their intentions but, while they delight in singing the praises of what they love, fear to be believed. Those, on the other hand, who endeavour to lead other people by reason do not act on impulse but kindly and benevolently, and their intentions are always consistent. Also, whatever we desire and do of which we are the cause in so far as we possess the idea of God—that is, know God—I set it down to *religion* (*religio*). The desire of doing good engendered by our living according to reason I call *piety* (*pietas*). Further, the desire on account of which somebody who lives according to reason is bound to associate others with themselves in friendship I call *honour* (*honestas*); by *honourable* (*honestum*) I mean what is praised by those who live according to reason, and by *base* (*turpe*) I mean that which runs counter to the gaining of friendship.

> Here Spinoza attempts to appropriate the common language of his culture while assigning it a different meaning. For example, the idea of religion, for Spinoza, is just acting from one's own essence, which is just acting itself. So eating when hungry is part of religion. This technique of appropriating the language of his society is common also in his earlier book, the *Theological-Political Treatise* (1670).

In addition, I have shown what are the foundations of a state. Also, the difference between true virtue and powerlessness can easily be gathered from what I have said, namely that true virtue is nothing other than living in accordance with reason; consequently, powerlessness is nothing but man's allowing himself to be led by things external to himself and to be determined by them to act in a manner demanded by the general constitution of the external things rather than in what is demanded by his own nature considered solely in itself. Such are the matters I promised to demonstrate in Prop. 18 of this part. From them it is plain that the law against the slaughtering of animals is founded rather on vain superstition and feminine pity than on sound reason. The rational quest of what is useful to us teaches us to associate ourselves with our fellow human beings, but not with beasts or things whose nature is different from human nature; on the contrary, we have the same rights in respect to them as they have in respect to us. Nay, as everyone's right is defined by their virtue, or power, humans have far greater rights over beasts than beasts do over humans. Still, I do not deny that beasts feel; what I deny is that because of it we ought to refrain from seeking our own advantage and using them as we please, treating them in the way that best suits us, since they do not agree with us in nature and their affects are naturally different from the human ones (Schol. Prop. 57 Pt. 3). It remains for me to explain the meaning of 'just' and 'unjust', 'sin' and 'merit'. On these points see the following Schol.

Spinoza argues in both the *Theological-Political Treatise,* and his late work, the *Political Treatise,* that right and power are coextensive. So if someone has the power to do it, and believes it to be in their own best interest, then one has the right to do it. If one is acting from reason, then the act really is in the person's best interest; if acting from affect, then it's a matter of chance whether the act is really in the person's best interest. Given that everything is necessary, according to Spinoza, the sense of 'right' here cannot be identical to our ordinary sense of moral right.

Some of these claims may strike a modern reader as quite problematic. It is useful to be clear about why, for example, Spinoza thinks persons have rights over animals, and do not concern themselves with what is good for animals, over what is good for persons. In this account, it is more than just unnecessary to concern oneself about what is good for animals; it is actually problematic to do so. Insofar as "beasts" are different from persons, what is good for them will be in conflict with what is good for persons. This must be so, since common goods exist insofar as things have common natures. Thus, to act in support of the animal's good is to act in opposition of one's own nature. This is irrational and hence not virtuous.

Scholium II. In the Appendix to Part 1 I promised to explain praise and blame, merit and sin, justice and injustice. Concerning praise and blame, I have discussed them in Schol. Prop. 29 Pt. 3. The time has now come to treat of the remaining terms. First, however, I must say a few words concerning *man's natural* (naturalis) *and social* (civilis) *state.*

Every human being exists by sovereign natural right and, consequently, by sovereign natural right each performs those actions that follow from the necessity of their nature. Therefore, by sovereign natural right everyone judges what is good and what is bad, provides for their own advantage according to their own disposition (Prop. 19 and 20 of this part), avenges the wrongs they have suffered (Coroll. 2 Prop. 40 Pt. 3), and endeavours to preserve what they love and to destroy what they hate (Prop. 28 Pt. 3). Now if human beings lived under the guidance of reason, everyone would hold on to this right without harming anyone else (Coroll. 1 Prop. 35 of this part).

One may wonder how we could avenge wrongs, and destroy what we hate, without harming anyone else. But on Spinoza's hypothesis, everyone is acting solely from reason (an impossibility). Thus, there are no wrongs, because everyone is acting in accord. In this world, the only things a person could hate would be things not like themselves.

However, since they are subject to their affects (Coroll. Prop. 4 of this part), which far surpass human power or virtue (Prop. 6), they are often drawn in different directions (Prop. 33) and are opposed to each other (Prop. 34), all while needing mutual help (Schol. Prop. 35). Thus, for people to be able to live in harmony and help one another, it is necessary for them to waive their natural right and give each other security that they will refrain from all actions that can injure others. The way in which this goal can be attained—that is, how people, who are necessarily subject to their affects (Coroll. Prop. 4), inconstant, and diverse (Prop. 33), should be able to give each other security and feel mutual trust—is evident from Prop. 7 of this part and Prop. 39 Pt. 3: an affect can only be restrained by another affect stronger than and contrary to the one to be restrained, and everybody refrains from doing harm through fear of a greater harm to themselves. On this law society (*societas*) can be established, so long as it claims as its own the right possessed by everyone to avenge misdeeds and pass judgment on good and evil; consequently, society must also possesses the authority to dictate a general way of living, to pass laws, and to have their respect guaranteed not by reason, which is unable to restrain the affects (Schol. Prop. 17 of this part), but by threats. Such a society established with laws and the authority to preserve itself is called a 'state' (*civitas*), and those who are protected by its law are called 'citizens' (*cives*). From this we can readily understand that in the state of nature there is nothing that is good or bad by universal consent, for everyone who is in the state of nature thinks solely of their own advantage and decides what is good or bad according to their own disposition and with reference only to their individual advantage, being bound by no law to accommodate anyone besides themselves. In the state of nature, therefore, sin (*peccatum*) is inconceivable; it can only exist in the social state, where good and evil are pronounced on by common consent and where everyone is bound to obey the state. Sin, then, is nothing but disobedience, which is therefore punished solely by the law of the state; obedience, on the other hand, is accredited to the citizen as merit, since by the very fact of this obedience they are deemed deserving of enjoying the advantages provided by the state. Also, in the state of nature no one is the owner of anything by common consent, nor is there anything in nature that can be said to belong to one person rather than another: all things are common to all. Hence, in the state of nature we can conceive of no wish to give to each their own or to deprive anybody of something that belongs to them; in other words, there is nothing in the state of nature that can be called 'just' or 'unjust'. Such ideas are possible only in the social state, where it is decreed by common consent what belongs to one person and what to another. From all these considerations it is evident that justice and injustice, sin and merit, are extrinsic notions, not attributes that display the nature of the mind. But enough on this topic.

> Spinoza's views here are quite similar to Hobbes's, with some notable differences. While not developed here, Spinoza sees the move from a state of nature to a social compact as a move from bondage to freedom. So, whereas for Hobbes, one is required to give up freedom in order to gain the security of the state, Spinoza does not require any renunciation of freedom, because we are not free in a state of nature. Instead, the state of nature is so chaotic that the affects are constantly aroused, making us unfree. Once the state is formed, people become more rational by obeying the law, and so everyone's freedom is enhanced. See the *Theological-Political Treatise*, Chapter 16, for more on this subject.

PROP. XXXVIII. *Whatever disposes the human body so as to make it capable of being affected in an increased number of ways or what makes it capable of affecting external bodies in an increased number of ways is useful to man, the more so the more capable it renders the body of being affected or affecting other bodies in an increased number of ways. Conversely, whatever makes the body less capable in this respect is harmful.*

Proof. Whatever thus increases the capabilities of the body increases also the mind's capability of perception (Prop. 14 Pt. 2); therefore, whatever thus disposes the body and renders it capable of such things is necessarily good, that is, useful (Prop. 26 and 27 of this part), the more so the more capable it can make the body in this respect. Conversely, something is harmful if it makes the body less capable in this respect (same Prop. 14 Pt. 2 in reverse and Prop. 26 and 27 of this part). *Q.E.D.*

> The term 'capacity' is unfortunate here because Spinoza's official view is that there are no capacities, only individual acts. So there is no capacity to understand, properly speaking, only individual acts of understanding. But this proposition can fit those claims if we take

capacity to mean something like "the number of ways of acting so long as the essence is maintained."

PROP. XXXIX. *Whatever brings about the preservation of the proportion of motion and rest that the parts of the human body have to one another is good; conversely, something is bad if it causes the parts of the human body to have a different mutual proportion of motion and rest.*

Proof. The human body needs many other bodies for its preservation (Post. 4 Pt. 2). Now what constitutes the form of a human body is the fact that its parts share their movement with one another in a certain fixed proportion (see Def. before Lemma 4 after Prop. 13 Pt. 2). Thus, anything that brings about the preservation of the proportion between motion and rest that the parts of the human body mutually possess preserves the form of the human body; consequently, it makes the human body capable of being affected in many ways and of affecting external bodies in many ways (Post. 3 and 6 Pt. 2); therefore, it is good (previous Prop.). Further, anything that causes the parts of the human body to have another proportion of motion and rest causes the human body to assume another form (same Def. Pt. 2), in other words, to be destroyed (which is self-evident, and which we pointed out in the Preface to this Part towards the end) and, consequently, totally incapable of being affected in an increased numbers of ways; therefore, it is bad (previous Prop.). *Q.E.D.*

Scholium. The extent to which such causes can injure or be of service to the mind will be explained in the Fifth Part. But here it should be noted that I consider a body to undergo death when its parts are so disposed as to have a different mutual proportion of motion and rest. For I do not venture to deny that a human body, while keeping the circulation of the blood and other properties that are thought to constitute the life of a body, can nonetheless be changed into another nature totally different from its own. There is indeed no reason that compels me to maintain that a body does not die unless it becomes a corpse; nay, experience itself would seem to point to the opposite conclusion. It sometimes happens that someone undergoes such changes that I can hardly call them the same person, as in the case of a certain Spanish poet I have heard about, who had fallen ill and, though he recovered from it, remained so oblivious of his past life that he would not believe that the plays and tragedies he had written were his own; indeed, he might have been taken for a grown-up infant if he had also forgotten his native tongue.[1] And if this story seems incredible, what should we say of infants themselves? A person of mature age deems an infant's nature so unlike their own that they would never be persuaded that they were once an infant, too, except by the analogy of other people. However, I prefer to drop such questions halfway through lest I give ground to the superstitious for raising new issues.

> It is interesting to try to guess which superstitions Spinoza has in mind here. Maybe something related to an immortal soul that constitutes the identity of a person. This passage is interesting, however, because it seems to suggest that there are individual essences as well as species-level essences. So not only does humanity exist as a given "proportion of motion and rest," but each individual has a particular way of meeting that "proportion of motion and rest," and so seems to have an individual essence. Given Spinoza's stated nominalism, it's somewhat difficult to make sense of this claim.

PROP. XL. *Anything that is advantageous to general human society, that is, causes people to live together in harmony, is useful; on the other hand, anything that brings discord into a state is bad.*

Proof. Whatever causes people to live in harmony also causes them to live according to reason (Prop. 35 of this part) and is therefore good (Prop. 26 and 27). Conversely, anything that brings about discord is bad (by the same reasoning). *Q.E.D.*

PROP. XLI. *Joy is, in itself, not bad but good; sadness, on the other hand, is bad in itself.*

Proof. Joy is an affect by which the body's power of action is increased or helped, whereas sadness is an affect by which the body's power of action is diminished or constrained (Prop. 11 Pt. 3 with Schol.). Thus, joy is in itself good (Prop. 38 of this part), etc. *Q.E.D.*

PROP. XLII. *Merriment cannot be excessive, but is always good; melancholy, on the other hand, is always bad.*

Proof. Merriment (see its Def. in Schol. Prop. 11 Pt. 3) is joy which, in so far as it relates to the body, consists in all parts of the

---

1 *Infans* in Latin means precisely "not speaking" (*in + fari*). (D.A.)

body being affected equally; that is, the body's power of action is increased or aided in such a manner that the several parts maintain their former proportion of motion and rest (same Prop.). Thus, merriment is always good and cannot be excessive (Prop. 39 of this part). Melancholy (see its Def. in the same Schol. Prop. 11 Pt. 3), on the other hand, is sadness that, in so far as it relates to the body, consists in the absolute decrease or hindrance of the body's power of action; therefore, it is always bad (Prop. 38 of this part). *Q.E.D.*

PROP. XLIII. *Stimulation can be excessive and bad; pain, on the other hand, can be good in so far as stimulation, or joy, is bad.*

Proof. Stimulation is joy that, in so far as it relates to the body, consists in one or some of its parts being affected more than the rest (see its Def. in Schol. Prop. 11 Pt. 3). This affect can be powerful enough to overcome other actions of the body (Prop. 6 of this part) and remain obstinately attached to it, thus making it incapable of being affected in a very many other ways; consequently, it can be bad (Prop. 38 of this part). Further, pain, which on the contrary is a form of sadness, cannot be good if considered in itself (Prop. 41). However, as its force and increase is defined by the power of an external cause compared to our own (Prop. 5), we can conceive of infinite degrees and modes of strength in this affect (Prop. 3); we can therefore conceive of it as being such as to be able to restrain stimulation so that it does not become excessive and to this extent hinder the body's capabilities (see the first part of this Proof). Thus, to this extent it will be good. *Q.E.D.*

So if a certain joy or pain is related only to one part of the body, then whether that is good for the whole is determined by how it alters the overall proportion of motion and rest.

PROP. XLIV. *Love and desire can be excessive.*

Proof. Love is joy accompanied by the idea of an external cause (Def. of affects, 6); consequently, stimulation accompanied by the idea of an external cause is love (Schol. 11 Pt. 3). Hence, love may be excessive (previous Prop.). Further, desire is stronger the stronger the affect from which it arises (Prop. 37 Pt. 3). Thus, as an affect can overcome all the rest of one's actions (Prop. 6 of this part), so desire arising from that very affect can overcome all other desires, too, and thus become excessive in just the same way that we showed in the last Proposition stimulation can become. *Q.E.D.*

Scholium. Merriment, which I have stated to be good, can be conceived more easily than it can be observed. For the affects by which we are daily assailed generally relate to some part of the body which is affected more than the rest; hence, the affects are generally excessive and fix the mind in the contemplation of one object to such an extent that it is unable to think of others; and although people are subject to many affects—so that very few are found who are always assailed by one and the same—there are cases where one and the same affect remains obstinately fixed. We sometimes see people so absorbed by one object that, although it is not present, they think they have it before them. When this is the case with somebody who is not asleep, we say that they are delirious or mad; nor do we regard as any less mad those who are inflamed with love and dream all night and all day about nothing but a lover or prostitute: they are usually the laughing-stock of others. But when a miser thinks of nothing but gain or money, or when an ambitious person thinks of nothing but glory, etc., they are not reckoned to be mad, because they are generally obnoxious and are thought worthy of hatred. In truth, however, greed, ambition, lust, etc. are forms of madness, although they are not generally reckoned among the diseases.

PROP. XLV. *Hatred can never be good.*

Proof. When we hate someone, we endeavour to destroy them (Prop. 39 Pt. 3); that is, we endeavour to do something that is bad (Prop. 37 of this part). Therefore, etc. *Q.E.D.*

Scholium. Please note that here and in what follows I mean by 'hatred' only hatred towards people.

Corollary I. Envy, derision, contempt, anger, revenge, and all the other affects that relate to hatred or arise from it are bad. This is also evident from Prop. 39 Pt. 3 and Prop. 37 of this part.

Corollary II. Whatever we desire on account of being affected with hatred is base and, in a state, unjust. This is also evident from

Prop. 39 Pt. 3 and from the definitions of 'base' and 'unjust' in Schol. Prop. 37 of this part.

Scholium. Between derision (which I have stated to be bad in Coroll. 1) and laughter I recognize a great difference. For laughter, as well as jokes, is merely joy; therefore, so long as it is not excessive, it is in itself good (Prop. 41 of this part). Assuredly, nothing forbids man to enjoy himself save grim and gloomy superstition. For why should it be more acceptable to satiate one's hunger and thirst than to drive away one's melancholy? I reason and have convinced myself as follows: No deity nor anyone else, save the envious, takes pleasure in my powerlessness and discomfort or counts as virtue the tears, sobs, fear, and other such things that are signs of the powerlessness of my mind; on the contrary, the greater the joy with which we are affected, the greater the perfection to which we pass, that is, the more we must partake of the divine nature.

> Spinoza here seems to have slipped into the vernacular language of his society and seems to be arguing with his religious contemporaries. By 'deity' here, Spinoza does not mean only the one infinite substance but also all of the (according to Spinoza, incoherent) deities of the various religions.

Therefore, to make use of things and enjoy them as much as possible (not to the point of sickness, though, for that would not be enjoyment) is a wise man's attitude. I say it is the attitude of a wise man to refresh and recreate himself with moderate and pleasant food and drink, and also with perfumes, with the pleasantness of flourishing plants, with dress, music, sports games, theatres, and all other such things of which each person can make use without any harm to another. For the human body is composed of very numerous parts of diverse nature, which continuously need new and varied nourishment so that the whole body may be equally capable of performing all the actions that can follow from its nature and, consequently, so that the mind may likewise be capable of understanding many things simultaneously. This choice of lifestyle, then, is the most consistent both with our principles and with general practice; therefore, the one we have mentioned, if any, is the best and to be commended in every way. There is no need for me to set forth the matter more clearly or in more detail.

PROP. XLVI. *If one lives under the guidance of reason, one endeavours, as far as possible, to requite someone else's hatred, anger, contempt, etc., towards oneself with love, that is, generosity.*

Proof. All affects of hatred are bad (Coroll. 1 previous Prop.). Therefore, whoever lives under the guidance of reason will endeavour, as far as possible, to avoid being assailed by affects of hatred (Prop. 19 of this part); consequently, they will also endeavour to prevent others from being acted upon by those same affects (Prop. 37). Now hatred is increased by being reciprocated and can, conversely, be quenched by love (Prop. 43 Pt. 3), so that hatred can change into love (Prop. 44 Pt. 3). Thus, whoever lives under the guidance of reason will endeavour to requite someone else's hatred, etc., with love, that is, with generosity (see its Def. in Schol. Prop. 59 Pt. 3). *Q.E.D.*

Scholium. Anyone who chooses to avenge wrongs with reciprocal hatred is certain to live a wretched life. Someone who, on the other hand, strives to conquer hatred with love certainly fights their battle with joy and confidence; they withstand many as easily as one and have very little need of fortune's aid. And those whom they defeat yield joyfully, not through lack of strength but through increase thereof. All these consequences follow so plainly from the mere definitions of 'love' and 'intellect' that there is no need to demonstrate them one by one.

PROP. XLVII. *Affects of hope and fear cannot in themselves be good.*

Proof. Affects of hope and fear do not exist without sadness. For fear is sadness (Def. of the affects, 13), and hope does not exist without fear (Def. of the affects, Explanation to 12 and 13); therefore, these affects cannot be good in themselves (Prop. 41 of this part), but only in so far as they can restrain excessive joy (Prop. 43). *Q.E.D.*

> It is interesting to note that directly after endorsing one influential Christian idea (to love our enemies), Spinoza then rejects another (that hope is a virtue).

Scholium. We may add that these affects show a defect of knowledge and powerlessness of the mind; and for the same reason confidence, despair, delight, and remorse too are signs of a powerless mind. For although confidence and delight are affects of joy, they nevertheless imply a preceding sadness, namely hope and fear. Thus, the more we endeavour to live a life guided by reason, the more we endeavour to depend less on hope, to free ourselves from fear, to dominate fortune as far as we can, and to direct our actions by the sure counsels of reason.

PROP. XLVIII. *The affects of partiality and scorn are always bad.*

Proof. These affects are repugnant to reason (see Def. of the affects, 21 and 22); therefore, they are bad (Prop. 26 and 27 of this part). *Q.E.D.*

PROP. XLIX. *Partiality is apt to make the person at whom it is directed prideful.*

Proof. If we see that someone thinks too highly of us out of love, we will easily glory (Schol. Prop. 41 Pt. 3), in other words, be affected with joy (Def. of the affects, 30), and we will readily believe the good attributed to us (Prop. 25 Pt. 3). Therefore, we will think too highly of ourselves out of self-love; in other words, we will easily become prideful (Def. of the affects, 28). *Q.E.D.*

PROP. L. *Pity is, in somebody who lives under the guidance of reason, in itself bad and useless.*

Proof. Pity is sadness (Def. of the affects, 18); thus, it is in itself bad (Prop. 41 of this part). The good effect that follows, namely our endeavour to free the person we pity from misery (Coroll. 3 Prop. 27 Pt. 3), is an action that we desire to do solely because it is dictated by reason (Prop. 37 of this part). Now it is only because of the dictates of reason that we are able to do the things that we know for certain to be good (Prop. 27); thus, in someone who lives under the guidance of reason, pity is in itself bad and useless. *Q.E.D.*

Corollary. It follows that anyone who lives under the guidance of reason endeavours, as much as they can, to avoid being touched by pity.

Scholium. Anybody who rightly realizes that all things follow from the necessity of the divine nature and come to pass in accordance with the eternal laws and rules of nature will not find anything worthy of hatred, laughter, or contempt, nor will they pity anyone, but they will endeavour *to act right*, as the saying goes, and *to rejoice* to the utmost extent of human virtue. We may add that somebody who is easily touched by an affect of pity and is moved by another's sorrow or tears, often does something they afterwards regret, partly because we do nothing out of affect which we know for sure is good, partly because we are easily deceived by false tears. I am in this place expressly speaking of someone who lives under the guidance of reason. For someone who is moved to help others neither by reason nor by compassion is rightly regarded as inhuman, for they seem unlike a human being <or to have discarded all humanity> (Prop. 27 Pt. 3).

PROP. LI. *Approval is not repugnant to reason, but can agree with it and arise from it.*

Proof. Approval is love towards one who has done good to another (Def. of the affects, 19); it can therefore relate to the mind in so far as the latter is said to act (Prop. 59 Pt. 3), that is, in so far as it understands (Prop. 3 Pt. 3). Consequently, it is in agreement with reason, etc. *Q.E.D.*

Another Proof. Whoever lives under the guidance of reason desires for others the good they seek for themselves (Prop. 37 of this part). Thus, from seeing someone doing good to another, their own endeavour to do good is aided; in other words, they will rejoice (Schol. Prop. 11 Pt. 3), which will be accompanied by the idea of the person who has done good to another (according to our hypothesis); consequently, they will approve of that person. *Q.E.D.*

Scholium. Indignation as we defined it (Def. of the affects, 20) is necessarily bad (Prop. 45 of this part); one should however note that when the sovereign power, being swayed by a desire to keep the peace, punishes a citizen who has injured another, I do not mean to say that it is indignant with the criminal, for it punishes them not because it is prompted by hatred to ruin them but because it is led by a sense of duty.

PROP. LII. *Self-contentment can arise from reason, and only that self-contentment which arises from reason is the highest that can exist.*

Proof. Self-contentment is joy arising from one's contemplation of oneself and one's own power of action (Def. of the affects, 25). Now somebody's true power of action, or virtue, is reason itself (Prop. 3 Pt. 3), which they clearly and distinctly contemplate (Prop. 40 and 43 Pt. 2); therefore, self-contentment arises from reason. Further, when someone is contemplating themselves, they perceive nothing clearly and distinctly—that is, adequately—save such things as follow from their power of action (Def. 2 Pt. 3), that is, from their power of understanding (Prop. 3 Pt. 3). Thus, the highest possible self-contentment arises from such contemplation alone. *Q.E.D.*

> There is a direct parallel here between the highest form of self-contentment (the contemplation of one's power), and our highest blessedness, as defined later in this work (the intellectual love of God).

Scholium. Self-contentment is truly the highest goal for which we can hope. For no one endeavours to preserve their being for the sake of any further goal (as we showed in Prop. 25 of this part). Also, as this self-contentment is more and more fostered and strengthened by praise (Coroll. 53 Pt. 3) and, conversely, is more and more disturbed by blame (Coroll. Prop. 55 Pt. 3), we are led chiefly by glory, and life under disgrace is almost unbearable.

PROP. LIII. *Humility is not a virtue, that is, it does not arise from reason.*

Proof. Humility is sadness arising from contemplating one's own powerlessness (Def. of the affects, 26). But in so far as one knows oneself by true reason, one is posited to understand one's own essence, that is, power (Prop. 7 Pt. 3). Therefore, if someone who is self-contemplating perceives any powerlessness in themselves, it is not because they understand themselves, but because their power of action is restrained (as we showed in Prop. 55 Pt. 3). Now if we posit that somebody perceives their own powerlessness by virtue of understanding something more powerful than themselves, by the knowledge of which they determine their own power of action, we are conceiving nothing other than that person understanding themselves distinctly, that is, their power of action being aided (Prop. 26 of this part). Thus, humility, that is, the sadness that arises from someone's contemplating their own powerlessness, does not arise from true contemplation—in other words, reason—and is not a virtue but a passion. *Q.E.D.*

PROP. LIV. *Repentance is not a virtue, that is, does not arise from reason, but whoever repents of an action is doubly wretched, that is, powerless.*

Proof. The first part of this Prop. is proved like the foregoing one. The second part is proved from the mere definition of the affect in question (Def. of the affects, 27). For that person first allows themselves to be overcome by an evil desire, then by sadness.

> In the last few propositions, Spinoza has rejected core Christian moral teaching; namely, he argues that pity for others, humility, and repentance are all bad. By contrast, seeking approval and contemplating our own strengths is good, so long as we don't go so far as to have a distorted understanding of reality. But then he modifies his view ...

Scholium. Since people seldom live under the guidance of reason, these two affects, humility and repentance, as well as fear and hope, bring more good than harm; hence, since we must sin, we had better sin in that direction. For if people who are powerless in mind were all equally prideful, were ashamed of nothing, and feared nothing—how, then, could they be joined together and constrained by bonds? The crowd instills fear when it is not in fear itself; hence, we need not wonder that the prophets, who provided for the good not of a few but of all, so strenuously commended humility, repentance, and reverence. Indeed, those who are subject to these affects can be led much more easily than others to eventually live under the guidance of reason, that is, to become free and enjoy the life of the blessed.

PROP. LV. *Extreme pride or self-abasement is extreme ignorance of self.*

Proof. This is evident from Def. of the affects, 28 and 29.

PROP. LVI. *Extreme pride or self-abasement indicates extreme powerlessness of the mind.*

Proof. The first foundation of virtue is the preservation of one's being (Coroll. Prop. 22 of this part) under the guidance of reason (Prop. 24). Therefore, whoever is ignorant of themselves is ignorant of the foundation of all virtues and, consequently, of all virtues. Further, to act virtuously is merely to act under the guidance of reason (Prop. 24); and someone who acts under the guidance of reason must necessarily know that they so act (Prop. 43 Pt. 2). Therefore, anyone who is in extreme ignorance of themselves—and, consequently, of all virtues (as we have just shown)—acts least in obedience to virtue; in other words, they are mentally most powerless (Def. 8 in this part). Thus, extreme pride or self-abasement indicates extreme powerlessness of the mind (previous Prop.). *Q.E.D.*

Corollary. Hence it most clearly follows that the prideful and the self-abased are the most subject to the affects.

Scholium. Yet self-abasement can be more easily corrected than pride, for the latter is an affect of joy whereas the former is one of sadness, so that the latter is stronger than the former (Prop. 18 of this part).

PROP. LVII. *The prideful loves the company of parasites—in other words, of flatterers—but hates that of generous people.*

Proof. Pride is joy arising from a person's over-estimation of themselves (Def. of the affects, 28 and 6). The prideful will endeavour to foster this opinion as much as they can (Schol. Prop. 13 Pt. 3); they will therefore love the company of flatterers or parasites (whose character is too well known to need defining here) and avoid the company of the generous, who estimate them truthfully. *Q.E.D.*

Scholium. It would be too long a task to enumerate here all the evil results of pride, seeing as the proud are subject to all the affects—to none of them, however, less than the affects of love and mercifulness. But I cannot pass over in silence the fact that one may be called 'prideful' for thinking too little of other people; thus, pride in this sense must be defined as joy arising from the false opinion of somebody who considers themselves superior to all others. The self-abasement opposite to this sort of pride would have to be defined as sadness that arises from the false opinion of someone who sees themselves as inferior to all others. And if we posit this, we can easily understand that the prideful is necessarily envious (Schol. Prop. 55 Pt. 3) and hates those people the most who are praised the most for their virtues; that the prideful's hatred is hard to overcome through love or favors (see Schol. Prop. 41 Pt. 3); and that such people only enjoy the presence of those who cater to their powerless mind and make them insane instead of merely foolish.

Although self-abasement is the affect contrary to pride, the self-abased is closest to the prideful. For since their sadness arises from the fact that they judge their own powerlessness based on other people's power, or virtue, their sadness will be alleviated—in other words, they will rejoice—if their imagination is busy contemplating other people's faults; hence comes the saying: "The unhappy are comforted by finding fellow sufferers."[1] Conversely, they will be saddened to the extent that they think themselves inferior to others; this is why nobody is so prone to envy as the self-abased; these endeavour more than anyone else to observe people's actions with a view to fault-finding rather than correction and, finally, they praise only self-abasement and glory therein—in such a way, however, as to still appear self-abased. These effects follow as necessarily from that affect as it follows from the nature of a triangle that its three angles are equal to two right angles.[2] I have already said that I call these and similar affects 'bad' solely with respect to what is useful to man. The laws of nature, however, refer to nature's general order, of which man is a part. I have decided to mention this, in passing, lest anyone think that I am here setting forth the faults and irrational deeds of human beings rather than nature and the properties of things. For as I said in the preface to Part 3, I regard human affects and their properties as on the same footing with other natural phenomena. And human affects no doubt point to the power and ingenuity, if not of human beings, of nature no less than other things that we wonder at and which we enjoy contemplating. Now, however, I go on to note about the affects of those elements that bring advantage to people or damage them.

This last sentence is interesting because it gives us a sense of the kind of normativity that Spinoza is concerned with in this book. Since everything is determined by logical necessity, Spinoza cannot be advo-

---

1 In other words, "misery seeks company." (D.A.)
2 See Schol. Prop. 17 Pt. 1 and p. 50, n. 1. (D.A.)

cating that we choose to behave in different ways. Instead, he is here only pointing out what is helpful and harmful without assigning blame (a concept that seems most naturally to be based on the ability to do otherwise). Nevertheless, as we see above, Spinoza also lapses into a moralizing tone, and seems to struggle to maintain his strict objectivity. It is also interesting to note that this is one of the times when the most important points are made in Scholia rather than in the propositions themselves. Some have interpreted Spinoza here as having written two books which are then intertwined: a geometrical demonstration and a more emotional and judgmental commentary. The tone of the two different types of passages is notable.

PROP. LVIII. *Glory is not repugnant to reason, but can arise from it.*

Proof. This is evident from Def. of the affects, 30, and also from the definition of an honourable person that you can find in Schol. 1 Prop. 37 of this part.

Scholium. What is known as vainglory (*vana gloria*) is self-contentment fostered only by the opinion of the populace; when this good opinion ceases, there ceases also self-contentment itself, that is, the highest good, which everybody loves (Schol. Prop. 52 of this part). Consequently, those who glory in popular approval must, day by day, anxiously strive, act, and try everything in order to retain their reputation. For the populace is variable and inconstant, so that, if a reputation is not kept up, it quickly withers away; indeed, since everyone wishes to catch popular applause for themselves, it easily happens that each tries to repress the fame of others; consequently, as the strife is about that which is regarded as the greatest of all goods, there arises a fierce desire to put one another down in every possible way, and the one who at last comes out victorious glories more in having done harm to others than in having done good to themselves. Thus, this sort of glory—that is, self-contentment—is really vain, since it is really non-existent.

The points to note concerning shame can easily be inferred from what I said on the subject of mercifulness and repentance. I will only add that shame, like pity, though not a virtue, is nonetheless good in so far as it shows that the person who feels shame has the desire to live honourably—in the same way as pain is said to be good in so far as it shows that the injured part is not yet rotten. Therefore, although somebody who is ashamed of having done something is actually sad, they are still more perfect than someone who is shameless and has no desire to live honourably.

Such are the points which I undertook to remark upon concerning the affects of joy and sadness. As for the desires, they are good or bad in so far as they arise from good or bad affects. However, they are, in truth, all blind in so far as they are engendered in us by affects that are passions (as is evident from what I said in Schol. Prop. 44 of this part) and would be useless if people could easily be induced to live by the guidance of reason only, as I will now briefly show.

PROP. LIX. *All the actions that we are determined to perform by an affect that is a passion we can be determined to perform by reason without affect.*

Proof. To act rationally is nothing but to do those things that follow from the necessity of our nature considered in itself alone (Prop. 3 Pt. 3 and Def. 2 Pt. 3). Now sadness is bad in so far as it diminishes or checks this power of action (Prop. 41 of this part); therefore, we cannot be determined by this affect to do anything we would be unable to do under the guidance of reason. Further, joy is bad only in so far as it hinders one's capability for action (Prop. 41 and 43 of this part); thus, to this extent too we cannot be determined by it to do anything we could not do under the guidance of reason. Lastly, joy, in so far as it is good, is in harmony with reason (for it consists in the fact that one's power of action is increased or aided), and it is not a passion except in so far as someone's power of action is not increased to the point that they adequately conceive of themselves and their actions (Prop. 3 Pt. 3 with Schol.). Therefore, if somebody who is affected with joy were brought to such a state of perfection as to gain an adequate conception of themselves and their actions, they would be equally—nay more—capable of those actions that they are already determined to perform by affects that are passions. Now all affects relate to joy, sadness, or desire (see Def. of the affects, 4, explanation), and desire is nothing other than the very endeavour to act (Def. of the affects, 1); consequently, all the actions that we are determined to perform by an affect that is a passion we can be led to perform by reason alone without affect. Q.E.D.

Another Proof. Any action is called 'bad' in so far as it arises from our being affected with hatred or some other bad affect (see Coroll. 1 Prop. 45 of this part). Now no action, considered in itself alone, is either good or bad (as we pointed out in the Preface to this part), but one and the same action is sometimes good, sometimes bad; thus, we can be led by reason to an action that is sometimes bad, that is, arises from some evil affect (Prop. 19 of this part). *Q.E.D.*

Scholium. An example will help clarify this point. The action of striking, in so far as it is considered physically and in so far as we merely look to the fact that one raises one's arm, clenches one's fist and moves one's whole arm violently downwards, is a virtue that is conceived out of the structure of the human body. If a person, then, moved by anger or hatred, is determined to clench their fist or to move their arm, this is because one and the same action can be associated with any mental images of things (as we showed in Pt. 2); therefore, we can be determined to perform one and the same action by the images of things we conceive confusedly just as well as by those we conceive clearly and distinctly. Hence it is evident that every desire that arises from an affect that is a passion would become useless if people could be guided by reason. Let us now see why we call desire that arises from an affect that is a passion 'blind'.

> The idea of desire arising from an affect may be difficult to grasp, given Spinoza's overall view. One way to see this is that affects increase or decrease some aspect of the body's internal self-maintaining motions. These motions are the bodies striving or endeavoring to exist, that is, desire. So the affective modifications of desire can cause someone to want something that they did not previously want. The smell of the cake makes me want to eat a piece even though I am currently dieting.

PROP. LX. *Desire arising from joy or sadness that relates not to the whole body but only to one or certain parts thereof does not consider the utility of the person as a whole.*

Proof. Let it be posited, for instance, that A, a part of a body, is so strengthened by the power of some external cause that it prevails over the remaining parts (Prop. 6 of this part). A will thus not endeavour to do away with its own strength in order that the other parts of the body may perform their duties, since this would require for it to have a force, or power, to lose its own strength, which is absurd (Prop. 6 Pt. 3). Thus, that part—and, consequently, the mind as well (Prop. 7 and 12 Pt. 3)—will endeavour to preserve that condition; therefore, a desire arising from this kind of affect of joy does not consider the utility of the person as a whole. If we posit, on the other hand, that part A is constrained so that the remaining parts prevail, it can be proved in the same manner that desire arising from sadness does not consider the utility of the person as a whole, either. *Q.E.D.*

Scholium. As joy generally relates to only one part of the body (Schol. Prop. 44 of this part), we generally desire to preserve our being without considering our health as a whole. To this it may be added that the desires that have the strongest hold on us consider the present and not of the future (Coroll. Prop. 9 of this part).

PROP. LXI. *Desire that arises from reason cannot be excessive.*

Proof. Desire, considered absolutely, is the actual essence of man in so far as it is conceived to be in any way determined to do something (Def. of the affects, 1). Hence, desire that arises from reason, that is, is engendered in us in so far as we act (Prop. 3 Pt. 3), is the actual essence, or nature, of man in so far as it is imagined as determined to do those things that are adequately conceived through man's essence only (Def. 2 Pt. 3). Now if such desire could be excessive, human nature considered in itself alone would be able to exceed itself, that is, would have more power than it actually has, which is an obvious contradiction. Therefore, such desire cannot be excessive. *Q.E.D.*

> In other words, since desire, the essence of man, the self-maintaining motions of the body, and reason are all one and the same thing, it makes no sense to say that desire arising from reason is excessive, because that would entail that a thing's essence is somehow "excessive," and that's incoherent.

PROP. LXII. *In so far as the mind conceives of things under the dictates of reason, it is affected equally, whether the idea is of a thing future, past, or present.*

Proof. Anything the mind conceives under the guidance of reason it conceives under the same form of eternity, or necessity (Coroll.

2 Prop. 44 Pt. 2) and is affected with the same certainty (Prop. 43 Pt. 2 with Schol.). Therefore, whether the idea is of a thing future, past, or present, the mind conceives the thing in question out of the same necessity and is affected with the same certitude; and whether the idea is of something future, past, or present, it will nonetheless be equally true (Prop. 41 Pt. 2); that is, it will always possess the same properties as an adequate idea (Def. 4 Pt. 2). Thus, in so far as the mind conceives things under the dictates of reason, it is affected in the same manner whether the idea is of a thing future, past, or present. *Q.E.D.*

> This proposition tells us something about how Spinoza understands time. Since reason considers things as they are, and it considers past, present, and future things equally, that would seem to suggest that Spinoza is an eternalist about time, whereby all modes past, present, and future are equally real and the passage of time is an illusion.

Scholium. If we could possess an adequate knowledge of the duration of things and determine through reason their periods of existence, we would contemplate things future and present with the same affect and the mind would desire as though it were present a good that it conceived as future. Consequently, it would necessarily neglect a lesser good in the present for the sake of a greater good in the future, and would in no way desire something that was good in the present but the cause of some ill in the future, as we shall prove in a moment. However, we can have but a very inadequate knowledge of the duration of things (Prop 31 Pt. 2); and we determine the periods of their existence only through imagination (Schol. Prop. 44 Pt. 2), which is not so powerfully affected by the image of something future as by that of something present. Hence, such true knowledge of good and evil as we possess is merely abstract, or universal, and the judgment we pass on the order of things and the connection of causes with a view to determining what is good or bad for us in the present is rather imaginary than real. Thus, it is no surprise if the desire arising from the knowledge of good and evil in so far as the latter looks into the future is more easily restrained than the desire of things that are agreeable at the present time (cf. Prop. 16 of this part).[1]

---

1 See that Prop. with p. 228, n. 1. (D.A.)

PROP. LXIII. *Anyone who is led by fear and does good in order to escape evil is not led by reason.*

Proof. All the affects that relate to the mind in so far as it acts, in other words, to reason (Prop. 3 Pt. 3), are nothing but affects of joy and desire (Prop. 59 Pt. 3). Therefore, anyone who is led by fear and does good for fear of evil is not led by reason (Def. of the affects, 13). *Q.E.D.*

Scholium. Superstitious people, who know better how to rail at vice than how to teach virtue and who strive not to guide others by reason but to restrain them with fear so that they might flee evil rather than love virtue, have no other goal than to make others as miserable as themselves. Thus, it is no surprise that they are generally troublesome and obnoxious to other people.

Corollary. Desire that springs from reason causes us to seek good directly and shun evil indirectly.

Proof. Desire that springs from reason can only arise from an affect of joy that is not a passion (Prop 59 Pt. 3), that is, from a joy that cannot be excessive (Prop. 61 of this part), and not from sadness. Therefore, this desire springs from the knowledge of good, not of evil (Prop. 8 of this part); hence, under the guidance of reason we seek good directly and shun evil only to this extent. *Q.E.D.*

Scholium. This Corollary may be illustrated by the example of a sick and a healthy person. The sick one eats what they dislike for fear of death; the healthy one, on the other hand, delights in the food and thus gets a better enjoyment out of life than if they were in fear of death and desired directly to avoid it. Similarly, a judge who condemns a criminal to death not out of hatred, anger or the like but out of love for the public well-being is guided solely by reason.

PROP. LXIV. *The knowledge of evil is an inadequate knowledge.*

Proof. The knowledge of evil is sadness itself in so far as we are conscious of it (Prop. 8 of this part). Now sadness is the transition to a lesser perfection (Def. of the affects, 3); therefore, it cannot be understood through man's nature itself (Prop. 6 and 7

Pt. 3). Thus, it is a passion (Def. 2 Pt. 3), thereby depending on inadequate ideas (Prop. 3 Pt. 3); consequently, the knowledge thereof, namely the knowledge of evil, is inadequate (Prop. 29 Pt. 2). *Q.E.D.*

Corollary. It follows that, if the human mind possessed only adequate ideas, it would form no conception of evil.

> There can be no adequate knowledge of what is evil, because evil is always fragmentary and adequate knowledge is not fragmented. An example might help here. Imagine that I am being eaten by a lion. From my limited perspective this is, surely, bad. But that's only because it cannot be understood solely through my own nature. But if we "zoom out" and see the lion and me together, then it no longer looks bad, but merely a change of one mode into another. If we "zoom out" still further and see how the whole ecosystem works, then we see no bad in it, only different interconnected processes. The more adequate our understanding, the less bad things are seen to be.

PROP. LXV. *Under the guidance of reason we will pursue the greater of two goods and the lesser of two evils.*

Proof. A good that prevents our enjoyment of a greater good is in reality an evil; for we apply the terms 'good' and 'bad' to things in so far as we compare them with one another (see Preface to this part). Therefore, evil is in reality a lesser good (by the same reasoning); thus, under the guidance of reason we will desire—that is, seek—only the greater good and the lesser evil (Coroll. Prop. 63 of this part). *Q.E.D.*

Corollary. Under the guidance of reason we will seek the lesser evil as a greater good and shun the lesser good because it is the cause of a greater evil. For the evil that is here called 'the lesser' one is really a good and, conversely, the lesser good is really an evil. Therefore, we will desire the former and shun the latter (Coroll. Prop. 63 of this part). *Q.E.D.*

PROP. LXVI. *Under the guidance of reason we will seek a greater good in the future in preference to a lesser one in the present and a lesser evil in the present in preference to a greater one in the future.*

Proof. If the mind could have an adequate knowledge of things future, it would be affected with the same affect towards something future as towards something present (Prop. 62 of this part).

Therefore, to the extent that we look merely to reason, as in this Proposition we are supposed to do, there is no difference whether the greater good or evil is assumed to be present or future; hence, we may seek a greater good in the future in preference to a lesser good in the present, etc. (Prop. 65). *Q.E.D.*

Corollary. We will under the guidance of reason seek a lesser evil in the present which is the cause of a greater good in the future; and we will shun a lesser good in the present which is the cause of a greater evil in the future. This Corollary is related to the foregoing Prop. as Coroll. Prop. 65 is related to Prop. 65 itself.

Scholium. If these statements are compared to what we have pointed out in this Part up to Prop. 18 concerning the strength of the affects, we will readily see the difference between someone who is led solely by affect or opinion and someone who is led by reason. The former, whether they want to or not, performs actions of which they are utterly ignorant; the latter accommodates no one but themselves and performs only such actions as they know are of primary importance in life and therefore chiefly desire. For this reason I call the former a slave and the latter free, and concerning the latter's disposition and manner of life it will be well to make a few observations.

PROP. LXVII. *A free person thinks of death least of all things; and their wisdom is a meditation not on death but on life.*

Proof. A free person, that is, one who lives exclusively under the guidance of reason, is not led by fear of death (Prop. 63 of this part) but desires directly what is good (Coroll. same Prop.), in other words, desires to act, to live, and to preserve their being on the basis of seeking their own advantage (Prop. 24). Consequently, they think of nothing less than of death, but their wisdom is a meditation on life. *Q.E.D.*

PROP. LXVIII. *If people were born free, they would, so long as they remained free, form no conception of good and evil.*

Proof. I have called 'free' those who are led solely by reason; therefore, anyone who is born free and remains free has only adequate ideas. Thus, they have no conception of evil (Coroll. Prop. 64 of this part) and, consequently, none of good either (as good and evil are correlate concepts). *Q.E.D.*

Spinoza now demonstrates this point with an interpretation of Genesis. This is a good example of Spinoza's "double speak" whereby he uses ordinary religious language to say something that is actually radical and subversive.

Scholium. It is evident from Prop. 4 of this part that the hypothesis of this Proposition is false and cannot be conceived except in so far as we look solely to the nature of man, or rather to God, not in so far as the latter is infinite but only in so far as he is the cause of man's existence. And this and other matters that we have already proved seem to have been signified by Moses[1] in his famous history of the first man. For in that narrative no other power of God is conceived save that by which he created man, that is, the power with which he provided solely for man's advantage. In this regard it is recounted that God forbade man, who was free, from eating of the tree of the knowledge of good and evil and that, as soon as man ate of it, he straightaway feared death rather than desiring to live. Further, it is recounted that when man had found a wife, who was in perfect agreement with his nature, he knew that there could be nothing in nature more useful to him than her, but after he started to believe the beasts to be like himself, he straightaway began imitating their affects (see Prop. 27 Pt. 3) and losing his freedom—freedom that was afterwards recovered by the patriarchs, led by the spirit of Christ, that is, by the idea of God, on which alone depends man's freedom and his desire for others to enjoy the good he desires for himself, as we have shown above (Prop. 37 of this part).

PROP. LXIX. *The virtue[2] of a free person is seen to be just as great in avoiding dangers as in overcoming them.*

Proof. An affect can only be restrained or removed by an affect contrary to itself and stronger than the affect to be restrained (Prop. 7 of this part). Now blind daring and fear are affects that can be conceived as equally great (Prop. 5 and 3); hence, an equally great virtue, or fortitude, of the mind (for whose Def. see

---

1 The traditional author of the first five books of the Old Testament. (D.A.)

2 The original meaning of Latin *virtus* is "courage" or "valor." (D.A.)

Schol. Prop. 59 Pt. 3) is required both to restrain daring and to restrain fear; in other words, a free person avoids dangers as well as strives to overcome them out of the same virtue of the mind (Def. of the affects, 40 and 41). *Q.E.D.*

Corollary. For a free person, therefore, timely retreat is ascribed to great courage just as much as combat is; in other words, a free person chooses retreat out of the same courage, or presence of mind, with which they choose to fight.

Scholium. What courage (*animositas*) is, or what I mean by it, is explained in Schol. Prop. 59 Pt. 3. By 'danger' I mean anything that can be the cause of any ill, such as sadness, hatred, discord, etc.

PROP. LXX. *A free person living among the ignorant strives, as far as they can, to decline their favours.*

Proof. Everyone judges what is good according to their own disposition (Schol. Prop. 39 Pt. 3). Therefore, an ignorant person who has conferred a benefit on another will estimate it according to their own disposition and, if they see it being estimated less highly by the receiver, they will be saddened (Prop. 42 Pt. 3). Now a free person strives to join others to themselves in friendship (Prop. 37 of this part) and does not want to repay their benefits with others of like value because of their affects, but to lead themselves and others by the free decision of reason, and strives to do only such things as they know to be of primary importance. Therefore, a free person, in order not be hated by the ignorant and, at the same time, to follow not the latters' desires but reason alone, will endeavour, as far as they can, to decline their favours. *Q.E.D.*

Scholium. I say *as far as they can*. For although people are ignorant, they are still people, and in cases of necessity they can afford us human aid, the most excellent of all aids. Therefore, it is often necessary to accept favours from them and, consequently, to thank them in the way they wish. As well, we must exercise caution in declining favours in order to avoid the appearance of despising those who bestow them or of being afraid, out of greed, to have to return them, so that, while we are trying to avoid their hatred, we end up offending them. Consequently, in declining favours we must look to the requirements of utility and courtesy.

Reading this passage it is important to remember that Spinoza himself lived a rather solitary life and seems to have only rarely socialized.

PROP. LXXI. *Only free people are fully grateful to one another.*

Proof. Only free people are fully useful to one another, are connected among themselves by the closest bonds of friendship (Prop. 35 of this part with Coroll. 1), and endeavour, with mutual zeal of love, to confer benefits on each other (Prop. 37 of this part). Therefore, only free people are fully grateful to one another (Def. of the affects, 34). *Q.E.D.*

Scholium. The bonds of gratitude that people who are led by blind desire have for one another are generally a bargaining, or rather an enticement, rather than actual gratitude. Moreover, ingratitude is not an affect. Yet it is base, as it mostly shows a person to be affected with excessive hatred, anger, pride, greed, etc. For someone who out of stupidity does not know how to repay gifts is not ungrateful, much less someone who is not moved by the gifts of a prostitute to serve her lust <and lewdness> or by those of a thief to conceal his thefts, or by those of anyone like that. In fact, one shows, conversely, a constant mind when one does not allow oneself to be corrupted by any gifts to the detriment of oneself or the community.

PROP. LXXII. *A free person never acts fraudulently, but always in good faith.*

Proof. If a free person were to do something fraudulently in so far as they are free, they would be doing it following the dictates of reason (for only in this respect do we call them 'free'); consequently, it would be virtuous to act fraudulently (Prop. 24 of this part) and, consequently, it would be more advisable for anybody, in order to preserve their being, to act fraudulently (same Prop.). In other words, it would be more advisable for people to agree in words only but be opposed to each other in fact (as is self-evident), which is absurd (Coroll. Prop. 31 of this part). Thus, a free person, etc. *Q.E.D.*

Scholium. If it be asked: What if one could free oneself from a present danger of death by breaking faith? Would not the principle of self-preservation entail that they must deceive? To this we shall respond in the same way: If reason entails this, it does so for everybody; consequently, it entails that people should not agree to unite their forces and to have common laws except fraudulently, in other words, that they should actually have no common laws at all. But this is absurd.

> Here Spinoza comes close to stating a version of Kant's "categorical imperative," namely, to act only according to those maxims that you can at the same time will to be a universal law.

PROP. LXXIII. *Someone who is guided by reason is more free in a state where they live following the dictates of the community than in solitude, where they obey only themselves.*

Proof. Somebody who is guided by reason is not led to obey by fear (Prop. 63 of this part) but, in so far as they endeavour to preserve their being according to the dictates of reason—that is, in so far as they endeavour to live in freedom (Schol. Prop. 66 of this part)—they desire to take account of the common good (Prop. 37) and, consequently, to live according to the dictates of the community (as we showed in Schol. 2 Prop. 37). Therefore, whoever is guided by reason desires, in order to enjoy greater freedom, to uphold the common laws of the state. *Q.E.D.*

Scholium. These and similar observations which we have made about man's true freedom relate to fortitude, that is, to courage and generosity (Schol. Prop. 59 Pt. 3). I do not think it worthwhile to prove separately all the properties of fortitude; much less need I show that whoever is strong (*fortis*) hates no one, gets angry with no one, envies no one, is indignant with no one, despises no one, and least of all is proud. These claims as well as all those others that have to do with the true way of life and religion are easily proved from Prop. 37 and 46 of this part, namely that hatred should be requited and overcome with love and that everybody who is guided by reason should wish for others to enjoy the good they desire for themselves. To this add what I pointed out in the Schol. Prop. 50 of this part and elsewhere, namely that a strong man has ever first in his thoughts that all things follow from the necessity of the divine nature, and thus anything he deems to be hurtful and evil, as well as anything that seems to him impious, horrible, unjust, and base, assumes that appearance owing to his own disordered, fragmentary, and confused view of things. For this reason, he endeavours above all else to conceive things as they really are and to remove the hindrances to true knowledge, such as hatred, anger, envy, derision, pride, and similar things that I have mentioned above. Thus, he endeavours, as we said before, to do right and to rejoice as much as he can. How far human virtue stretches to attain these things, and what it is able to do, I will show in the following Part.

Here Spinoza provides a helpful summary of some of the most important conclusions from Parts III and IV.

APPENDIX

What I have said in this Part concerning the right way of life is not arranged in such a way as to provide the reader with a quick overview of it, but I have expounded it in a piecemeal fashion, depending on how my points could most easily be deduced from each other. Therefore, I have undertaken to gather those points here and to bring them under general headings.

I. All our endeavours—in other words, desires—follow from the necessity of our nature in such a way that they can be understood either through it alone, as their proximate cause, or in so far as we are a part of nature which cannot be adequately conceived through itself without considering other individual things.

II. Desires that follow from our nature in such a way that they can be understood through it alone are those that relate to the mind in so far as the latter is conceived as consisting of adequate ideas; the other desires, on the other hand, do not relate to the mind except in so far as it conceives things inadequately, and their force and increase must be defined not by human power but by the power of things external to us. Therefore, the former are rightly called actions, the latter passions, for the former always indicate our power, whereas the latter show our powerlessness and fragmentary knowledge.

III. Our actions, in other words, those desires that are defined by man's power, that is, reason, are always good; the others, on the other hand, can be either good or bad.

IV. Thus, in life it is above all useful to perfect the intellect, or reason, as much as we can, and in this alone consists man's highest happiness, or bliss. Indeed, bliss is nothing but the very contentment of the mind that arises from the intuitive knowledge of God. Now perfecting the intellect is nothing other than to understand God, God's attributes, and the actions that follow from the necessity of his nature. For this reason, the ultimate goal of somebody who is led by reason—in other words, their highest desire, through which they seek to control all others—is that by which they are brought to the adequate conception of themselves and of all things within the scope of their intelligence.

> This claim is an important one and will be central to Part V of the book.

V. Therefore, without intelligence there is no rational life, and things are only good in so far as they help us enjoy the life of the mind, which is defined by intelligence. Conversely, we call 'evil' only those things that impair man's ability to perfect his reason and enjoy the rational life.

VI. As, however, all things of which man is the efficient cause are necessarily good, no evil can befall man except through external causes, namely in so far as he is a part of the whole of nature, whose laws human nature is compelled to obey and to which it is forced to conform in nearly infinite ways.

VII. It is impossible for man not to be a part of nature and not to follow its common order; however, if one is among such individuals as agree with one in nature, one's power of action will by this very fact be aided and fostered. If, on the other hand, one is among such individual things as do not agree with one in nature, one will hardly be able to accommodate oneself to them without undergoing a great change oneself.

VIII. Whatever in nature we deem to be evil, that is, capable of impairing our ability to exist and enjoy the rational life, it is permissible to remove in whatever way seems safest; on the other hand, whatever is there that we deem to be good, that is, useful for preserving our being and enjoying the rational life, we are allowed to appropriate for our benefit and make of it any use we want. And absolutely, everyone is allowed, by sovereign right of nature, to do anything they think will advance their own interest.

IX. Nothing can agree with the nature of any given thing more than other individual things of the same species; therefore, for man to preserve his being and enjoy the rational life there is nothing more useful than a human being who is led by reason (see above, 7). Further, as among the existing individual things none is known that is more excellent than a human being who is led by reason, in no way can anyone better display the power of their skill and disposition than in educating people in such a manner that they come at last to live under the dominion of their own reason.

X. In so far as people are turned against each other by envy or any kind of hatred, they are to that extent opposed to each other, and are therefore to be feared the more they surpass in power all others individual things in nature.

XI. Yet minds are not conquered by force, but by love and generosity.

> This claim seems new, and it's not self-evident what Spinoza means by "conquered" here, but he could be referring to the rational man's returning hatred with love.

XII. It is above all useful for human beings to associate their ways of life, to bind themselves with such bonds as are most fitted to gather them all into unity and to do absolutely anything that serves to strengthen friendship.

XIII. To this end, however, skill and watchfulness are needed. For people are diverse (seeing as there are few who live under the guidance of reason), yet generally envious and more prone to revenge than to mercifulness. Thus, no small force of character is required to take everyone as they are and to restrain oneself from imitating the affects of others. But those who snipe at mankind, are more skilled in railing at vice than in teaching virtue, and know how to break people's spirit rather than strengthen it—such people are irksome both to themselves and to everybody else. Thus, many have been driven by excessive impatience of spirit or misguided religious zeal to choose to live among brutes rather than among humans, just as boys or youths who cannot endure the chidings of their parents with an even mind will seek refuge in the military and choose the hardships of war and the orders of a tyrant over the comforts of home and the admonitions of their father, letting themselves be saddled with any burden as long as they may take revenge on their parents.

XIV. Therefore, although people for the most part direct everything according to their own lusts, their being unified in a society brings many more advantages than drawbacks. Therefore, it is better to bear patiently the wrongs they may do one and to strive to promote whatever serves to bring about harmony and friendship.

XV. Those things that beget harmony are such as relate to justice, equity, and honourable living. For people bear unwillingly not only what is unjust or unfair, but also what is considered base or that someone should slight the received customs of society. But in order to win love, those qualities are especially necessary which have regard to religion and piety (cf. Schol. 1 and 2 Prop. 37, Schol. Prop. 46 and Schol. Prop. 73 Pt. 4).

XVI. Further, harmony is often the result of fear, but then it is unsafe. Add that fear arises from the powerlessness of the mind, which is why it does not pertain to the exercise of reason. The same is true of pity, although this latter seems to bear some resemblance to piety.

XVII. Further, people are gained over by liberality, especially those who lack the means to buy what is necessary to sustain life. However, to give aid to every poor person is far beyond the power and the advantage of any private man, for the riches of any private man are wholly inadequate to meet such a call. Also, an individual man's resources are too limited for him to be able to make friends with everybody; hence, providing for the poor is a duty that falls on society as a whole and pertains only to the common advantage.

XVIII. In accepting favours and in returning gratitude, our concern must be wholly different (see Schol. Prop. 70 and Schol. Prop. 71 Pt. 4).

XIX. Further, meretricious love, that is, the lust of generation arising from bodily beauty, and absolutely every sort of love that recognizes as its cause anything save freedom of the mind, readily turns into hate—unless, what is worse, it is a form of madness; and then it is fostered more by discord than by harmony (cf. Schol. Prop. 31 Pt. 3).

XX. As far as marriage is concerned, it is certain that it is in harmony with reason if the desire for physical union is not engendered solely by bodily beauty but also by the love of begetting children and educating them wisely; and also if the love of both, the man and the woman, is not caused solely by bodily beauty but mainly by freedom of the mind.

XXI. Furthermore, flattery begets harmony, but only through the vile offence of slavishness or treachery. Nobody, in fact, is more readily taken in by flattery than proud people who wish to be first but are not.

XXII. There is in self-abasement a spurious appearance of piety and religion. And although self-abasement is the opposite of pride, someone who abases themselves is closest to the proud (see Schol. Prop. 57 Pt. 4).

XXIII. Also, shame brings about harmony only in such matters as cannot be kept secret. Furthermore, as shame is itself a form of sadness, it does not concern the exercise of reason.

XXIV. The remaining affects of sadness towards people are directly opposed to justice, equity, honour, piety, and religion; and although indignation seems to bear a certain resemblance to equity, life is lawless where everyone may pass judgment on another's deeds and vindicate their own or another's rights.

XXV. Moderation (*modestia*), that is, the desire to please people that is determined by reason, relates to piety (as we said in Schol. 1 Prop. 37 Pt. 4). But if it springs from affect, it is ambition, that is, the desire that prompts people, under the false cloak of piety, to often stir up discords and seditions. For somebody who desires to help others either in word or in deed, so that they may together enjoy the highest good, will above all else strive to gain their love, not to instill them with wonder so as to have a school of thought named after oneself, nor to give any cause for envy. Further, in common conversations one will avoid talking of other people's faults and be careful to speak but sparingly of human powerlessness; but one will dwell at length on human virtue, or power, and in which way it can be perfected, in order that people may thus, not out of fear or aversion, but only out of an affect of joy, endeavour to live in obedience to reason as much as they can.

XXVI. Aside from human beings, we know of no particular thing in nature in whose mind we can delight and with which we can associate ourselves in friendship or any sort of fellowship. Therefore, a regard for our advantage does not call on us to preserve whatever there is in nature besides man but teaches us to preserve, destroy or in any way adapt it according to its various utility.

We cannot be friends with our pets.

XXVII. The main utility that we derive from things external to us, besides the experience and knowledge that we acquire from observing them and from transforming them from their present shape into new ones, is the preservation of our body; and from this point of view those things are most useful which can feed and nourish the body in such a way that all of its parts may rightly fulfil their functions. For the more capable the body is of being affected in a great variety of ways and of affecting external bodies in very many ways, the more capable the mind is of thinking (see Prop. 38 and 39 Pt. 4). Now there seem to be very few things of this kind in nature, so that to nourish our body as it requires we must use many foods of diverse nature. For the human body is composed of very many parts of a different nature, which need continual and varied nourishment in order for the whole body to be equally capable of doing everything that can follow from its own nature and, consequently, for the mind to be equally capable of forming many concepts as well.

XXVIII. Now the strength of each individual would hardly suffice to provide these nourishments if people did not lend one another mutual aid. Money, however, has provided us with a token for everything, which is why the mind of the multitude is chiefly engrossed with it: they can hardly imagine any kind of joy unless accompanied with the idea of money as cause.

XXIX. However, this vice belongs only to those who seek money not because they are poor or for the sake of satisfying their needs, but because they have learned the arts of profit, with which they puff themselves up to great splendour. Apart from this, they nourish their bodies out of habit, but scantily, believing that they lose as much of their wealth as they spend on the preservation of their body. But those who know the true use of money and moderate their wealth based solely on their actual needs live content with little.

XXX. As, therefore, those things are good which assist the various parts of the body and enable them to perform their functions and as joy consists in a person's power being helped or increased in so far as they are composed of mind and body, all those things that bring joy are good. Yet since things do not work with the object of giving us joy, their power of action is not regulated to suit our advantage, and, lastly, joy mostly relates specifically to one part of the body, the affects of joy and, consequently, also the desires that arise from them tend for the most part (unless reason and vigilance are applied) to become excessive, which is compounded by the fact that the affects prompt us to pay most regard to what is agreeable in the present, while we cannot estimate things future with an equal affection of the mind (see Schol. Prop. 44 and Schol. Prop. 60 Pt. 4).

XXXI. Superstition, on the other hand, seems to declare all that brings sadness to be good and all that brings joy to be bad. However, as we said above (Schol. Prop. 45 Pt. 4), none but the envious take delight in my powerlessness and trouble. For the greater the joy by which we are affected, the greater the perfection to which we pass and, consequently, the more we partake of God's nature; and joy can never be bad if it is regulated by a true regard for our advantage. On the other hand, whoever is led by fear and does good only to avoid evil is not guided by reason.

XXXII. But human power is extremely limited and is infinitely surpassed by the power of external causes; therefore, we have no absolute power to adapt to our use those things that lie outside of us. Nevertheless, we will bear with an even mind all that happens to us that runs counter to what consideration of our advantage requires so long as we are conscious that we have done our duty, that the power we possess has been insufficient to enable us to avoid those evils, and that we are a part of the whole of nature and follow its order. If we understand this fact clearly and distinctly, that part of us which is defined by intelligence, that is, the better part of us, will be fully content with it and endeavour to persist in such contentment. For in so far as we understand, we cannot desire anything except for what is necessary, nor can we be content with anything at all except for what is true; thus, to the extent that we understand these things correctly, the endeavour of the better part of ourselves agrees with the order of nature as a whole.

In closing Part IV, it is interesting to note here that Spinoza has developed an "ethical" system that would have been largely agreeable to his contemporaries and yet did it in an entirely naturalistic metaphysical system.

End of Part 4.

PART V
OF THE POWER OF THE INTELLECT, OR OF HUMAN FREEDOM

PREFACE

Finally, I pass to the remaining portion of my Ethics, which is concerned with the way, or procedure, that leads to freedom. Thus, in it I will treat of the power of reason, showing how much power it has over the affects, and then what is the nature of the mind's freedom, or bliss; from these things we will be able to see how much more excellent the wise is than the ignorant. The questions, however, how and by what means the intellect must be perfected or through what discipline the body needs to be tended so as to be able to perform its functions correctly, do not belong here: the latter pertains to medicine, the former to logic. Here, therefore, as I have said, I will treat only of the power of the mind, or of reason, and I will above all else show the extent and nature of its control over the affects, with which it can restrain and moderate them. For I have already shown that we do not have absolute control over them. Yet the Stoics thought that they depended absolutely on our will and that we could absolutely govern them. However, they were compelled, by the protest of experience, not from their own principles, to admit that no small amount of practice and zeal is needed to restrain and moderate them; and someone endeavoured to illustrate this by the example (if I remember correctly) of two dogs, the one a house dog and the other a hunting dog: he had been able, through long practice, to get the house dog accustomed to hunting and the hunting dog accustomed to refraining from running after hares. Descartes agrees with this view a great deal; for he maintained that the soul, or mind, is specially united to a particular part of the brain, namely that part called 'pineal gland', with the aid of which the mind feels all the movements that are set in motion in the body as well as external objects, and which the mind can move in various ways through a simple act of volition. He asserted that this gland is so suspended in the midst of the brain that it could be moved by the slightest motion of the animal spirits;[1] further, that this gland is suspended in the midst of the brain in as many different manners as the animal spirits can impact on it and has as many different marks impressed on it as there are different external objects pushing the animal spirits

---

1 *Spiritus* means primarily "blow" or "wind." (D.A.)

towards it; on account of this, if the will of the soul, moving the gland in various ways, suspends it in one or another manner in which it has already been suspended once before by the animal spirits driven one way or another, the gland will in turn push those spirits and determine them in the same manner in which they were repulsed before by a similar position of the gland. He further asserted that every act of mental volition is united by nature to a certain given motion of the gland. For instance, if someone has the volition to look at a remote object, this act of volition will cause the pupil of the eye to dilate, whereas, if the person in question had only thought of the dilation of the pupil, it would not help simply to will it since nature has not associated the motion of the gland, which serves to push the animal spirits towards the optic nerve in a way conducive to the dilation or contraction of the pupil, with the wish to dilate or contract it but only with the wish to look at remote or very near objects. Lastly, he maintained that, although every motion of the aforesaid gland seems to have been united by nature, from the very beginning of our life, to one particular thought out of the whole number of our thoughts, it can nevertheless become associated with other thoughts through habit; this he endeavours to prove in the Passions of the Soul, art. 50 pt. 1. *From this he concludes that there is no soul so weak as not to be able, under proper direction, to acquire absolute power over its passions. For these, as defined by him, are* perceptions, or feelings, or disturbances of the soul, which relate to it as a species and which (mark the expression) are produced, preserved, and strengthened through some movement of the spirits *(Passions of the Soul, art. 27 pt. 1). However, seeing as we can join any motion of the gland and, consequently, of the spirits, to any volition, and the determination of the will depends entirely on our own powers—if, therefore, we determine our will with sure and firm decisions according to which we wish to direct our actions and associate the motions of the passions we wish to acquire with said decisions, we will acquire absolute control over our passions. Such is the doctrine of this illustrious author (in so far as I gather it from his own words); it is one which, had it been less ingenious, I could hardly believe to have proceeded from so great a man. Indeed, I am lost in wonder that a philosopher who had firmly asserted that he would draw no conclusions that did not follow from self-evident premises and would affirm nothing that he did not clearly and distinctly perceive, and who had so often taken to task the scholastics for wishing to explain obscurities through occult qualities, could maintain a hypothesis more occult than any occult quality. What, I ask, does he understand by the union of the mind and the body? What clear and distinct conception does he have of thought in most intimate union with a certain particle of extended matter? I truly wish he had explained this union through its proximate cause. But he conceived the mind to be so thoroughly distinct from the body that he could not assign any particular cause to the union between the two or to the mind itself, but was forced to resort to the cause of the whole universe, that is, God. Further, I would very much like to know how many degrees of motion the mind can impart on this pineal gland and with how much force it can hold it suspended. For I do not know whether this gland is driven about more slowly or more quickly by the mind than by the animal spirits, and whether the motions of the passions that we have closely joined to firm decisions cannot again be disjoined from them by bodily causes; in which case it would follow that, although the mind firmly intended to face a given danger and had joined to this decision the motions of daring, the gland might at the sight of the danger become suspended in such a way that the mind could not think of anything except fleeing. In truth, since there is no standard of measurement for volition in relation to motion, there is no way to compare the powers of the mind with the power, that is, strength of the body, either; consequently, the strength of the latter cannot in any wise be determined by the strength of the former. We may also add that no gland is found in the midst of the brain which is so placed that it can be driven around this easily and in so many ways, as well as that not all nerves are prolonged all the way up to the cavities of the brain. Lastly, I omit all the assertions he makes concerning the will and its freedom, as I have abundantly proved that they are false. Therefore, since the power of the mind, as I have shown above, is defined solely by the intelligence, we will determine the remedies against the affects, which I believe everybody experiences but does not accurately observe or distinctly see, solely through the knowledge of the mind, and from it we will also deduce all that has to do with the mind's bliss.*

Having examined the basic nature of reality (Part I), the nature of the mind (Part II), the nature of emotions/affects (Part III), and human weakness to control emotions (Part IV), Spinoza then turns to the power of reason (Part V). Many have noted that Spinoza's discussion of Descartes in this opening seems out of place. Why begin Part V with a long complaint about Descartes's views which he has criticized numerous times before? We leave this question as an exercise for the reader to consider.

AXIOMS

I. If two contrary actions are started in the same subject, a change must necessarily take place either in both or in one of the two, until they cease to be contrary.

II. The power of an effect is defined by the power of its cause in so far as its essence is explained or defined by the essence of its cause. (This axiom is evident from Prop. 7 Pt. 3.)

PROPOSITIONS

PROP. I. *In the way that thoughts and the ideas of things are arranged and concatenated in the mind, precisely in the same way the modifications (*affectiones*) of the body, that is, the images of things, are arranged and concatenated in the body.*

Proof. The order and connection of ideas is the same as the order and connection of things (Prop. 7 Pt. 2) and, conversely, the order and connection of things is the same as the order and connection of ideas (Coroll. Prop. 6 and 7 Pt. 2). Therefore, just as the order and connection of ideas in the mind takes place according to the order and concatenation of the modifications of the body (Prop. 18 Pt. 2), the order and connection of the modifications of the body takes place, conversely, in the same way that the thoughts and the ideas of things are arranged and concatenated in the mind (Prop. 2 Pt. 3). *Q.E.D.*

PROP. II. *If we remove a disturbance of the mind, or affect, from the thought of an external cause and unite it to other thoughts, then the love or hatred towards that external cause will be destroyed, and so will the vacillations of mind that arise from these affects.*

Proof. What constitutes the form of love or hatred is joy or sadness accompanied by the idea of an external cause (Def. of the affects, 6 and 7); therefore, when this cause is removed (*tollere*), the form of love or hatred is removed with it. Consequently, these affects and those that arise from them are destroyed. *Q.E.D.*

PROP. III. *An affect that is a passion ceases to be one as soon as we form a clear and distinct idea of it.*

Proof. An affect that is a passion is a confused idea (general Def. of the affects). If, therefore, we form a clear and distinct idea of the affect itself, this idea will be distinguished from the affect itself, in so far as it relates solely to the mind, by reason only (Prop. 21 Pt. 2 with Schol.). Consequently, the affect will cease to be a passion (Prop. 3 Pt. 3). *Q.E.D.*

Corollary. Therefore, an affect becomes more under our control, and the mind is acted upon by it to a lesser extent, the better it is known to us.

> The transformation of passive affects into active understandings, in order to gain better control over them, is one of the Spinoza's core "therapeutic" ideas in Part V. Since an idea and the idea of that idea are one and the same thing, it follows that if we turn the idea of the idea into an adequate idea, then the original idea becomes adequate too. Or, in another way, since understanding is an active process and something that we do, when we understand an emotion, then we go from being passive (experiencing it) to being active (contemplating it). Because understanding is joyful, we can take joy in understanding even our negative emotions.

PROP. IV. *There is no modification of the body of which we cannot form some clear and distinct conception.*

Proof. Whatever is common to all things cannot be conceived except adequately (Prop. 38 Pt. 2); therefore, there is no modification of the body of which we cannot form some clear and distinct conception (Prop. 12 Pt. 2 and Lemma 2 after Schol. Prop. 13 Pt. 2). *Q.E.D.*

> Since a clear and distinct conception would seem to require a complete knowledge of its causes, this passage may seem to contradict what Spinoza said in Part II. But Spinoza seems to hold that we can consider modifications of the body solely insofar as they relate to human nature; and, in that sense, we can have an adequate idea of them. Nevertheless, it is hard to reconcile these competing claims about adequacy.

Corollary. It follows that there is no affect of which we cannot form some clear and distinct conception. For an affect is the idea of a modification of the body (general Def. of the affects), which must therefore involve some clear and distinct conception (previous Prop.).

Scholium. Seeing as there is nothing from which there does not follow some effect (Prop. 36 Pt. 1) and we clearly and distinctly understand whatever follows from an idea that is adequate in ourselves (Prop. 40 Pt. 2), it follows that everyone has the power to understand themselves and their affects clearly and distinctly—if not absolutely, at least in part—and consequently to become such as to be acted upon by them to a lesser degree.

It's noteworthy that Spinoza distinguishes "clear and distinct" understanding here from understanding "absolutely."

Thus, we must focus our efforts on acquiring, as far as possible, a clear and distinct knowledge of every affect in order that the mind may thus, through affect, be determined to think of the things that it clearly and distinctly perceives and in which it fully acquiesces and, consequently, in order that the affect itself may be separated from the thought of an external cause and associated with true thoughts.

The claim seems to be that an affect can be separated from its original idea (an inadequately understood external cause) and associated with true ideas (the affective change in the body). In this way we can come to understand an emotion through our own nature, and so have some kind of an adequate understanding of it. As bodies are finite, the change to the body is finite. As such this change can be clearly and distinctly understood—unlike the cause, which requires understanding an infinite causal series. Though the finitude of an effect on a body might seem like something that could be fully comprehended, Spinoza cannot claim that this effect can be absolutely understood given that "the idea of an effect depends on and involves the idea of a cause" (Ax IV Part I). One way to think about this is to think of adequacy as a continuum. When we understand our emotions, our relation to them becomes more of an action and less of a passion. Perhaps we can never have a perfectly adequate (absolute) understanding, but we can have a more adequate one. One might also think about this as understanding our emotions intuitively—in accord with the third kind of knowledge identified in Part II. In intuitive knowledge of this kind, we understand something adequately by seeing immediately, in some sense, how it follows from the essence of substance.

As a consequence of this, not only will love, hatred, etc. be destroyed (Prop. 2 of this part), but also the appetites—or desires—that are wont to arise from such an affect will become incapable of being excessive (Prop. 61 Pt. 4). For it must be especially remarked that the appetite through which man is said to act and the one through which he is said to be acted upon are one and same. For instance, we have shown that human nature is so constituted that each of us desires everyone else to live according to our preference (see Schol. Prop. 31 Pt. 3); and this appetite, in somebody who is not guided by reason, is a passion called 'ambition' and does not greatly differ from pride; in someone who lives by the dictates of reason, on the other hand, it is an action, or virtue, which is called 'piety' (see Schol. 1 Prop. 37 Pt. 4 and Proof 2 of the same Prop.). Similarly, all appetites, or desires, are passions only in so far as they spring from inadequate ideas, whereas the same results are accredited to virtue when they are aroused or generated by adequate ideas. For all those desires that determine us to do something can just as easily arise from adequate ideas as from inadequate ones (Prop. 59 Pt. 4). And—to return to the point from which I started—no more excellent remedy for the affects (among all the things that depend on our power) can be devised than this one, namely the true knowledge of them. For the mind has no other power save that of thinking and of forming adequate ideas, as we have shown above (Prop. 3 Pt. 3).

PROP. V. *An affect towards a thing that we conceive simply and not as necessary, as possible, or as contingent is, all else being equal, the strongest of all.*

Proof. An affect towards something that we imagine to be free is stronger than one towards something necessary (Prop. 49 Pt. 3) and, consequently, all the much stronger still than one towards something we imagine as possible or contingent (Prop. 11 Pt. 4). Now imagining a thing as free can be nothing other than imagining it simply while we are in ignorance of the causes that have determined it to act (see what we have shown in Schol. Prop. 35 Pt. 2); therefore, an affect towards something we imagine simply is, all else being equal, stronger than one we feel towards something necessary, possible, or contingent and, consequently, it is the strongest of all. *Q.E.D.*

This recalls Spinoza's "therapeutic" insight that imagining things in isolation increases our emotional reaction to them. So if we imagine a wrong that someone has done to us and focus intensely on the wrong out of context with no other relevant information—just focusing on the harmful act itself—then our anger is going to be the strongest, because we will have the idea of a harm and the cause of the harm with no other related or associated ideas. If we view the harm in a broader context, however, and remember that the person's actions are fully determined by an infinite series of causes, then our anger is mitigated.

PROP. VI. *The mind has greater power over the affects, that is, is less acted upon by them, to the extent that it understands all things as necessary.*

Proof. The mind understands all things to be necessary (Prop. 29 Pt. 1) and to be determined to exist and operate by an infinite chain of causes (Prop. 28 Pt. 1); therefore, to this extent it causes itself to be less acted upon by the affects arising from them (previous Prop.) and to be less affected towards the things themselves (Prop. 48 Pt. 3). *Q.E.D.*

Scholium. The more this knowledge, that things are necessary, revolves around particular things which we imagine more distinctly and vividly, the greater is the power of the mind over the affects, as experience also testifies. For we see that the sadness arising from the loss of some good is mitigated as soon as the person who has lost it comes to think that it could not have been preserved by any means. Likewise, we see that no one pities an infant because it cannot speak, walk, or reason or, lastly, because it passes so many years, as it were, unaware of itself, whereas, if most people were born full-grown and only a few as infants, everyone would pity the infants, because infancy would then not be looked on as something natural and necessary but as a fault or sin of nature. We could note several other instances of the same sort.

> Spinoza's infant analogy is insightful. We see harms that cannot be avoided, and which have clear causes, as less bad than harms that seem avoidable or pointless. But on Spinoza's view, every event is necessary, and so every harm or loss that we endure is as necessary as anything can be. We can't even clearly and distinctly understand things occurring differently than they do. In this way, all "harms" are akin to the many years of painful and difficult growing an infant must "endure" before it reaches adulthood. Though it is unpleasant to lose one's baby teeth, for example, we understand that these difficulties are natural and unavoidable. Accordingly, the suffering involved upsets us far less than it would if only some people had to endure such challenges.

PROP. VII. *Affects that arise from or are set in motion by reason, if we take account of time, are more powerful than those that relate to particular objects that we regard as absent.*

Proof. We do not regard something as absent because of the affect with which we imagine it, but because the body is affected by another affect that excludes the existence of said thing (Prop. 17 Pt. 2). Therefore, the affect that relates to a thing that we regard as absent is not of such a nature as to overcome the rest of someone's actions and power (about which see Prop. 6 Pt. 4) but is, on the contrary, of such a nature that it can in some way be restrained by the affects that exclude the existence of its external cause (Prop. 9 Pt. 4). Now an affect that arises from reason necessarily relates to the common properties of things (see the Def. of 'reason' in Schol. 2 Prop. 40 Pt. 2) that we always regard as present (for there can be nothing that excludes their present existence) and which we always imagine in the same manner (Prop. 38 Pt. 2). Therefore, an affect of this kind always remains the same; consequently, affects that are contrary to it and are not fostered by their external causes will have to adapt themselves to it more and more until they are no longer contrary to it (Ax. 1 of this part); to this extent the affect that arises from reason is more powerful. *Q.E.D.*

An example may help here. If we imagine that someone has wronged us in some particular way in the past, but that person is now gone, then we will feel anger at this harm. But someone who is fascinated by human psychology in general, and enjoys observing how humans think and feel, will find joy in thinking about facts about human minds. So the fascination with human psychology can cause the person to wonder about the motives, unconscious causes, etc. of the person who caused the harm, and the joy of that reflection will—all else being equal—be stronger than the anger related to the absent person.

PROP. VIII. *The more simultaneously concurring causes set an affect in motion, the stronger it is.*

Proof. Many simultaneous causes are more powerful than if they were fewer (Prop. 7 Pt. 3); thus, the more simultaneous causes arouse an affect, the more powerful it is (Prop. 5 Pt. 4). *Q.E.D.*

Scholium. This Proposition is also evident from Ax. 2 of this part.

PROP. IX. *An affect that relates to many and diverse causes which the mind regards as simultaneous with the affect itself is less hurtful and we are acted upon by it to a lesser extent and are less affected towards each of its causes than if it were a different and equally strong affect that relates to a single cause or to fewer causes.*

Proof. An affect is only bad, or hurtful, in so far as it hinders the mind from being able to think (Prop. 26 and 27 Pt. 4); therefore, the affect by which the mind is determined to contemplate several things at once is less hurtful than another equally strong one which so engrosses the mind in the single contemplation of one object or a few objects that it is unable to think of anything else. This was our first point. Next, as the mind's essence, in other words, its power (Prop. 7 Pt. 3), consists solely in thought (Prop. 11 Pt. 2), the mind is acted upon by an affect that determines it to think of several things at once to a lesser extent than by an equally strong affect that keeps it engrossed in the contemplation of one object or a few objects. This was our second point. Lastly, this affect, in so far as it relates to several causes, is less strong toward each of them (Prop. 48 Pt. 3). *Q.E.D.*

> Obsession over a single thing stops us from thinking about other things and so is harmful. This fixation results in emotions that are more powerful, insofar as the intellect fails to move on to other related ideas.

PROP. X. *So long as we are not assailed by affects contrary to our nature, we have the power of arranging and concatenating the modifications of our body according to order for the understanding.*

Proof. The affects that are contrary to our nature—that is, are bad (Prop. 30 Pt. 4)—are bad in so far as they hinder the mind from understanding (Prop. 27 Pt. 4). Thus, so long as we are not assailed by affects contrary to our nature, the mind's power through which it endeavours to understand things (Prop. 26 Pt. 4) is not hindered; therefore, it is able to form clear and distinct ideas and to deduce them from one another (see Schol. 2 Prop. 40 and Schol. Prop. 47 Pt. 2). Consequently, so long as this is the case, we have the power to arrange and concatenate the modifications of the body according to order for the understanding (Prop. 1 of this part). *Q.E.D.*

Scholium. Through this power to arrange and concatenate the bodily modifications in the right way we can guard ourselves from being easily affected by bad affects. For a greater force is needed to restrain affects that are arranged and associated according to order for the understanding than when they are uncertain and unsettled (Prop. 7 of this part). Therefore, the best we can do so long as we do not possess a perfect knowledge of our affects, is to come up with a system of right conduct, that is, fixed practical precepts, to commit them to memory, and to apply them continually to the particular circumstances that now and again meet us in life, so that our imagination may become extensively imbued with them and that they may be always ready to our hand. For instance, we have laid down among the rules of life that hatred should be overcome with love, or generosity, not requited with hatred (see Prop. 46 Pt. 4 with Schol.). Now in order that this precept of reason may always be ready to our hand when we need it, we must often think about and reflect upon the wrongs generally committed by people and in what manner and with what procedure they can best be warded off by generosity; in this way we will associate the idea of a wrong with the imagining of this precept, which accordingly will always be ready for use when a wrong is done to us (Prop. 18 Pt. 2). If we keep ready the notion of our true advantage, too, and of the good that follows from mutual friendship and common fellowship; if we further remember that from the right way of life arises supreme contentment of the mind (Prop. 52 Pt. 4) and that people, just like everything else, act by the necessity of their nature—then the wrong, or the hatred that commonly arises from it, will engross a very small part of our imagination and thus be easily overcome. Or if anger, which is wont to spring from the most egregious wrongs, is not so easily overcome, it will nevertheless be overcome (though not without a vacillation of spirit) far sooner than if we had not thus reflected on the subject beforehand (as is evident from Prop. 6, 7, and 8 of this part). As for courage as a means of doing away with fear, we must reflect in the same way: we must enumerate and frequently imagine the common dangers of life, as well as how best we can avoid and overcome them through readiness and strength of mind. We have to note, however, that in arranging our thoughts and mental images we must always bear in mind what is good in every individual thing (Coroll. Prop. 63 Pt. 4 and Prop. 59 Pt. 3) in order that we may always be determined to act by an affect of joy. For instance, if one sees that one is too keen in the pursuit of glory, one should think about its right use, to what end it ought to be pursued, and by what means it can be attained; but one should not think of its misuse, and its emptiness, the fickleness of mankind and the like, things no one thinks about except through a sickness of the mind. For it is with thoughts like these that the most ambitious torment themselves the most, when they despair of gaining the honour they are after, and want to appear wise while they are just venting their anger. Therefore, it is certain that those people who cry out the loudest against the misuse of glory and the vanity of the world are those who most greedily covet it. And this is not peculiar to the ambitious, but is common to all who are ill-used by fortune and weak in spirit. Indeed, a miser who happens to be poor will talk incessantly of the misuse of wealth and of the vices of the rich, and in this way they merely torment themselves and show the world that they do not bear with equanimity not only their own poverty, but also other people's wealth. Likewise, those who have been ill-received by their girlfriend think of nothing but the fickleness and duplicitousness of women and other stock faults of the fair sex, all of which they consign to oblivion the moment they are again taken into favour by their sweetheart. Thus, anyone who seeks to govern their affects and appetites solely through the love of freedom strives, as far as they can, to gain a knowledge of the virtues and their causes and to fill their mind with the delight that arises from the true knowledge thereof; on the other hand, they will in no way desire to dwell on people's faults or to snipe at them or to delight in a false show of freedom. Whoever will diligently observe and practise these precepts (which indeed are not difficult) will verily, in a short space of time, be able mostly to direct their actions according to the dictates of reason.

This passage is a complex one, but it is a good summary of Spinoza's practical approach to a joyful life. By frequently connecting the practical rules for living with different situations in our minds, we can hope that when the situations arise, the related general rules which best promote human thriving will immediately occur. For, when the difficulty is faced, if one's frequent reflections on how the opposite good supports one's flourishing, the difficulty will trigger thoughts of that opposite good. The joyful affect of the opposing good is thus immediately available to counteract the harmful/sad affect. This response is the opposite of focusing on, and emphasizing, the evil. Such an emphasis merely increases the harm through the obsession which fosters it. In focusing on the evil of a harm, the affect is strengthened rather than resisted. Spinoza thinks if one has embedded the rules that are connected to joy, then those rules will prepare one for responding to harmful occurrences, in such a way that one will be less subject to their affects. The free life is thus regular meditation on health and life, not on weakness and death.

PROP. XI. *The more things a mental image relates to, the more frequent, that is, the more often vivid it is and the more it occupies the mind.*

Proof. The more objects a mental image—that is, an affect—relates to, the more are the causes by which it can be aroused and fostered, all of which (according to our hypothesis) the mind contemplates simultaneously out of the affect itself. Thus, the affect is all the more frequent, that is, all the more often in full vigour, and occupies the mind more (Prop. 8 of this part). *Q.E.D.*

PROP. XII. *The images of things are more easily associated with the images that relate to things we clearly and distinctly understand than with others.*

Proof. The things that we clearly and distinctly understand are either the common properties of things or what is deduced from them (see Def. of reason in Schol. 2 Prop. 40 Pt. 2); consequently, they are more often aroused in us (previous Prop.). Therefore, it is easier for us to contemplate other things in conjunction with these than in conjunction with others and, consequently, for them to be more often associated with these than with others. *Q.E.D.*

PROP. XIII. *The more other images some mental image is associated with, the more often it is vivid.*

Proof. The more other images some mental image is associated with, the more causes there are by which it can be aroused (Prop. 18 Pt. 2). *Q.E.D.*

PROP. XIV. *The mind can cause all bodily modifications, that is, images of things, to relate to the idea of God.*

Proof. There is no modification of the body of which the mind cannot form some clear and distinct conception (Prop. 4 of this part). Thus, the mind can cause all of them to relate to the idea of God (Prop. 15 Pt. 1). *Q.E.D.*

The ground for this proposition has been carefully laid and it is perhaps one of the core ideas of the whole of the *Ethics*. We are able to associate any idea to the idea of God and, in so doing, change the character of the idea itself. If we are considering some wrong that has been done to us, for example, we can associate this idea to the idea of

God, and see it as a natural event which follows from the laws of nature. This way of thinking of the wrong is very different from associating this idea with fantasies of revenge, or with other wrongs that have been committed against us.

PROP. XV. *Anybody who clearly and distinctly understands themselves and their affects loves God, the more so the more they understand themselves and their affects.*

Proof. Anyone who clearly and distinctly understands themselves and their affects rejoices (Prop. 53 Pt. 3), and this joy is accompanied by the idea of God (previous Prop.). Therefore, such a person loves God (Def. of the affects, 6), the more so the more they understand themselves and their affects (by the same reasoning). *Q.E.D.*

PROP. XVI. *This love towards God must occupy the mind the most.*

Proof. This love is associated with all the modifications of the body (Prop. 14 of this part) and is fostered by all of them (Prop. 15). Consequently, it must occupy the mind the most (Prop. 11). *Q.E.D.*

PROP. XVII. *God is without passions and is affected with no affect of joy or sadness.*

Proof. All ideas, in so far as they relate to God, are true (Prop. 37 Pt. 2), that is, adequate (Def. 4 Pt. 2); therefore, God is without passions (general Def. of the affects). Also, God cannot pass either to a greater or to a lesser perfection (Coroll. 2 Prop. 20 Pt. 1); thus, he is not affected with any affect of joy or sadness (Def. of the affects, 2 and 3). *Q.E.D.*

Corollary. Strictly speaking, God does not love or hate anyone. For God is not affected with any affect of joy or sadness (previous Prop.); consequently, he does not love or hate anyone (Def. of the affects, 6 and 7).

As affects always relate to inadequate ideas of external causes, God can suffer no affects. As such, God feels neither love nor hate.

PROP. XVIII. *No one can hate God.*

Proof. The idea of God that is in us is adequate and perfect (Prop. 46 and 47 Pt. 2); therefore, in so far as we contemplate God, we act (Prop. 3 Pt. 3). It follows that there can be no sadness accompanied by the idea of God (Prop. 59 Pt. 3); in other words, no one can hate God (Def. of the affects, 7). *Q.E.D.*

> The proof here is interesting. Since the idea of God is always adequate, thinking about God is always the most powerful type of mental act. The idea cannot be inadequate because the idea of the essence of God (space or consciousness) is as much in the whole as in the part. Thus, however fragmentary, the idea of God is always adequate. To hate God, one would have to have the idea of God cause a decrease in activity or health in the mind. This is impossible. Thus, hate is impossible.

Corollary. Love towards God cannot turn into hate.

Scholium. It may be objected that, as we understand God as the cause of all things, by that very fact we regard God as the cause of sadness. To this I respond that, to the extent that we understand the causes of sadness, it ceases to be a passion (Prop. 3 of this part), that is, it ceases to be sadness (Prop. 59 Pt. 3). Thus, to the extent that we understand God to be the cause of sadness, we rejoice.

PROP. XIX. *Whoever loves God cannot endeavour for God to love them in return.*

Proof. If someone should so endeavour, they would desire for God, whom they love, not to be God (Coroll. Prop. 17 of this part); consequently, they would desire to be saddened (Prop. 19 Pt. 3), which is absurd (Prop. 28 Pt. 3). Therefore, whoever loves God, etc. *Q.E.D.*

> This proof recalls Spinoza's claims about why one always desires the good for an object of love. As the object of love brings us joy (i.e., empowers our striving), we want the love-object's good so that we can be maximally empowered. For God to feel any affect, however, would require God to be less powerful, since God would need to have inadequate ideas to feel affects. Thus, if one loves God, then one cannot desire for God to love one in return because this would require that one desire for an object of love to be less powerful.

PROP. XX. *This love towards God cannot be stained by the affect of envy or jealousy; on the contrary, it is fostered all the more the greater a number of people we imagine to be joined to God by the same bond of love.*

Proof. This love towards God is the highest good we can seek for under the guidance of reason (Prop. 28 Pt. 4), is common to everybody (Prop. 36 Pt. 4), and we desire everyone to delight therein (Prop. 37 Pt. 4). Therefore, it cannot be stained by the affect of envy (Def. of the affects, 23) or of jealousy (Prop. 18 of this part as well as Def. of 'jealousy' in Schol. Prop. 35 Pt. 3). On the contrary, it must be fostered all the more the greater a number of people we imagine to delight therein (Prop. 31 Pt. 3). *Q.E.D.*

Scholium. In the same way we can show that there is no affect directly contrary to this love by which this love can be destroyed; therefore, we can conclude that this love towards God is the most constant of all the affects and that, in so far as it relates to the body, it cannot be destroyed unless together with the body itself. As for its nature, in so far as it relates solely to the mind, we will inquire into it later. I have now gone through all the remedies against the affects, that is, all that the mind, considered in itself alone, can do against them.

Spinoza now provides a helpful summary of the power that reason has over the affects.

From this it appears that the mind's power over the affects consists:

I. in the actual knowledge of the affects (Schol. Prop. 4 of this part);

II. in the fact that it separates the affects from the thought of an external cause that we imagine confusedly (Prop. 2 and Schol. Prop. 4 of this part);

III. in the time when the modifications that relate to things we understand surpass those that relate to things we conceive in a confused and fragmentary manner (Prop. 7 of this part);

IV. in the multitude of causes by which those modifications that relate to the common properties of things or to God are fostered (Prop. 9 and 11 of this part);

V. lastly, in the order in which the mind can arrange its affects and concatenate them with one another (Schol. Prop. 10 as well as Prop. 12, 13, and 14 of this part).

In summary, we have power over our emotions by: knowing them, by separating the affect from the confused idea of the external cause, by focusing on how we are affected, as opposed to the cause of the affect, and by developing the habit of emphasizing contrary positive affects.

But in order that this power of the mind over the affects may be better understood, it should be specially observed that we call the affects 'strong' when we compare the affect of one person with that of another and see that one of them is more strongly assailed than the other by the same affect, or when we are comparing the various affects of the same person with each other and find that they are more affected, that is, stirred by one affect more than by another. For the strength of every affect is defined by a comparison of the power of an external cause with our own power (Prop. 5 Pt. 4). Now the power of the mind is defined by knowledge only, and its powerlessness—in other words, passion—is measured solely by the privation of knowledge, that is, by that through which ideas are called inadequate; from this it follows that the mind which is acted upon the most is the one whose greatest part is made up of inadequate ideas, so that it can be characterized more easily by its passions than by its actions, whereas the mind that acts the most is the one whose greatest part is made up of adequate ideas, so that, even if it should contain as many inadequate ideas as the former mind, it can still be more easily characterized by ideas that are ascribed to human virtue than by ones that tell of human powerlessness. It must further be observed that spiritual illnesses and misfortunes most often originate in an excessive love for something that is subject to many variations and of which we can never become masters. For no one is agitated or anxious over anything they do not love, nor do wrongs, suspicions, enmities, etc. arise except from the love for things of which no one can really be master. We can thus readily conceive the power that clear and distinct knowledge, and especially the aforementioned third kind of knowledge (on which see Schol. Prop. 47 Pt. 2), founded on the actual knowledge of God, holds over the affects: if it does not absolutely remove (*tollit*) them in so far as they are passions (see Prop. 3 with Schol. Prop. 4 of this part), it causes them, at any rate, to constitute the smallest part of the mind (Prop. 14). Further, it begets a love towards something that is immutable and eternal (Prop. 15) and of which we really are masters (Prop. 45 Pt. 2)—a love that, because of that, cannot be defiled by any of the faults inherent in the common kind of love but can grow from strength to strength (Prop. 15 of this part) and occupy the greatest part of the mind (Prop. 16) and affect it to a large extent.

And with these explanations I have finished dealing with all that concerns this present life. Indeed, that I have encompassed in a few words all the remedies against the affects as I promised I would do in the beginning of this Schol. is plain for everyone to see who has paid attention to what I have expounded in the present Schol. as well as to the Def. of the mind and its affects and, lastly, to Prop. 1 and 3 Pt. 3. Therefore, it is now time to move on to those matters that concern the duration of the mind without relation to the body.

> The following is generally considered the most obscure and difficult part of the book. Spinoza here talks about the duration of the mind without the body, which he argued in Part II were one and the same thing conceived in two ways. Reconciling these two claims has been a challenge for scholars. Spinoza was certainly aware of the tension and did not think that it constituted a problem for him. A close reading of these passages is thus required.

PROP. XXI. *The mind cannot imagine anything or remember what is past except as long as the body endures.*

Proof. The mind does not express the actual existence of its body, nor does it conceive the modifications of the body as actual except while the body endures (Coroll. Prop. 8 Pt. 2); consequently, it does not conceive any body as actually existing except while its own body endures (Prop. 26 Pt. 2). Thus, it cannot imagine anything (see Def. of 'imagination' in Schol. Prop. 17 Pt. 2) or remember things past except as long as the body endures (see Def. of 'memory' in Schol. Prop. 18 Pt. 2). *Q.E.D.*

> This claim seems to follow immediately from Part II's identification of mind and body. The mind is just an idea of the body, so if there is no body then there is no mind.

PROP. XXII. *In God there is nonetheless necessarily an idea that expresses the essence of this or that human body under the form of eternity.*

Proof. God is the cause, not only of the existence of this or that human body, but also of its essence (Prop. 25 Pt. 1). This essence, therefore, must necessarily be conceived through the very essence of God (Ax. 4 Pt. 1), and out of a certain eternal necessity (Prop. 16 Pt. 1), and this concept must necessarily exist in God (Prop. 3 Pt. 2). *Q.E.D.*

So within the infinite intellect of God there is an idea of the body from the perspective of eternity or understanding it as it relates only to the essence of God. So there are two ways to understand the body: first inadequately (as humans generally do) and second as adequately (the way God does). But the adequate idea that exists in God's mind also exists in the human's mind and so ...

PROP. XXIII. *The human mind cannot be absolutely destroyed with the body, but there remains of it something that is eternal.*

Proof. There is necessarily in God a concept, or idea, which expresses the essence of the human body (previous Prop.), which, therefore, is necessarily something that pertains to the essence of the human mind (Prop. 13 Pt. 2). But we have not assigned to the human mind any duration definable by time, except in so far as it expresses the actual existence of the body, which is explained through duration and can be defined by time—that is, we do not assign to it duration except while the body endures (Coroll. Prop. 8 Pt. 2). Yet, as there is nonetheless something that is conceived out of a certain eternal necessity through the very essence of God (previous Prop.), this something that pertains to the essence of the mind will necessarily be eternal. *Q.E.D.*

This is a dense and difficult proof, but the outline of the argument seems reasonably clear. Within the human mind there are ideas of the body conceived both temporally (inadequately) and "under the form of eternality" (adequately). The idea of the body from the perspective of eternity is God's idea of the body. Remember that the human mind is just a tiny bit of the infinite intellect of God. So if we conceive of the ideas in the human mind as a bundle of ideas, then the adequate ideas in that bundle are also God's ideas. The inadequate ones are also God's ideas, of course, but they are inadequate because they are isolated and fragmentary. Since the ideas that are adequate in our mind are literally just God's ideas, they cannot in principle be destroyed. They cannot be destroyed because God is eternally thinking everything that can be thought. An analogy may be helpful. If we are Platonists about mathematics so that numbers are real things that exist in God's mind, then the more math that we know as human beings, the more part of our mind is literally identical to the mathematical ideas in God. That knowledge is eternal because math does not change over time.

Scholium. This idea that expresses the essence of the body under the form of eternity is, as we have said, a certain mode of thinking that belongs to the essence of the mind and is necessarily eternal. It is not possible, however, for us to remember existing before our body, for our body can bear no trace of such existence and eternity cannot be defined in terms of time or have any relation to time. Now, all this notwithstanding, we perceive and experience that we are eternal. For the mind perceives those things that it conceives by understanding no less than those it remembers; the eyes of the mind, through which it sees and observes things, are the proofs themselves. Thus, although we do not remember existing before the body, we perceive that our mind, in so far as it involves the essence of the body under the form of eternity, is eternal and that thus its existence cannot be defined in terms of time, in other words, explained through duration. Consequently, our mind can only be said to endure, and its existence can only be defined by a fixed time, to the extent that it involves the actual existence of the body. Only to this extent does it possess the power to determine the existence of things by time and conceive them under the category of duration.

> The argument here is dense and difficult, but Spinoza is focusing on the two ways of conceiving of a fragment. Bodies are mere fragments of infinite substance. As such, ideas of such fragments are necessarily inadequate ideas (ideas of things that are finite and limited). Ideas of a body as such are only of the fragment, and thus exist only as long as the body does. Yet, insofar as the body is a fragment, it can be conceived of *as* a fragment. When conceiving a body *as* a fragment, the fragment is only understood in reference to its portion of the whole. This relation is eternal—though the thing itself is not.

PROP. XXIV. *The more we understand individual things, the more we understand God <or we also have more understanding of God>.*

Proof. This is evident from Coroll. Prop. 25 Pt. 1.

> It may seem like a contradiction that we could ever know God better, since our idea of God is necessarily adequate. But we come to know God better, it seems, by drawing out the logical implications of God's essence (namely, everything that exists).

PROP. XXV. *The highest endeavour of the mind and its highest virtue is to understand things through the third kind of knowledge.*

Proof. The third kind of knowledge proceeds from an adequate idea of certain attributes of God to an adequate knowledge of the essence of things (see its Def. in Schol. 2 Prop. 40 Pt. 2); and the more we understand things in this way, the better we understand God (previous Prop.). Therefore, the highest virtue of the mind— in other words, its highest power, that is, nature (Def. 8 Pt. 4), or the highest endeavour of the mind (Prop. 7 Pt. 3)—is to understand things through the third kind of knowledge (Prop. 28 Pt. 4). *Q.E.D.*

To understand something by the third kind of knowledge is to know it as God knows it.

PROP. XXVI. *The more capable the mind is of understanding things through the third kind of knowledge, the more it desires to understand things through that kind.*

Proof. This is evident; for to the extent that we conceive the mind to be capable of understanding things through this kind of knowledge, we conceive it as determined to understand things through that same kind of knowledge. Consequently, the more capable the mind is of this, the more it desires to do so (Def. of the affects, 1). *Q.E.D.*

PROP. XXVII. *From this third kind of knowledge arises the mind's highest possible contentment.*

Proof. The mind's highest virtue is to know God (Prop. 28 Pt. 4), that is, to understand things through the third kind of knowledge (Prop. 25 of this part), and this virtue is greater the more the mind knows things through said kind of knowledge (Prop. 24 of this part). Consequently, whoever knows things through this kind of knowledge passes to the summit of human perfection and is therefore affected by the highest joy (Def. of the affects, 2), and this joy is accompanied by the idea of themselves and their own virtue (Prop. 43 Pt. 2). Thus, from this kind of knowledge arises the highest contentment that can exist (Def. of the affects, 25). *Q.E.D.*

As the affirmation of adequate ideas is the most powerful activity of a mind, the mind is best functioning/striving when thinking adequate ideas. Accordingly, the more adequate ideas one has, the more able is one's striving (health under the attribute of thought). Thus, to get more adequate ideas is to increase one's joy. Thus, the greatest joy follows the greatest number of adequate ideas.

PROP. XXVIII. *The endeavour, or desire, to know things through the third kind of knowledge cannot arise from the first, but it can from the second kind of knowledge.*

Proof. This Proposition is self-evident; for whatever we understand clearly and distinctly we understand either through itself or through something else that is conceived through itself; that is, the ideas that are clear and distinct in us—in other words, the ideas that relate to the third kind of knowledge (see Schol. 2 Prop. 40 Pt. 2)—cannot follow from ideas that are fragmentary and confused, which relate to knowledge of the first kind (same Schol.), but must follow from adequate ones, that is, ideas of the second and third kind of knowledge (same Schol.). Therefore, the desire to know things through the third kind of knowledge cannot arise from the first kind but it can from the second (Def. of the affects, 1). *Q.E.D.*

PROP. XXIX. *Whatever the mind understands under the form of eternity it does not understand by virtue of conceiving the present actual existence of the body, but by virtue of conceiving the essence of the body under the form of eternity.*

Proof. To the extent that the mind conceives the present existence of its body, it conceives duration, which can be determined by time, and only to that extent does it possess the power to conceive things in relation to time (Prop. 21 of this part and Prop. 26 Pt. 2). Now eternity cannot be explained in terms of duration (Def. 8 Pt. 1 with explanation). Therefore, to this extent the mind lacks the power to conceive things under the form of eternity, but it possesses it because it is in the nature of reason to conceive things under the form of eternity (Coroll. 2 Prop. 44 Pt. 2), and also because it is in the nature of the mind to conceive the essence of the body under the form of eternity (Prop. 23 of this part), and besides these two there is nothing that belongs to the essence of the mind (Prop. 13 Pt. 2). Therefore, this power to conceive things under the form of eternity does not belong to the mind except in so far as it conceives the essence of the body under the form of eternity. *Q.E.D.*

Given that understanding things temporarily is necessarily inadequate and only conceiving of things "under the form of eternity" is adequate, a good case can be made that time is in some sense unreal in Spinoza.

Instead of being something real, temporal passage is an illusion that arises from inadequate ideas.

Scholium. Things are conceived by us as actual in two ways: either in so far as we conceive them as existing in relation to a given time and place or in so far as we conceive them as contained in God and following from the necessity of the divine nature. Whatever we conceive in this second way as true, or real, we conceive under the form of eternity, and its ideas involve the eternal and infinite essence of God, as we showed in Prop. 45 Pt. 2 (see also Schol. same Prop.).

PROP. XXX. *To the extent that our mind knows itself and the body under the form of eternity, it necessarily possesses a knowledge of God and knows that it is in God and is conceived through God.*

Proof. Eternity is the very essence of God in so far as it involves necessary existence (Def. 8 Pt. 1). Therefore, to conceive things under the form of eternity is to conceive things in so far as they are conceived through the essence of God as real entities, in other words, in so far as they involve existence through the essence of God. Thus, to the extent that our mind conceives itself and the body under the form of eternity, it necessarily possesses a knowledge of God and knows, etc. *Q.E.D.*

PROP. XXXI. *The third kind of knowledge depends on the mind as its formal cause in so far as the mind itself is eternal.*

Proof. The mind does not conceive anything under the form of eternity except in so far as it conceives its own body under the form of eternity (Prop. 29 of this part), that is, except in so far as it is eternal (Prop. 21 and 23). Therefore, in so far as it is eternal, it possesses the knowledge of God (previous Prop.), which is necessarily adequate (Prop. 46 Pt. 2). Hence, the mind, in so far as it is eternal, is capable of knowing everything that can follow from this given knowledge of God (Prop. 40 Pt. 2), in other words, of knowing things by the third kind of knowledge (see its Def. in Schol. 2 Prop. 40 Pt. 2), and accordingly the mind, in so far as it is eternal, is the adequate, or formal, cause of such knowledge (Def. 1 Pt. 3). *Q.E.D.*

For "formal cause" here Spinoza could mean formal in contrast to the Aristotelian final, efficient, and material causes, or in contrast to objective causes in the Cartesian sense. If the latter sense, then the third kind of knowledge arises not from the representational content of our ideas, but from the idea understood by way of its part/whole relationship with the infinite intellect (ignoring the meaning or content of it).

Scholium. Consequently, the more potent one is in this kind of knowledge, the more conscious one will be of oneself and of God, in other words, the more perfect and blessed, as will appear even more clearly in the following. Here, however, we must observe that, although we are already certain that the mind is eternal in so far as it conceives things under the form of eternity, in order that what we wish to show may be more easily explained and better understood, we will consider the mind as though it had just begun to exist and to understand things under the form of eternity, as indeed we have done so far. We can do so without any danger of error so long as we are careful not to draw any conclusion unless our premises are plain.

PROP. XXXII. *Whatever we understand by the third kind of knowledge we take delight in, and this delight is accompanied by the idea of God as cause.*

Proof. From this kind of knowledge arises the highest possible contentment of the mind (Prop. 27 of this part), that is, joy (Def of the affects, 25), and this contentment is accompanied by the idea of the mind itself and, consequently, also by the idea of God as cause (Prop. 30). *Q.E.D.*

Corollary. From the third kind of knowledge necessarily arises the intellectual love of God. For from this kind of knowledge arises joy accompanied by the idea of God as cause (previous Prop.), that is, the love of God (Def. of the affects, 6), not in so far as we imagine him as present (Prop. 29) but in so far as we understand him to be eternal; this is what I call the intellectual love of God.

PROP. XXXIII. *The intellectual love of God, which arises from the third kind of knowledge, is eternal.*

Proof. The third kind of knowledge is eternal (Prop. 31 of this part and Ax. 3 Pt. 1); therefore, the love that arises from it is also necessarily eternal (same Axiom). *Q.E.D.*

Scholium. Although this love towards God had no beginning (previous Prop.), it possesses all the perfections of love just as though it had arisen, as we pretended it did in Coroll. previous Prop. Nor is there any difference here except that the mind possesses as eternal those same perfections that we pretended accrued to it with the accompanying idea of God as eternal cause. For if joy consists in the transition to a greater perfection, assuredly bliss must consist in the mind's being endowed with perfection itself.

PROP. XXXIV. *The mind is not subject to those affects that relate to passions except as long as the body endures.*

Proof. Imagination is the idea through which the mind contemplates a thing as present (see its Def. in Schol. Prop. 17 Pt. 2); yet this idea indicates the present disposition of the human body rather than the nature of the external thing (Coroll. 2 Prop. 16 Pt. 2). Therefore, an affect is imagination in so far as it indicates the present disposition of the body (see the general Def. of the affects); thus, the mind is not subject to those affects that relate to passions except as long as the body endures (Prop. 21 of this part). *Q.E.D.*

Corollary. It follows that no love save intellectual love is eternal.

Scholium. If we look to people's general opinion, we will see that they are indeed conscious of the eternity of their mind, but that they confuse eternity with duration and ascribe the latter to the imagination, or memory, which they believe to remain after death.

PROP. XXXV. *God loves himself with an infinite intellectual love.*

Proof. God is absolutely infinite (Def. 6 Pt. 1), that is, God's nature delights in infinite perfection (Def. 6 Pt. 2), a delight accompanied by the idea of himself (Prop. 3 Pt. 2), that is, the idea of his own cause (Prop. 11 and Def. 1 Pt. 1). Now this is what we have described as intellectual love (Coroll. Prop. 32 of this part).

> This proposition is hard to fit with Spinoza's earlier claim that God cannot love or hate anyone because it experiences no affects. God can't experience affects because it cannot increase or decrease in perfection. So "intellectual love" in this context is delight in something

perfect, not the perception of one's body passing from lower to greater health.

PROP. XXXVI. *The mind's intellectual love for God is that very love of God by which God loves himself, not in so far as he is infinite, but in so far as he can be explained through the essence of the human mind regarded under the form of eternity; in other words, the mind's intellectual love for God is part of the infinite love by which God loves himself.*

Proof. This love of the mind must relate to the actions of the mind (Coroll. Prop. 32 of this part and Prop. 3 Pt. 3); it is, consequently, an action by which the mind contemplates itself with the accompanying idea of God as cause (Prop. 32 of this part with Coroll.); in other words, it is an action by which God, in so far as he can be explained through the human mind, contemplates himself with the accompanying idea of himself (Coroll. Prop. 25 Pt. 1 and Coroll. Prop. 11 Pt. 2). Thus, this love of the mind is part of the infinite love by which God loves himself (previous Prop.). *Q.E.D.*

Corollary. It follows that God, in so far as he loves himself, loves human beings; consequently, God's love for human beings and the mind's intellectual love for God are identical.

It is important here again to carefully distinguish "intellectual love" from the kind of love Spinoza was discussing in Part IV. But to love a mode of God is to love God expressed in that way.

Scholium. From what has been said we clearly understand wherein our salvation, or bliss, or freedom consists, namely in the constant and eternal love for God—that is, in God's love for human beings. This love, or bliss, in the Holy Scriptures is called 'glory', and not undeservedly. For whether this love relates to God or to the mind, it can rightly be called contentment of the mind, which is not really distinct from glory (Def. of the affects, 25 and 30). For in so far as it relates to God, it is joy—if we may still use that term—accompanied by the idea of himself (Prop. 35 of this part), and so is it in so far as it relates to the mind (Prop. 27). Further, since the essence of our mind consists solely in knowledge, whose beginning (*principium*) and foundation is God (Prop. 15 Pt. 1 and Schol. Prop. 47 Pt. 2), it becomes clear to us in what way and by what logic our mind follows from the divine nature as regards its essence and existence and constantly depends on God. I have thought it worthwhile here to call attention to this fact in order to show through this example how powerful the knowledge of particular things, which I have called 'intuitive' or 'of the third kind' (Schol. 2 Prop. 40 Pt. 2), is and that it is preferable to the universal knowledge, which I have named 'knowledge of the second kind'. For although in Part 1 I showed in general terms that everything (and, consequently, the human mind as well) depends on God for its essence and existence, that demonstration, though legitimate and placed beyond the chances of doubt, does not affect our mind so much as when the same conclusion is derived from the actual essence of some particular thing, which we say depends on God.

PROP. XXXVII. *There is nothing in nature that is contrary to this intellectual love, in other words, that can remove it.*

Proof. This intellectual love follows necessarily from the nature of the mind in so far as the latter is regarded through the nature of God as an eternal truth (Prop. 33 and 29 of this part). If, therefore, there were anything contrary to this love, that thing would be contrary to what is true; consequently, the thing that should be able to remove this love would cause what is true to be false, which is absurd (as is self-evident). Therefore, there is nothing in nature, etc. *Q.E.D.*

Scholium. The Axiom of Part 4 refers to individual things in so far as they are regarded in relation to a given time and place. Of this, I think, no one has any doubt.

PROP. XXXVIII. *The more things the mind understands by the second and third kind of knowledge, the less it is acted upon by those affects that are bad and the less it fears death.*

Proof. The mind's essence consists in knowledge (Prop. 11 Pt. 2); therefore, the more things the mind understands by the second and third kinds of knowledge, the bigger is the part of it that remains (Prop. 29 and 23 of this part) and, consequently, the bigger is the part that is not touched by affects that are contrary to our nature (previous Prop.), in other words, are bad (Prop. 30 Pt. 4). Thus, the more things the mind understands by the second and third kinds of knowledge, the bigger will be the part of it that remains uninjured and, consequently, the less the mind is acted upon by affects, etc. *Q.E.D.*

Scholium. Hence we understand what I touched on in Schol. Prop. 39 Pt. 4 and promised to explain in this Part, namely that death becomes less hurtful the greater the mind's clear and distinct knowledge is and, consequently, the more the mind loves God. Further, since from the third kind of knowledge arises the highest possible contentment (Prop. 27 of this part), it follows that the human mind can be of such a nature that the part of it that we have shown to perish with the body (Prop. 21) becomes of no importance when compared with what remains. But I will soon treat of the subject at greater length.

PROP. XXXIX. *Whoever possesses a body capable of the greatest number of actions also possesses a mind whose greatest part is eternal.*

Proof. Whoever possesses a body capable of the greatest number of actions is least agitated by those affects that are bad (Prop. 38 Pt. 4)—that is, by those affects that are contrary to our nature (Prop. 30 Pt. 4). Therefore, such a person possesses the power to order and concatenate the modifications of the body according to order for the understanding (Prop. 10 of this part) and, consequently, to cause all the modifications of the body to relate to the idea of God (Prop. 14); as a consequence, they will be affected with love towards God (Prop. 15), a love that must occupy—in other words, constitute—the greater part of the mind (Prop. 16). Thus, such a person will possess a mind whose greatest part is eternal (Prop. 33). *Q.E.D.*

> It would seem that Spinoza is committed here to the idea that younger people with healthier bodies—and hence minds—have a greater eternal part of the mind than the elderly whose bodies—and hence minds—are declining. But Spinoza could hold that while certain bodily activities become harder for the elderly, other brain activities (whatever the correlates are to adequate thinking) are more robust.

Scholium. Since human bodies are capable of the greatest number of actions, there is no doubt that they can be of such a nature as to relate to minds that possess a great knowledge of themselves and of God and whose greatest, that is, main part is eternal, so that they hardly fear death. But in order that this may be understood more clearly, we must here call to mind that we live in a state of perpetual variation and, depending on whether we change for the better or the worse, we are called successful or unsuccessful. For someone who from being an infant or a child becomes a corpse is called unsuccessful, whereas it is counted as success if we have been able to live through the whole period of life with a sound mind in a sound body.[1] And in truth, whoever, as in the case of an infant or a child, has a body capable of very few actions and depending, for the most part, on external causes has a mind which, considered in itself alone, is barely conscious of itself, or of God, or of things; whoever, on the other hand, has a body capable of very many actions has a mind which, considered in itself alone, is highly conscious of itself, of God, and of things. In this life, therefore, we primarily endeavour to make the body of infancy, in so far as its nature allows and is conducive to it, change into another that is capable of very many activities and relates to a mind that is highly conscious of itself, of God, and of things; and we desire to change it in such a way that all that relates to its memory, or imagination, may become insignificant in comparison with its intellect, as I have already said in Schol. previous Prop.

PROP. XL. *The more perfection each thing possesses, the more it acts and the less it is acted upon; and vice versa, the more it acts the more perfect it is.*

This is perhaps a useful place to recall some of Spinoza's complex identity claims. As knowledge = power = activity = perfection = existing, the more knowledge one has, the greater one's existence. Likewise, since inadequate ideas relate to those ideas involving external causes, the more ideas relate to one's own actions, the more adequate are one's ideas. If one is significantly acted upon, however, then one's knowledge of oneself will necessarily involve many inadequate ideas. Thus, the more one is acted upon, the more inadequate are one's ideas, and hence the weaker and sadder one is.

Proof. The more perfect each thing is, the more reality it possesses (Def. 6 Pt. 2) and, consequently, the more it acts and the less it is acted upon (Prop. 3 Pt. 3 with Schol.). This demonstration also proceeds in the same way in reverse order and thus proves that, conversely, the more a thing acts, the more perfect it is. Q.E.D.

Corollary. From this it follows that the part of the mind which endures, regardless of its size, is more perfect than the rest. For

---

1 *Mens sana in corpore sano*: from Juvenal (10.356).

the eternal part of the mind is the intellect (Prop. 23 and 29 of this part), through which alone we are said to act (Prop. 3 Pt. 3); the part that we have shown to perish is imagination itself (Prop. 21 of this part), through which alone we are said to be acted upon (Prop. 3 Pt. 3 and general Def. of the affects). Therefore, the former, regardless of its size, is more perfect than the latter (previous Prop.). *Q.E.D.*

Scholium. These are the doctrines that I decided to set forth concerning the mind in so far as it is regarded without relation to the existence of the body. From these, as well as from Prop. 21 Pt. 1 and other places, it is plain that our mind, in so far as it understands, is an eternal mode of thinking, which is determined by another eternal mode of thinking, and this other by a third, and so on to infinity—so that all of them taken together constitute God's eternal and infinite intellect.

PROP. XLI. *Even if we did not know that our mind is eternal, we would still consider as of primary importance piety and religion and generally everything that we showed in Part 4 to relate to courage and generosity.*

Proof. The first and only foundation of virtue—that is, the rule of living right—is seeking one's own interest (Coroll. Prop. 22 and Prop. 24 Pt. 4). Now we took no account of the mind's eternity in determining what reason prescribes as advantageous, in fact, its eternity has only become known to us in this Fifth Part. So although at that point in time we did not know that the mind is eternal, we nevertheless regarded what relates to courage and generosity as of primary importance. Therefore, even if we still did not know about this doctrine, we would still put those same precepts of reason in the first place. *Q.E.D.*

> Spinoza's language in this proof suggests that he may have changed his mind on the eternality of the mind since writing those parts of the books.

Scholium. The general belief of most people seems to be different. Most people seem to believe that they are free to the extent that they are allowed to obey their lusts and that they give up their rights to the extent that they are bound to live according to the commandments of the divine law. Therefore, they believe that

piety, religion, and absolutely everything that relates to the fortitude of the mind are burdens, which they hope to lay aside after
death and receive the reward for their bondage, that is, for their
piety and religion; and it is not only by this hope but also, and
chiefly, by the fear of being punished with terrible torments after
death that they are induced to live according to the divine commandments, so far as their feeble and infirm spirit will carry
them. If people lacked this hope and this fear and believed
instead that the mind perishes with the body and that no prolonged life is in store for the wretches who are broken down with
the burden of piety, they would return to their own inclinations,
directing everything in accordance with their lusts and desiring to
obey fortune rather than themselves. Such behaviour appears to
me no less absurd than if someone who does not believe that they
can sustain their body through wholesome food for all eternity
should wish to cram themselves with poisons and deadly substances; or if, because they see that the mind is not eternal, or
immortal, they should prefer to be out of their mind and live
without the use of reason. These ideas are so absurd as to be
hardly worth refuting.

PROP. XLII. *Bliss is not the reward of virtue but virtue itself; and we
do not delight in it because we restrain our lusts but, on the contrary,
we are able to restrain our lusts because we delight in it.*

Proof. Bliss consists in love for God (Prop. 36 of this part with
Schol.), a love that arises from the third kind of knowledge
(Coroll. Prop. 32); therefore, this love must relate to the mind in
so far as it acts (Prop. 59 and 3 Pt. 3); consequently, it is virtue
itself (Def. 8 Pt. 4). This was our first point. Further, the more
the mind delights in this divine love, or bliss, the more it understands (Prop. 32 of this part), that is, the more power it has over
the affects (Coroll. Prop. 3) and the less it is acted upon by those
affects that are bad (Prop. 38). It follows that the mind, because
it delights in this divine love, or bliss, has the power to restrain its
lusts. And since a human being's power to restrain the affects
consists solely in the intellect, it follows that no one delights in
bliss because they have restrained their affects but, on the contrary, their power to restrain their lusts arises from this bliss itself.
Q.E.D.

Scholium. I have thus completed all that I wished to set forth regarding the mind's power over the affects and the mind's freedom. From this it appears how powerful the wise are and how much preferable to the ignorant, who are driven only by their lusts. For the ignorant, besides being agitated in various ways by external causes and never gaining the true contentment of the mind, live, as it were, unwitting of themselves, of God, and of things, and as soon as they cease to be acted upon they also cease to be. The wise, on the other hand, in so far as they are regarded as such, are barely disturbed in spirit but, being conscious of themselves, of God, and of things by some eternal necessity, never cease to be but always possess the true contentment of the mind. If the way which I have shown to lead to this result seems exceedingly hard, it can nevertheless be discovered. And certainly, something so seldom found must be hard. How could it be the case, if salvation were readily available and could be found without great effort, that it is neglected by most everybody? But everything excellent is as difficult as it is rare.

The End.

INDEX

Footnotes are indicated by "n" followed by the note number.

supreme perfection, 67

thankfulness, 178, 207, 270, 275
Theological-Political Treatise (Spinoza), 9–10, 245
Thirty Years' War (1618–48), 10
time
    eternalism, 29, 264
    eternity, 29, 51, 54, 297–99, 301–04, 309
    as illusory, 127, 301–02
    impact of affects and, 158–59
    strengths of affects and, 263–64
timidity, 208
tollitur, 93, 148, 165, 180, 217, 296
truth
    false ideas and, 217–19
    ideas as true, 30, 103–05, 115–16, 124–26

"unconscious" mind, 108, 197

value, theory of
    desire and, 204
    perfection and imperfection, 212–15
virtue
    defined, 217, 230, 268n2
    in avoiding dangers, 268–69
    bliss as, 310
    striving and, 232–35

wonder, 185–86, 198–99

About the Publisher

The word "broadview" expresses a good deal of the philosophy behind our company. Our focus is very much on the humanities and social sciences—especially literature, writing, and philosophy—but within these fields we are open to a broad range of academic approaches and political viewpoints. We strive in particular to produce high-quality, pedagogically useful books for higher education classrooms—anthologies, editions, sourcebooks, surveys of particular academic fields and sub-fields, and also course texts for subjects such as composition, business communication, and critical thinking. We welcome the perspectives of authors from marginalized and underrepresented groups, and we have a strong commitment to the environment. We publish English-language works and translations from many parts of the world, and our books are available world-wide; we also publish a select list of titles with a specifically Canadian emphasis.

broadview press

This book is made of paper from well-managed FSC® - certified forests, recycled materials, and other controlled sources.

 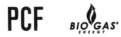